D0983880

CRISIS MANAGEMENT

*Confrontation and Diplomacy
in the Nuclear Age*

CRISIS MANAGEMENT

*Confrontation and Diplomacy
in the Nuclear Age*

PHIL WILLIAMS

A Halsted Press Book

JOHN WILEY & SONS
New York

First published in Great Britain 1976 by Martin Robertson & Co. Ltd., 17 Quick Street, London N1 8HL.

Published in the U.S.A. by Halsted Press, a Division of John Wiley & Sons, Inc., New York.

ISBN 0 470–98899–1

LC 76–40605

Printed in Great Britain

Contents

Preface

The purpose of this essay is to provide an introduction to the notion of crisis management as it has been developed in the academic literature and practised by the United States, the Soviet Union and, to a lesser extent, Communist China during the Cold War. It is hoped that it will be of particular interest to those who are concerned with the evolving superpower relationship, as well as to students of foreign policy analysis and strategic studies. The following chapters do not pretend to break any new frontiers in knowledge; rather are they intended to offer comments and reflections upon a mode of behaviour that has been crucial to the avoidance of nuclear war. The essay also leads the reader into a large and wide-ranging body of literature that is concerned not only with the details of particular crises, but also with establishing general propositions about crisis behaviour.

The formidable difficulties encountered even in this relatively limited and straightforward task are discussed in chapter one. It seems appropriate, however, to enter an additional caveat at the outset. For stylistic purposes it has been necessary to adopt certain conventions that involve considerable over-simplification. The use of capital cities, for example, is a helpful short-hand means of expression, but it glosses over many complexities, some of which are explored in chapter five. Similarly, the term policy-makers is used frequently to describe those who make the decisions in crisis situations, even though crisis management does not involve policy in the normal sense of the word. Despite its drawbacks, 'policy-makers' appeared to be preferable to 'crisis-managers'.

For these and other shortcomings, I alone bear the responsibility. For any merit the work may have, however, friends and colleagues who have been generous with their time and energy must take much of the credit. My interest in crisis management has in fact been sustained over a lengthy period during which time I have accumulated an enormous debt of gratitude to many people. I would like to express my appreciation to John Garnett, Ken Booth and Robbie Purnell of the Department of International Politics, University College of Wales, Aberystwyth, for their help and encouragement during the time when I was first exploring crisis management. My thanks are also due to Professor Philip Reynolds for his helpful comments on some of the earlier chapters.

Students and colleagues in the Department of Politics at Aberdeen University have provided a stimulating and congenial atmosphere within which the work was completed. In particular Clive Archer, David Capitanchik, Jean Houbert, John Main and Harvey Starr (now at Indiana University) have provided critical but refreshing ideas that have improved the arguments presented here in a variety of ways. In addition, Professor Frank Bealey has provided constant encouragement and on many occasions has helped to restore my sagging spirits in his own distinctive way. Special mention must be made of David Greenwood, who not only read the complete manuscript and offered invaluable suggestions for its improvement, but brought to our many discussions on the subject a clarity and incisiveness that were badly needed. It also gives me immense pleasure to thank Professor Jack Spence, of the Department of Government, Leicester University, both for his comments on the manuscript and for his help and inspiration ever since he first aroused my interest not only in crisis management but in international politics as a whole.

The manuscript went through several successive drafts and I would like to thank Mrs Freda Rennie, who typed one complete version, as well as Miss Janice Fraser, Mrs Elizabeth Eyres, Miss Lily Findlay and Miss Liz Weir, all of whom provided crucial secretarial assistance at various junctures.

Finally, I would like to acknowledge the indispensable contribution of my wife Avis, without whose love, patience and understanding this book would never have been completed.

To my
Mother and Father

PART ONE

Crisis Management: Background and Development

CHAPTER ONE

Introduction

I Purpose and Scope

During the late 1940s and the 1950s the term 'Cold War' was used so often that it became virtually a cliché. Yet the label was, in many senses, an appropriate one and described very graphically the conflict relationship between the United States and the Soviet Union that developed in the aftermath of the Second World War. On the one hand, Soviet–American hostility was sufficiently acute and the competition between them sufficiently intense to merit the term 'war'. On the other hand, it was not war in the more usual sense of the word: the conflict did not involve continual or unremitting violence. Although the Cold War was punctuated by local or regional hostilities, its weapons were not solely, and perhaps not even primarily, the tank and the machine gun but were more subtle means of influence such as the propaganda leaflet, economic aid and diplomatic manoeuvres. There were occasions, however, when it appeared as if the situation might be transformed from this relatively subdued mode of conflict into much more overt and large-scale violence involving the two superpowers themselves. Indeed, one of the major features of the Cold War was the sporadic occurrence of direct confrontations between the United States and the Soviet Union (and, to a slightly lesser extent, between the United States and Communist China), confrontations that threatened to initiate a process of 'hot war' between the protagonists.

The present work examines some of these crises in an attempt both to understand and to highlight the way in which they were managed and ultimately defused or resolved by the protagonists. It focuses mainly on the actions of the two superpowers in an effort to discover, describe and elucidate the major features of

3

their confrontations, and in particular the methods or procedures they have devised for controlling and regulating such crises. Is it possible, for example, to see general and recurring patterns of behaviour, or was each crisis handled on an individual and entirely *ad hoc* basis? Can one legitimately talk of 'rules' of crisis management and, if so, what is the basis for such 'rules'? In addition to dealing with these questions, the following essay also tries to assess the extent to which crisis management is a novel phenomenon and one unique to the period since 1945. It does not pretend to add anything substantially new to the story of individual crises, but by providing a synthesis of the existing literature may add a fresh perspective and, it is hoped, some useful insights into the crisis behaviour of the superpowers.

II Difficulties of Analysis

Even this relatively limited task of reflecting and commenting upon the crisis management techniques of the United States and the USSR encounters formidable difficulties, not all of which can be overcome. Perhaps the most serious problem is that of obtaining reliable data. Any analysis of relatively recent events cannot avoid resting in large part upon scattered insights and fragmentary and inconclusive evidence. In the case of superpower crises there is, of course, the added problem of a marked asymmetry between our knowledge of United States decision-making processes and the information that we have about the calculations and influences that proved decisive in the Soviet Union. Commentary in the West about Soviet crisis behaviour is almost invariably speculative and uncertain, not least because there are few 'inside' or participant accounts of the decision-making process within the Kremlin during superpower confrontations. Put at its simplest, there is no equivalent on the Soviet side of, for example, Robert Kennedy's very personal but highly illuminating analysis of the Cuban Missile Crisis as seen by an influential and knowledgeable member of the United States decision-making group. Although it may be true that those who make history are sometimes prone to rewrite it, participant accounts of such events are of considerable value and provide insights that would otherwise be unobtainable. In the case of the Soviet Union – and, indeed, Communist China – such insights are either non-existent or inaccessible. Not surprisingly this is reflected in the relative paucity of literature about the crisis decisions of the Soviet Union. As one very thorough review of the available material concluded:

> In contrast to the rich accumulation of United States foreign policy case studies, the literature on Soviet foreign policy in particular crises or periods is small, fragmented, and underdeveloped. Clearly, data constraints have discouraged growth of a Soviet case study literature . . . even of the conventional non-theoretically oriented type.[1]

The problem is exacerbated by the fact that the present writer has no knowledge of the Russian language and therefore has to rely exclusively on Western sources.

There are two consequences of this. In the first place it ensures that the essay is uneven. There is an almost unavoidable bias towards an analysis of superpower crisis management from a United States perspective, and far more attention is given to the American decision-making process than to that of the Soviet Union. Secondly, it means that statements about Soviet behaviour are necessarily more tentative than those relating to the United States. It is possible to draw inferences from Soviet actions about the considerations that may have been important to Soviet decision-makers; it is impossible to establish unequivocally that these inferences are the correct ones. Any conclusions that are derived from such an analysis, therefore, must be treated with a considerable degree of caution.

Another kind of difficulty arises in deciding which crises are to be examined and which omitted. On what criteria is such a choice to be based? There is no simple or systematic answer to this question and, as a result, there is inevitably something arbitrary about the selection that is made here. Indeed, it may suffer from both sins of omission and sins of commission. As a guiding principle, however, it takes into account those confrontations that appeared to involve a distinct possibility that large-scale military hostilities might erupt – either between the United States and the Soviet Union or between the United States and Communist China.

Some of the crises examined here fall very clearly into this category. The Berlin Crises of 1948 and 1961 and the Cuban

Missile Crisis of 1962 are obvious examples. So too is the Taiwan Crisis of 1958, although in this case the Chinese People's Republic was the principal opponent of the United States. The Soviet–American interactions that occurred simultaneously, however, are also worthy of analysis and demonstrate that the two superpowers were entirely aware of the dangers inherent in the situation. Attention is also given to the brief superpower crises that developed as a result of the hostilities in the Middle East in 1967 and 1973. In both crises, a clash of superpower forces, although not imminent, was certainly not sufficiently remote that Soviet and American decision-makers felt able to ignore the possibility. Perhaps a more surprising inclusion is the outbreak of the Korean War and the American decision to commit ground forces to the aid of South Korea in June 1950. Although this is not usually considered as a superpower crisis, it did contain some of the elements of such a confrontation, largely because the relationship between North Korea and the Soviet Union was extremely close. In fact, the decision-makers in Washington saw the North Korean attack not only as something that was inspired and supported by Moscow, but also as symbolic of the new, more aggressive foreign policy being adopted by Stalin. Consequently, the American response was directed far more towards the Soviet Union than towards North Korea, being designed primarily to demonstrate the costs and risks inherent in such a policy. In the event, Soviet–American hostilities were avoided. China and the United States, however, were less fortunate. Thus the events leading to the Chinese intervention in the Korean War are explored briefly in order to highlight more clearly dangers that, in the other confrontations since 1945, have on the whole been moderated or overcome. In addition, occasional references are made to the crisis of July 1914, especially where it seems that the contrast with contemporary crisis behaviour is illuminating or emphasises particular problems with which decision-makers still have to contend.

It could be objected, of course, that this selection omits situations like the conflict over Iran in 1946, the Suez episode of 1956 or the United States intervention in the Middle East in 1958. The crucial point, however, is that none of these events appears to meet the criterion for inclusion. In 1946 the dispute over Iran was conducted solely on the diplomatic level and there seems to have been little prospect of it escalating towards military hostilities between the superpowers. In relation to the Suez intervention the United States and the Soviet Union were not even on opposing sides. Although the criticisms by the United States of the Anglo–French military action against Egypt were far more muted and restrained than the savage verbal denunciations issued by the Soviet Union, the fundamental positions of the two superpowers were not that far apart. The intervention in the Lebanon in 1958 is slightly different in that the United States did use its military power to eliminate what was seen as a threat of a Communist takeover in a pro-Western state. At the same time, though, it was not a situation that threatened to bring the United States into direct military conflict with the opposing superpower, and seems to have been of only marginal importance to the Soviet Union. It is, of course, impossible to eliminate a residual uncertainty about the accuracy of such judgements, but it seems reasonable to suggest that these episodes are very different from those referred to in the previous paragraph and do not warrant inclusion in the following discussion.

Their exclusion has the added advantage of reducing the analysis to more manageable proportions. Several problems remain outstanding, however. Not the least of these concerns the extent to which valid and reliable generalisations can be made about crisis behaviour. It is sometimes argued that each crisis is historically unique or, in the words of one analyst, a 'one-time event'.[2] The thesis is very persuasive. Postwar confrontations between the United States and the Soviet Union have varied substantially in terms of their geographical location, the issues at stake, the personalities most directly concerned and the military capabilities at the disposal of the participants. Such differences, particularly when coupled with the relatively small number of case studies being examined, set obvious and definite limits to the degree of confidence with which generalisations or predictions about crisis behaviour can be made. Indeed, this is another reason why the conclusions to emerge from a study of this kind should be treated with caution. But care must also be taken not to go to the opposite extreme and ignore the fact that, as well as having many idiosyncratic features, crises share certain common characteristics.

One way to cope with this dilemma is to adopt what has been described by Alexander George and Richard Smoke as the method of 'focused comparison', a method that enables the analyst to go beyond the particular and unique without ignoring the existence of differences between events that may be as crucial as any similarities.[3] By looking in depth at eleven case studies relating to the operation of deterrence and asking the same set of questions in each case, George and Smoke ensure that the same variables are employed throughout their investigation. Because of the limited number of cases and the fairly rich detail of their analysis, however, they are able to account explicitly for the variation in these factors from case to case. 'With this method the investigator is able . . . to uncover similarities among cases that suggest possible generalizations, but he is also able to investigate the differences among cases in a systematic manner.'[4] Consequently, it is possible to identify the differing circumstances or causes that led to variations in outcomes, and proceed from these to note 'contingent generalisations' regarding the conditions under which deterrence is likely to succeed or fail.[5]

The approach adopted here is far less systematic in that it does not try to isolate and assess particular variables by explicitly asking the same set of questions in relation to each crisis. Nor does it formally analyse each crisis as a distinct case study. Indeed, it was felt that to describe and discuss a number of case studies in detail and then try to extrapolate general principles from them would lead in the present work to a compartmentalised analysis divided far too rigidly between empirical material and theoretical conclusions. The alternative adopted here attempts to blend together the empirical and the theoretical, but this also has its drawbacks. Perhaps most significantly, it involves a certain degree of repetitiveness as each situation is examined from several distinct perspectives in an attempt to identify and describe different facets of crisis behaviour. The impression of repetitiveness tends to be reinforced by the fact that the same decision or action sometimes fulfils several functions and contributes in a variety of different ways to the control of superpower crises – with the result that it has to be discussed at several stages in the analysis.

Fortunately these difficulties are not such as to preclude or prohibit all attempts at generalisation. Where this is done, though, it is only after careful and detailed examination of the crises specified in search of what can appropriately be described as counter-examples – that is, instances of behaviour that deviate markedly from the overall pattern suggested by the bulk of the available evidence. So long as no counter-examples are discovered, then it appears reasonable to argue that certain modes of action are more likely than others or that certain conditions make one outcome as opposed to another more probable.

No attempt is made to accord these tentative generalisations the status of scientific laws, and, in this sense, what is largely a methodological problem clearly has substantive implications. In so far as it may be possible to discern or discover 'rules' of behaviour, for example, they should not be regarded as rules from which no deviation is possible. This point is emphasised by Professor Laurence Martin in his warning that 'any attempt to develop a general technique for crisis management inevitably runs the risk of establishing rules that are too crude to do justice to the rich variety of reality'.[6] Not only is this a valid objection against regarding crisis management as an exact science in which it is possible to formulate immutable rules for statesmen to follow unquestioningly, but it is also an indispensable antidote to any temptation to conceptualise and rationalise the actions of decision-makers to a greater extent than is warranted. It may be that in parts of the following analysis this temptation has proved overwhelming. Thus it is essential to keep constantly in mind that crisis management, far from being a science, is an art in which the traditional qualities of statesmanship – wisdom, diplomatic skill and incisive judgement – can prove decisive, either through their presence or through their absence. Although crises cannot be analysed solely and exclusively in terms of the personalities involved, neither can any satisfactory account omit such considerations. It must be acknowledged at the outset therefore that decision-makers are guided more by their own experience and an intuitive 'rule of thumb' than by any precise formula. Consequently any attempt to develop a detailed blueprint for crisis management or to reduce it to a set of simple axioms and preordained rules can only prove sterile. It is the decision-makers who ultimately have to make the difficult choices, and any account that reduces them to the position of automatons following preconceived and pre-programmed options is almost certainly untenable.

This kind of caveat about crisis management probably applies with particular force to the behaviour of the Soviet Union. Indeed, it could be argued that the idea of crisis management is a peculiarly Western concept – developed amidst the general euphoria that followed the peaceful resolution of the Cuban Missile Crisis – and that the Soviet Union acknowledges neither its relevance nor its importance, and perhaps not even its existence. Against this, however, must be set the fact that the Soviet Union has been engaged in occasional confrontations with the United States and, in practice, has probably learned to cope with such situations in a manner that is not entirely dissimilar to that of its adversary. Merely because there is no formal Soviet recognition of crisis management as a distinct type of behaviour does not necessarily mean that the Soviet leaders have not developed procedures and techniques designed to contain within tolerable limits their confrontations with the opposing superpower. In short, the danger of over-conceptualisation is a significant but not overwhelming problem.

It may be objected, however, that the sum total of all these difficulties is such as to render any investigation a perilous undertaking of dubious value. Yet there are very compelling reasons for going ahead with such an analysis despite its attendant disabilities and deficiencies. The present work in fact rests upon certain assumptions about the importance of crises as a focus of attention which must now be made explicit.

III   The Importance of International Crises

The first, although in many respects the least intellectual, reason for examining crises is that they have a curiously macabre fascination – for policy-makers and publics as well as academic analysts. Indeed, an international confrontation is one of the few occurrences that, temporarily at any rate, can jolt mass publics out of their traditional apathy towards foreign policy and international politics. Furthermore, such crises provide the supreme challenge to the wisdom, resourcefulness and courage of the decision-makers involved. It may be that the test of combat for the warrior finds an equivalent in the test of nerve for the diplomat. Just as a general's reputation rests ultimately upon his skill in military campaigns, a statesman's reputation depends in large part upon his ability to lead the way through the intricacies and dangers of crisis diplomacy. The names Chamberlain and Munich, for example, are almost synonymous, and whatever the British prime minister's other achievements, his standing – at least in the popular mind – has been damaged perhaps beyond repair by what appears as a paralysis of the will when faced with the formidable challenge of Nazi Germany. Conversely, John Kennedy's reputation has retained considerable prestige through what is often regarded as his superb handling of the Cuban confrontation in 1962. Such judgements are not necessarily accurate. Nevertheless, they illustrate the symbolic importance that may be attached to international crises.

A more substantial consideration underlying the present study is the belief that crises are one of the most significant phenomena in interstate relations, and deserve and demand attention as such. As a focus for research and analysis, crises may yield fruitful insights into several aspects of international politics and foreign policy-making. Glenn Snyder has put the point very well:

> An international crisis is international politics in microcosm. That is to say, a crisis tends to highlight or force to the surface a wide range of factors and processes which are central to international politics in general. Such elements as power configurations, interests, values, risks, perceptions, degrees of resolve, bargaining, and decision-making lie at the core of international politics; in a crisis they tend to leap out at the observer, to be combined and related in a revealing way, and to be sharply focused on a single, well-defined issue.[7]

Indeed, the very occurrence of international crises is symptomatic of the anarchic nature of interstate politics. In a situation where there is no central authority to control the behaviour of a large number of autonomous political units, conflicts of interest are perennial. Blatant and direct military clashes are often avoided, of course, through mutual accommodation and restraint and careful calculations of self-interest. Nevertheless, some conflicts of interest are so intense that crises in which threats of force figure prominently are impossible to avoid. As a result, the possibility of hostilities which is always latent in international politics becomes far less remote. 'The element of potential war is elevated from an underlying to a central and imminent position.'[8]

It is because crises lie at the crucial threshold between peace and war that they are of profound interest to strategic analysts. Almost invariably they provide clear and dramatic examples of statesmen using force or the threat of force in support of their foreign policy objectives. Consequently, any balanced assessment of the role of military force in contemporary international politics must include some reference to the postwar crises identified above and consideration of the part played by 'coercive diplomacy' in their resolution. Furthermore, an empirical study of crisis behaviour may prove a useful counter-weight to some of the more abstract theories of bargaining and risk-taking presented in the strategic studies literature. Options such as escalation and commitment, which appear highly attractive for a hypothetical 'strategic man' concerned with maximising his gains, may have far less appeal for the real-world decision-makers caught up in the midst of a crisis and acutely conscious of the disastrous results of a wrong move.[9] Thus the present study may be a useful opportunity to assess the utility and the limitations of the coercive bargaining techniques made familiar by analysts like Thomas Schelling and Herman Kahn, and particularly the extent to which such tactics have actually been adopted by decision-makers in the United States and the Soviet Union.[10]

More generally, the study of international crises may contribute to our understanding of, and knowledge about, war. This is not to suggest that the outbreak of hostilities between states can be explained solely in terms of the crisis that may have preceded it. Such an assertion would be both foolish and misleading. Merely because an analysis of crises cannot provide a full explanation for the occurrence of war, however, makes it neither irrelevant nor superfluous. The causes of war are many and varied: they are general and highly specific, long-term and immediate. Nevertheless, it would be impossible to provide a wholly satisfactory analysis of the causes of the First World War, for example, without devoting considerable attention to the crisis of July 1914 which precipitated hostilities. Popular nationalism, inflexible military alliances and a series of intense arms races were all factors that increased tension and set the European states on the road towards war; but the final decisive steps were taken in the diplomatic crisis resulting from the assassination of the Archduke Franz Ferdinand. An examination of the calculations and miscalculations of the great powers in the July Crisis is therefore indispensable to any account of the origins of the 1914–18 war.

The converse of all this is also true: an analysis of crisis behaviour – particularly for the period since 1945 – can help to explain the maintenance of peace as well as the outbreak of war. Nor should it be thought that crises cease to be important merely because they punctuate periods of peace rather than highlight the transition from peace to war. An international crisis almost invariably has a pronounced impact on the relationship of the protagonists.[11] On the one hand, it might crystallise and solidify their hostility, thereby making future confrontations more likely. Alternatively, the crisis could resolve some of the outstanding issues dividing the participants and thus prepare the way for the establishment of a more stable and harmonious long-term relationship. The Berlin Crisis of 1948 had consequences of the first kind: it was an important landmark in the intensification of the Cold War and East–West rivalry. Although there had been some tentative moves towards greater Western cohesion prior to the crisis, it was the confrontation over Berlin that evoked quick decisive action and hastened the signing of the North Atlantic Treaty. The Cuban Missile Crisis probably had the second type of consequence, at least to the extent that it helped promote *détente* and the mellowing of superpower conflict. Although crises are not always distinct turning points in international politics, at a minimum they tend to strengthen pre-existing trends. Furthermore, the behaviour of the participants in a crisis will affect not only their images of each other – and thereby their future attitudes and behaviour towards one another – but also the images that other states hold of them. Once conceived, these images may be difficult to change. Even when a crisis is resolved without open hostilities, therefore, its repercussions will usually be pervasive if not always immediately dramatic.

Another attraction of crises as a focus for attention is that they can also be approached from the perspective of the foreign policy analyst.[12] The emphasis in this approach is placed not on the interactions of the protagonists but on the internal decision-making procedures and mechanisms of the states involved. A crisis is essentially a self-contained occurrence with a distinct and identifiable beginning, middle and end. Thus it may be possible to analyse the whole sequence of activities involved in the formulation and execution of policies by the participants. The decision-makers' initial assessments of the situation, their discussions of alternative proposals for dealing with it, the detailed implementation of the option finally chosen as well as any modifications or alterations resulting from the adversary's response can all be examined in considerable depth – on the American side at least. Nor is this the only advantage of such an approach. A high level of stress is almost inevitably an integral feature of international crises. Consequently, the study of crisis decision-making provides an excellent opportunity to assess the effects of stress on political systems, and may yield useful insights into their resilience and adaptability. It may also enable the analyst to examine whether or not statesmen can think and act rationally when exposed to a high level of stress. A most useful and rewarding exercise, in fact, would be to compare and contrast decision-making in a crisis with the formulation of policy under normal conditions. Not only would this facilitate a more balanced assessment of the impact of stress, it might also enable the analyst to discern whether or not crisis decision-making tends to be more efficient than routine foreign policy-making.

The implication of all this is that the sustained and systematic analysis of international crises has much to recommend it, a conclusion that is perhaps no less valid merely because there has been a transition from Cold War to *détente*. Although both the frequency and intensity of superpower crises have decreased in the last decade this does not necessarily mean that they will cease to be a recurring feature of international politics in the forseeable future. East–West *détente* does not preclude occasional confrontation, carrying with it the risk of nuclear holocaust. Indeed, it would be foolish to suggest that all the potential conflicts of interest in the superpower relationship either have been, or can be, eliminated. Although a concern with 'crisis prevention' is perhaps becoming a more significant element in superpower calculations, this is no guarantee that dramatic and dangerous confrontations can be avoided. Nor can the possibility of crises between lesser states be eliminated. The changing constellation of power and alignment, more intense competition for energy resources, widespread nuclear proliferation and increased militancy in the underdeveloped nations add great uncertainties to the future, and augur ill for a world free of international crises.

Furthermore, as was suggested above, crises are almost certainly endemic to the state system. To prevent them altogether would necessitate extensive and unrealistic changes in the nature of international politics. Whereas complete crisis prevention would be a radical measure involving a thorough restructuring of the international system, crisis management is far more a palliative, designed to deal with the existing state of affairs. It is concerned in part with the control and regulation of crises once they have occurred, and the procedures whereby a peaceful outcome can more readily be achieved.

This preoccupation with the management as opposed to the prevention or avoidance of crises can be criticised, of course, on the grounds that it is merely a temporary expedient offering little opportunity for long-term improvement in the international system. There is some justification for such arguments, but it is important to remember that survival is the first prerequisite of change and that, although the techniques of crisis management can offer no guarantee that nuclear war will be avoided, without them the likelihood of such a war would be far greater. As John Garnett has argued, it is little use trying 'to abolish that which cannot be abolished'. The important thing is 'to manage it success-fully so that wars . . . become less rather than more frequent occurrences in international politics'.[13] The present work reflects this bias in its preoccupation with the way superpower crises since 1945 have been managed and resolved. It touches on some of the other aspects of international crises discussed above, but explores them at length only when they relate to the major theme. The way this theme is developed must now be outlined.

IV   A Preliminary Overview

The essay is divided broadly into two parts. The first section sets out, initially, to analyse the concept of crisis management and then attempts to place it in context as one of the modes of behaviour adopted by the superpowers in their attempt to come to terms with the dangers and opportunities of the nuclear age. The second and much more detailed section examines crisis management *in action*. It elaborates, so far as is possible, the way decisions have been made in superpower confrontations as well as the techniques that have been used by the participants in their efforts to control or dampen down such conflicts, resolve their differences and restore, if not a harmonious relationship, at least one in which the dangers and risks are not wholly unacceptable. This is, of course, a very general summary and it may be useful, therefore, to provide a slightly more detailed account of the contents before proceeding further.

The main concern in chapter two is with exploring the concepts of 'crisis' and 'crisis management'. As well as examining some fairly well-established distinctions between different types of crisis, the chapter outlines the major features of superpower confrontations and attempts to assess the implications of the various characteristics. Perhaps the most important consideration to emerge from this discussion is the sheer intractability of such crises and the enormity of the task faced by decision-makers charged with the responsibility for their control and management. The specific nature of this task is identified more fully in the subsequent analysis of crisis management. As part of this analysis, the diverse meanings given to the concept are discussed and an effort made to synthesise and reconcile some of the conflicting interpretations propounded in the literature.

The following two chapters examine, albeit in a cursory manner, the process whereby crisis management has become a matter of major concern. That it was not always so is suggested by the discussion in chapter three, particularly the brief analysis of the Sarajevo Crisis. As attitudes towards the use of military force in international politics have changed, however, so has the peaceful resolution of crises become much more significant. This transformation of attitudes is outlined further in chapter four, which – like the previous chapter – is based on the premise that beliefs about the legitimacy and efficacy of military force are a vital factor in government deliberations during international crises. The differences between pre-nuclear and nuclear crises are examined in relation to these changes, and it is suggested that in the nuclear age both Soviet and American decision-makers constantly have to reconcile the desire to attain their policy objectives with the need to avoid large-scale hostilities against the adversary. This has significant implications for the willingness of the superpowers to take risks, but has not prohibited such behaviour. Indeed, it is suggested that, on occasion, the United States and the USSR have been prepared to take actions liable to precipitate a showdown with the opponent. Nor are they wholly unwilling to continue their risk-taking behaviour during the crisis itself as part of the attempt to secure their objectives. At the same time they do not want the confrontation to end in war. Thus, when crises occur risks must be controlled and dangers moderated.

The dangers of war, in fact, stem from three distinct aspects of crises and crisis behaviour. There are first of all the dangers that arise from possible defects and deficiencies in the decision-making processes of the governments involved. Secondly, there are certain dangers that are intrinsic to crisis situations and encompass risks and uncertainties that are neither intended nor entirely controlled by the participants. Finally, there are the risks that are deliberately created during the bargaining process, whereby the superpowers try to gain certain advantages and further promote their interests. Although these dangers are not unrelated to each other, the division is a useful one for analytical purposes, and forms the basis for the three main chapters in part two.

Chapter five examines the way decisions are made in superpower crises and suggests that, although there are several problems such as stress that threaten to impair or disrupt the decision-making process, their impact should not be overestimated. The problems cannot be dismissed as insignificant, but in past superpower crises at least they do not seem to have been overwhelming. In the American case (and it is in the context of decision-making that the asymmetry of information discussed above is most pronounced and particularly onerous) crisis decision-making appears to demonstrate a fairly high degree of rationality in which political and bureaucratic factors intrude to a lesser extent than is usual in foreign policy-making. Decisions tend to emerge from a small, select, top-level command group formed specifically to handle the crisis and, seemingly, able to operate in a relatively efficient manner.

A major problem for such groups is the need to maintain control over events and prevent them from developing a logic or momentum of their own. Thus chapter six looks initially at the possible ways in which events could become uncontrollable. After this speculative survey of potential dangers, it examines the available counter-measures and describes the means whereby, in practice, the superpowers have retained their freedom of choice and avoided becoming locked into a situation that could degenerate rapidly and inexorably into war. Perhaps the most significant point to emerge is the importance that the superpowers seem to have attached to the distinction between coercion and violence. Although the Soviet Union and the United States have been prepared to threaten one another, they have been far less willing to resort to overt violence, largely because of a feeling that once this threshold has been crossed the prospects for avoiding large-scale war diminish drastically. They have also attempted to minimise the possibility of accidental or unauthorised violence in the belief that even a localised violent incident could spark off a potentially uncontrollable escalation. In addition, it appears that decision-makers in Washington and Moscow alike have been loathe to allow either their subordinates or allied governments the kind of discretion that could undermine their own freedom of choice and manoeuvre.

Even if such problems are overcome, however, there remain the dangers involved in the bargaining process. These are examined in chapter seven. As in the previous chapter, the discussion begins with a speculative analysis of potential difficulties and dangers. In this instance though this is done by creating what could almost be described as a 'model' of an *unrestrained bargaining process*, based on the tactics discussed by Schelling and Kahn and those that were adopted by Hitler in the 1930s. Although there is something slightly artificial about this, it provides a useful way of highlighting some of the dangers and enables us better to understand the actual moves made by the superpowers. Indeed, it appears that in practice the superpowers have not only avoided the more dangerous techniques but have devised tactics that are both more acceptable and more effective. Mutual recognition of the basic structure of the crisis, the introduction of conciliatory gestures and the use of both formal and informal communication channels have all been important in this connection. They are discussed at some length in chapter seven. Finally, the major conclusions derived from the analysis are presented in chapter eight.

CHAPTER TWO

The Concept of Crisis Management

I Foreign Policy Crises and International Crises

In the analysis of international politics, it is sometimes very easy to become obsessed with semantics at the expense of substance. Although it is necessary to clarify the terms being used, an excessive preoccupation with definitional problems can lead to sterile discussion in which analysis of substantive issues tends to be peripheral if not non-existent. Furthermore, it has to be recognised that many of the phenomena of international politics are too complex to be encapsulated in a single definition, however neat and logical. On the other hand, clarity, precision and a degree of consistency in the terms being adopted are essential. Consequently, the present chapter aims to define both the concepts of 'crisis' and 'crisis management' as a precursor to a more detailed examination of how the superpower crises of the postwar world have been handled and mishandled. It is hoped that the discussion will further establish the boundaries of the present work and also provide a basis for the arguments contained in subsequent chapters.

The task is not an easy one. Any attempt to define the notion of crisis encounters formidable problems. Yet it is these very problems that make it imperative that the attempt be made. A major difficulty arises from an excessive and indiscriminate use of the word. Seldom has any term been asked to carry so many meanings or serve so many different purposes as the word 'crisis'. Because it carries powerful emotional connotations, for example, it can be used by governments as a device to rally support or silence dissent. In times of crisis or national emergency a government may acquire wider powers and the public tolerate actions or policies that, under normal conditions, it would have rejected decisively. Thus a situation may be defined as a crisis in the hope that this will secure acquiescence in options that might otherwise be unpalatable or unacceptable.

This instrumental use of the term is merely one cause of its linguistic proliferation. Equally important is the fact that it can be used to describe such a wide variety of different situations. It is possible, for example, to talk of an emotional crisis or a financial crisis – the former perhaps precipitated by the latter in some instances. Furthermore, the term can be applied equally well on the global level as on the individual level. The crisis of capitalism, the crisis of civilisation, the energy crisis and the environmental crisis are all terms used in relation to problems that have a global or near-global range. In addition to varying in scope, however, crises appear to vary enormously in duration. Thus, one very eminent historian has described international politics during the interwar period as 'The Twenty Years Crisis', while for other analysts the term denotes an event or situation that is confined within a much shorter period of time, and is measured in days or weeks rather than years.[1] The fact that the term is so elastic in its interpretation almost certainly contributes to its over-zealous adoption.

This widespread use, if not abuse, of the word 'crisis' to describe very disparate events and situations has often been coupled with a tendency to regard it as virtually self-explanatory. As one analyst has pointed out: 'everybody' knows when a crisis occurs.[2] The results of this have not been entirely beneficial for academic research into crises and crisis behaviour. Because a crisis is easily recognisable, the term has tended all too often 'to be used without explanation and with the tacit assumption that its general meaning will somehow be understood. Unfortunately, the assumption does not appear to be a safe one, and the result is a great deal of confusion about the precise meaning of the concept.'[3] The development of interest in international crises stimulated by the Cuban Missile Crisis of 1962 and sharpened by the appearance in 1968 of Oran Young's seminal work, *The Politics of Force*, has done something to rectify this. Indeed, it has led to a series of systematic attempts to endow the concept with a greater degree of precision.[1] Such efforts, though, have been impaired by the fact that different analysts tend to approach crises from different perspectives. Although the availability of different 'analytical perspectives' may be one of the attractions of studying crises, it is not without significant drawbacks and has been a major hindrance to the attainment of a greater degree of consistency in the use of the term than has yet been achieved.[5]

To suggest that the perspective problem is unique to the analysis of crises, however, would be misleading. It is a more general difficulty that may be inherent in the study of international politics. The term 'limited war', for example, is sometimes used to refer to hostilities that, from the viewpoint of the global system, are circumscribed in both scope and impact, even though they may be anything but limited from the perspective of one or other of the participants. American involvement in Vietnam clearly illustrates this. Looked at from the vantage point of the international system, the hostilities fell squarely into the category of limited war: they were, on the whole, contained within a carefully defined geographical area. For the United States too it was a limited war, fought for limited political objectives and employing limited, although far from insubstantial, means. For Hanoi, on the other hand, the war was virtually total in its intensity. The North Vietnamese objective was total victory and, although the means at its disposal were absolutely far smaller than the American war effort, as a proportion of the total resources available to the combatants they probably represented a far greater effort. Whether or not the war could be regarded as limited, therefore, depended in part upon whether one was sitting in Hanoi or Washington. The war looked very different too, depending on whether it was examined from inside or outside the immediate area of hostilities.

Similar, if not identical, problems face the analyst of crises. The difficulty is that what provides a crisis for one state may not be a crisis for another, or be regarded as such by outside observers. Thus it seems important to establish a distinction between what could most appropriately be called a *foreign policy crisis*, and an *international crisis*.[6] The distinction should not be overdrawn. Nevertheless, it is a significant if a subtle one. Perhaps the best way of clarifying it is to suggest that a foreign policy crisis involves an urgent problem facing a *single* government, whereas an international crisis involves certain kinds of stresses and strains in the relationship *between* governments.

Although the two kinds of crisis are not synonymous, neither are they mutually exclusive. A foreign policy crisis can be – although it need not be – part of an international crisis, whereas an international crisis invariably involves at least two foreign policy crises. The difference, therefore, is partly a matter of substance. It is also a matter of conceptualisation, however, and depends on whether one adopts a bird's-eye view, which focuses on the overall relationship and pattern of interaction among the participants, or a decision-making perspective, in which the situation is examined through the eyes of the policy-makers themselves.

The term 'foreign policy crisis' then is both broader and narrower than 'international crisis'. It is broader in the sense that it is less specific and is applicable to a greater variety of situations than those usually encompassed by the term 'international crisis'. It is narrower in that it applies only to the predicament of a single state. A foreign policy crisis has been defined as a situation facing the decision-makers of a particular government which poses a high threat to their values and objectives, takes them by surprise and gives them little time in which to formulate a response.[7] The international situation can be seen as providing the 'occasion for decision' and is treated analytically as a crucial input to the decision-making process.[8] This is a crisis in much the same way as a natural disaster such as an earthquake or a flood is a crisis. The problem it presents for policy-makers is how to respond quickly and effectively. They must ensure that its worst effects are ameliorated and its potential for damage and disruption is contained or reduced.

Looked at in this way, the notion of a foreign policy crisis admits of situations going well beyond the idea of a crisis as involving a deliberate challenge from, or provocative actions by, a rival power. The element of confrontation is a possible, and perhaps even a probable, ingredient of many foreign policy crises; it is certainly not a prerequisite for one. The revolution in the Dominican Republic in 1965 provides a useful example of a foreign policy crisis – in this instance for the United States – in which the element of showdown between two governments was completely absent.[9] Indeed, it was events within Santa Dominica that were perceived in Washington as constituting sufficient *threat* to require the intervention of about twenty thousand American troops. Not only did the uprising take the Johnson

Administration by *surprise*, but it was regarded as the precursor to the establishment of a left-wing government on the island. The United States was particularly sensitive to this possibility since it would have signalled the end of Cuba's isolation as the only communist state in Latin America, and further undermined the American objective of keeping the western hemisphere free of communism.[10] Coupled with this, of course, was the *short time* available for the United States to decide upon an appropriate and effective response. If the apparent threat to American interests was to be eliminated, intervention had to be quick and decisive. Thus the three essential elements of a classic foreign policy crisis were present.

Many other examples could readily be given. The 1956 uprising in Hungary is one. The difficulties faced by Moscow in this crisis were not entirely different from those with which the United States had to contend in the Dominican Republic. Indeed, the threat to the Soviet political system was probably far more real, and certainly more far-reaching in its implications, than that posed to American objectives by the Dominican revolt. It is hardly surprising, therefore, that the response it elicited was even more forceful and dramatic than President Johnson's. The present purpose, however, is not to compare and contrast the two situations or the superpower reactions, but merely to illustrate what is meant by the term 'foreign policy crisis'.

An international crisis, on the other hand, is broader in that it is concerned with a particular type of relationship between *two* or more states. Having said this, it is obvious that, conceptually at least, any international crisis can be broken down into several discrete foreign policy crises, with each side's action being treated as a problem for the opponent. This kind of exercise has much merit. It creates an awareness that an international crisis may differ in its intensity from one participant to the next. The threat to the values and objectives of one of the protagonists may be greater than the threat it in turn presents to its adversary. Similarly, the time pressures may be far less acute for one side than the other. Throughout the following analysis, therefore, it is kept in mind that an international crisis tends to look very different from the vantage points of the rival capitals. Nevertheless, such a crisis can be understood fully only if seen in terms of the interaction of the participants. The central concern must be the way their relationship develops and the kind of exchanges that take place between them.

It is in this sense that the term 'international crisis' is narrower and more select than 'foreign policy crisis'. Indeed, it has very distinct connotations, the most important of which are the elements of direct confrontation – of challenge and provocation. These features are always implied by the term 'international crisis'. It is not a matter of events causing problems but of two or more states coming into direct and dramatic conflict. As Coral Bell has written:

> The essence of true crisis in any given relationship is that the conflicts within it rise to a level which threatens to transform the nature of the relationship . . . The concept is of normal strain rising to the level of breaking strain.[11]

This is deliberately a very general description of crises, concerning most areas of activity, and it can usefully be applied to other disciplines as well as international politics. It is also extremely valuable within the discipline itself, of course, and Professor Bell uses it as the basis for distinguishing between two types of international crisis: those between allies and those between adversaries. The breaking strain in 'intra-alliance' or 'intra-mural' crises refers to a possible transformation in the relationship of the states involved from friendship to enmity; in 'adversary' crises to the possible transition from peace to war.[12] The scope of the present study, however, encompasses only the latter type of situation. It concentrates exclusively on crises between adversaries or potential enemies.

The main reason for this is that, although 'intra-mural' and 'adversary' crises share some common features, the differences between them may be even more significant. Stresses and strains in a relationship among states with similar goals and values, a relatively high degree of trust and a tradition of co-operation are very different in degree, and perhaps even in kind, from the increased strain and tension that periodically occur in a relationship based on mutual suspicion, hostility and consistent, although sometimes muted, opposition to one another's goals and ambitions. Thus it may be as well to treat 'intra-mural' conflicts as problems of *alliance management* rather than crisis management, reserving the latter term exclusively for adversary crises.[13]

Indeed, when the term 'international crisis' is used in the

present study it refers only to a confrontation between adversaries, or what one analyst has called 'the acute international
crisis'.[14] An attempt must now be made, therefore, to provide a
fuller and more specific definition of such situations. Oran
Young has taken the following definition for operational
purposes:

> A crisis in international politics is a process of interaction occurring
> at higher levels of perceived intensity than the ordinary flow of
> events and characterized by: a sharp break from the ordinary
> flow of politics; shortness of duration; a rise in the perceived
> prospects that violence will break out; and significant implications
> for the stability of some system (or pattern of relationships) in
> international politics.[15]

While this definition is carefully thought out and has much to
recommend it, the following might be considered as a possible
alternative: *an international crisis is a confrontation of two or
more states, usually occupying a short time period, in which the
probability of an outbreak of war between the participants is
perceived to increase significantly.*

Whether there is any real, as opposed to merely a perceived,
increase in the likelihood of war during a crisis is, of course,
uncertain. Young has suggested that 'the rise in the perceived
prospects that violence will break out' tends to stimulate such
vigorous actions by the decision-makers involved to prevent it
that the probability of an outbreak may diminish rather than
increase.[16] Herman Kahn has argued in a very similar vein that
'nobody really knows what the probability of war is under
different circumstances. We do not even know whether it goes
up or down in a tense situation. It is, for example, quite conceivable that the extra care or concern associated with a tense
situation might more than make up for the seeming extra
danger'.[17]

Nevertheless, it would be foolish to overlook the need for this
extra care and concern. There are several features of international crises, including those between the superpowers, that
make them potentially explosive.[18] The very fact that an international crisis involves a high threat to important values and
objectives of the participants is of the utmost significance.
Furthermore, the protagonists may believe that the outcome of
the crisis will have far-reaching import for their future rela-

tionship *and* their future power and status in the international community. If so it is not only their immediate objectives that will be jeopardised but also their long-term aspirations. In such circumstances the use of force may become a less unattractive option than under more normal conditions, particularly if it appears that other possible ways of settling the issue in dispute are exhausted, ineffective or inappropriate.

In addition, the feeling of being threatened may evoke a hasty and ill-considered response. This is made more likely by several other characteristics usually associated with crisis situations. The increased rapidity of events, for example, almost inevitably means that decision-makers are faced with great uncertainties and imponderables in their efforts to assess the situation and devise alternative courses of action for dealing with it. Sensitive both to the seriousness of the problem with which they are faced and the need for a quick solution or decision, therefore, it seems likely that the participants will feel a strong sense of urgency.[19] This in turn could lead to a high degree of stress and anxiety, something that could impair their judgement and discrimination.

The sense of urgency and the scope for miscalculation are also likely to be increased by another vitally important characteristic of a crisis: namely that it involves reduced control over events and their effects. At the same time, this should not be exaggerated. One of the most basic facts of life in international politics is that, at the best of times, statesmen have only a very tenuous control over events.[20] Even if they foresee certain problems or dangers looming ahead, for example, there is often nothing they can do to avoid them.[21] In this respect the difference between a crisis and non-crisis situation is one of degree rather than kind. It remains significant, though, and helps to differentiate a crisis from the ordinary flow of international politics. Indeed, where the degree of control is already limited, any further reduction can have damaging consequences. Thomas Schelling has put the point very well in his argument that one of the hallmarks of an international crisis is its sheer unpredictability. The participants, far from being in control of events, have to take steps and make decisions in a realm where the risks and uncertainties are almost overwhelming.[22]

Not surprisingly, therefore, the peaceful resolution of an international crisis is an awesome task. A crisis situation by its very nature is intractable and far from amenable to precise manipulation and control. Yet it is manipulation and control that lie at the heart of most discussions of crisis management. And it is to this concept that attention must now be given.

II Crisis Management

The problems attendant upon the notion of management are far less pronounced than those that encrust the concept of crisis. They are not totally absent, however, and, as Oran Young has asserted, the word 'management' is 'seldom defined precisely or employed consistently'.[23] Although Young is referring to its use in the wider and more general field of conflict management, his remark has considerable relevance to the present discussion. Indeed, Glenn Snyder has observed that 'the term crisis management has been used rather vaguely in the literature with a variety of meanings and emphases'.[24] Rather than elaborating what are often very subtle differences between the various interpretations, however, it seems more useful for present purposes to polarise the interpretations into two main schools of thought.

The first school consists of those who equate crisis management purely and simply with the peaceful resolution of confrontations. Success is *wholly* dependent upon the avoidance of war. Implicit in this view is the notion of a crisis as a *pathological* occurrence to be ended or defused as quickly as possible. The aim is to control the situation and dampen down the conflict. High risks must be avoided. It is argued that the central question for those involved is 'will this action make war more likely?' If the answer is 'yes', then less dangerous alternatives have to be found. The crisis itself is the real enemy, and the participants are actually partners in the task of eliminating the dangers of war and restoring things to normal. It is fully acknowledged that the fate of each state depends not only on its own behaviour but also on that of its opponent. Consequently, considerable emphasis is placed on the common interests of the participants.

The second school of thought about crisis management lies at the opposite extreme and interprets crisis management solely as an exercise in winning. The objective is to make the enemy back down, to gain concessions from him, and thereby to further one's ambitions in the international arena. Crises are not regarded as pathological or distasteful but rather as an opportunity for aggrandisement. It is the opposing state and not the crisis itself that is the enemy. Far from being a partnership, there is fierce competition or rivalry in which every attempt is made to manipulate or influence the adversary's behaviour in desired directions. The crucial question is not 'will this action increase the probability of war?' but 'will it force the adversary to capitulate?' If higher risks are necessary to achieve desired results then so be it. This is a far more parochial or selfish viewpoint in which successful crisis management is defined as maximum concessions by the adversary and minimum concessions by oneself: the ratio of gains to losses is the essential measure of performance. To put it slightly differently – and make the almost obligatory genuflection to game theory – it appears that this school of thought regards a crisis as a zero-sum situation in which the gains accruing to one side automatically mean a loss for the opponent. There is no conception of common interest uniting the participants, only of the conflicting interests that divide them. And crisis management is the art of ensuring that in this conflict of interests one's will prevails.

These two interpretations of crisis management are almost diametrically opposed, and it seems inconceivable that there could be any possible meeting ground between them. Yet this may not be so. The central problem with each of these analyses is that it completely ignores the other and provides only one part of the overall picture. Each interpretation offers considerable insight into crisis management, but the insight is incomplete and as a result gives a distorted view. Indeed, the essential point about crisis management is that it involves elements of *both* the activities just described.

To some extent, of course, this is reflected in the definitions that have actually appeared in the literature, as opposed to the deliberately more formal and extreme interpretations presented above. But even these definitions have generally leaned heavily to one side or the other. Leslie Lipson, for example, has defined crisis management as 'reaching a solution acceptable to both sides without resorting to war'.[25] This crystallises some of the central features of crisis management. Yet it gives insufficient attention to other equally important aspects. By virtually reducing the activity to a joint exercise in tension-reduction and problem-solving, it underplays the conflict that not only brought about the confrontation, but will tend to perpetuate or intensify it. The difficulty is that the participants do not readily agree on an acceptable solution. Each state usually attempts, at least initially, to impose a solution or engineer an outcome that is more favourable to itself than to the opponent.

If the element of conflict is underemphasised in Lipson's definition, however, it is given far more prominence in that enunciated by Kintner and Schwarz. They see crisis management as 'winning a crisis while at the same time keeping it within tolerable limits of danger and risk to both sides'.[26] But this goes too far in the opposite direction. Although fully acknowledging the competitive aspects, it pays barely more than lip service to the problem of controlling the crisis and bringing it to a peaceful conclusion. Indeed, there must be considerable doubt as to whether the notion of 'winning' is at all applicable to the concept of crisis management, let alone the very essence of it. Statesmen on both sides obviously must try to secure the objectives at stake in a confrontation; but if they want to prevent it escalating into war they cannot aim for total victory. To anticipate or strive for a complete surrender by the opponent could lead to disaster.

In other words, both definitions of crisis management are slightly misleading. Yet they complement and supplement one another very well. Lipson's emphasis on the avoidance of war and the resolution of the dispute has to be balanced against the emphasis placed by Kintner and Schwarz on obtaining national objectives. Nor is it surprising that crisis management encompasses both these activities when the dual nature of crises is considered. For as well as being periods of opportunity, crises, particularly in the nuclear age, are also times of danger.[27] Consequently they involve a strange mixture of *bilateral competition*, in which the primary purpose is to attain one's goals, and *shared danger*, in which priority is given to the reduction of risks and the avoidance of disaster.[28] Crisis management is essentially an attempt to balance and reconcile these diverse elements. There is almost inevitably a kind of schizophrenic quality about it, as those involved create risks while simultaneously trying to ensure that their risk-taking behaviour has no uncontrollable or unintended consequences that might result in war. As the present writer has argued elsewhere:

> . . . crisis management is concerned on the one hand with the procedures for controlling and regulating a crisis so that it does not get out of hand and lead to war, and on the other with ensuring that the crisis is resolved on a satisfactory basis in which the vital interests of the state are secured and protected. The second aspect will almost invariably necessitate vigorous actions carrying substantial risks. One task of crisis management, therefore, is to temper these risks, to keep them as low and as controllable as possible, while the other is to ensure that the coercive diplomacy and risk-taking tactics are as effective as possible in gaining concessions from the adversary and maintaining one's own position relatively intact.[29]

Perhaps the best way of looking at it is as an extension of traditional diplomacy, where the purpose is 'to obtain what one wants without recourse to violence'.[30]

It is worth emphasising further that the outbreak of violence need not be deliberately initiated, and can erupt despite the best efforts of statesmen to prevent it. One aim of crisis management, therefore, is to ensure that the crisis remains under control and that war does not break out through a series of miscalculations and mistakes by the participants. The *Oxford Dictionary* defines management as control, and it is possible to argue that the attempt to maintain control over events and not allow them to get out of hand or develop a logic and momentum of their own is one of the major tasks of the 'crisis-managers'. Even those who are generally very sceptical about the concept appear to be in agreement with this aspect of it. Laurence Martin, for example, has stated that 'crisis management is no more than a phrase to describe the aim of remaining as much in control of events as possible'.[31]

Yet it is important not to underrate the complexities involved. Indeed, given the characteristics of crises described above, it seems almost inevitable that any attempt at the management of superpower confrontations will prove troublesome. In one sense, therefore, the notion of crisis management is almost a contradictory one. It is an attempt to manage what may be unmanageable, to control the uncontrollable. Manipulating and influencing the opponent while simultaneously controlling events and avoiding war is a daunting task. But it is a task that must be carried out, since the only alternatives in the contemporary world may be annihilation or surrender. This was not always the case in the past, and in the next two chapters it is suggested that crisis management as it is understood here is perhaps unique to the nuclear age.

CHAPTER THREE

Crises in the Prenuclear Age

1 Introduction

Having clarified the notion of crisis management, the background to its development and the reasons for its emergence as one of the most vital tasks facing foreign policy decision-makers in the contemporary era must now be examined. This is all the more important because the peaceful resolution of great power crises has not always been so crucial or so formidable a problem as it is today. Indeed, so long as men regarded war as advantageous rather than abhorrent, romantic rather than repugnant, there was little interest in channelling international confrontations away from open hostilities. A number of developments during the twentieth century, however, have profoundly transformed this situation and contributed towards a growing distaste for large-scale war as an instrument of national policy. The most fundamental, and indeed the most obvious, of these developments has been the revolutionary advances in the technology of mass destruction. Largely (although not exclusively) because of the constantly increasing destructiveness of military power, attitudes towards the use of force and violence in international politics have changed drastically. Consequently, crisis management has attained an unprecedented urgency and importance – especially for the superpowers.

The present chapter attempts to identify these changing attitudes towards war. It also examines the way they were manifested in the July Crisis of 1914 and the Munich Crisis of 1938. Although there may be something suspect about any survey of this kind that does not include a much wider range of historical case studies, these two crises have been chosen as particularly illuminating examples of the way crises were handled in the past.

Both may be extreme cases, with the one resulting in war and the other having a peaceful but very one-sided outcome. Nevertheless, neither crisis was entirely atypical of its era. The great powers may have been more intransigent and slightly less cautious in the Sarajevo Crisis than during the preceding ten years, but their behaviour did not mark a pronounced departure from earlier exercises in crisis diplomacy. Tendencies present in previous crises were exaggerated but not caricatured in July 1914. Similarly, the Munich Crisis did not deviate significantly from the pattern of crisis behaviour established by Britain, France and Germany throughout the latter half of the 1930s. Thus both crises can usefully be analysed as a preliminary to the discussion of the period since 1945 contained in chapter four.

II From Crisis to War : July 1914

It was quite conceivable in the years up to 1914 for the leaders of a state to envisage calmly the prospect of going to war in pursuit of national ambitions. War was still regarded as a rational instrument of state policy, or as one writer has put it 'a possible and profitable activity for nations'.[1] There were various reasons for this, ranging from deep and pervasive beliefs about international politics to plain military short-sightedness. In the decades before the First World War, for example, ideas of 'social Darwinism' were widespread: struggle was emphasised as a means of eradicating those species not worthy to survive, and by implication such a belief was extended to nations.[2] Acceptance of these ideas was made easier by the fact that recent wars in Europe either had been relatively minor affairs or, when the great powers were involved, had been over very quickly. Bismarck's wars in particular had been short decisive campaigns and there was widespread expectation among both civilian and military leaders that this would be the pattern for the future. The influence of Clausewitz and Norman Angell also worked in the same direction and helped popularise the short-war concept throughout Europe. 'Quick decisive victory was the German orthodoxy; the economic impossibility of a long war was everybody's orthodoxy.'[3]

What such expectations and beliefs ignored was that the century after the Napoleonic era had been one of the most fateful in the evolution of warfare. Trends that had manifested themselves during the Revolutionary and Napoleonic Wars were all greatly intensified as the nineteenth century wore on: the administrative apparatus of the state grew rapidly, thus enabling governments to harness the energies of entire nations when involved in hostilities; the Industrial Revolution continued unabated, ensuring that the wars of the future would very likely be fought by advanced industrial nations utilising all the vast resources at their disposal; and the twin forces of democracy and nationalism developed to such an extent that, if and when war did occur, it could only be fought with an unprecedented passion and intensity. This last point in particular was emphasised by Clausewitz, writing in the early nineteenth century. Almost alone among his contemporaries, he understood the implications of the European conflict of 1789–1815 for the future of warfare. Realising that war had been transformed from 'a mere Cabinet affair in which the people only took part as a blind instrument' into a phenomenon in which 'the people on each side weighed in the balance', he argued that it would become increasingly irrational and uncontrollable.[4]

The First World War was the vindication of this analysis. It was also the culmination of all three trends described above. Yet prior to the actual experience of the war, few people appreciated the significance of these developments. The nineteenth century justifiably can be characterised as a century of unnoticed if not 'silent' development. The handful of perceptive and far-sighted people like H. G. Wells, Ivan Bloch and Conan Doyle, who realised the decisive impact that increasing industrialisation and the advances of science were likely to have on the shape of war, found themselves voices in the wilderness.[5] Their arguments and theories were either scorned or ignored by the military professionals.

Indeed, this was symptomatic of the failure of the military to assess correctly the importance of the various trends. Although many European observers had gone to America to see what lessons could be learned from the Civil War, they concentrated on specific issues and missed its wider significance as 'the first total war fought with the tools and weapons of the Industrial Revolution'.[6] The almost general failure to assimilate and digest this basic fact was to have far-reaching consequences. The Civil War was dismissed as an aberration arising from unique conditions; in fact, it was a precedent setting a broad pattern of the future. Little wonder, therefore, that for most people in authority the nature of the First World War proved to be what Aron has termed a 'technical surprise'.[7] The gap between 'expectation and event' was enormous. It was also understandable. Indeed, one writer has suggested that the failure to foresee the form of future conflict was the result of 'the now familiar time lag between the rapid develop-ment of technology and the belated abandonment of ideas, mental habits, and social attitudes that the new machines and the new industries had rendered out of date'.[8] Belief in the romance and glamour of war was not to die until 1915 or 1916. The tragedy was that by 1914 it had already lived many years too long. Such is the strength and resilience of deeply embedded attitudes, how-ever, that very often it is only the most traumatic events or circumstances that can change them. In relation to this we should keep in mind the relatively long interlude of peace that reigned in Europe throughout the last part of the nineteenth century. Little occurred during this period to highlight the redundancy of the prevailing attitudes. Beliefs about war stagnated, with the result that both policy-makers and publics became complacent: 'the sense of the tragic' was lost.[9]

The divorce between image and reality had dire consequences in July 1914. Indeed, it goes far towards explaining why the leaders of the various nations were prepared to take the risks they did. Thus when Bernadotte Schmitt criticises the German leaders, particularly Kaiser Wilhelm and his Chancellor, Bethmann-Hollweg, for 'accepting the risk of war with unbelievable nonchalance', he almost completely overlooks the important role of these attitudes.[10] The German leaders, like most of the other participants in the crisis, were supremely confident of victory in a war. All over Europe the armies commenced hostilities expecting to march straight to the enemy's capital and return home 'before the autumn leaves had fallen from the trees'.[11] The misconception was enormous, its results tragic. Although there was some fear of war and attempts at mediation, particularly by the British foreign secretary, Lord Grey, these were only sporadic and of secondary importance. The protagonists generally put their own particular interests far before the preservation of peace and attempts at maintaining it. As the foremost authority on the July Crisis has put it, 'In those tragic days, the first concern of those in charge of the foreign policy of all the Great Powers should have been not to consider the immediate advantage or disadvantage of their friends and allies, on the assumption that war was coming, but to see that war did not break out.'[12] Although no one, with the possible exception of the German General Staff, consciously desired and consistently worked towards a European or a world war, most of the states involved were prepared to risk such a possibility.[13]

Their willingness to do this was heightened by their perceptions of the stakes at issue. Almost all the European governments regarded the crisis in 1914 as a test of will, power and prestige far surpassing in importance any of their previous encounters. Coral Bell has suggested that such views were largely a result of the 'crisis slide' that had occurred from 1906 onwards. The essential characteristic of such a slide is that 'the decision-makers of one or more of the dominant powers believe that they see the options available to them steadily closing down to the single option of war or unlimited defeat'.[14] Indeed, each of these earlier crises had a substantial impact on the international system, and together they helped cement Europe into two inflexible and fully armed camps. It was this rigidity of the international system that ensured that in neither alliance did the great powers have much freedom of choice. In fact, by 1914 the European state system exhibited many of the less attractive aspects of 'bipolarity' while lacking the more appealing features of such a structure. Power and responsibility were not distributed evenly within the system. Militarily, Europe was divided into two while the centres of independent decision-making were far more numerous. Thus an issue that initially was of intrinsic importance to only a few states became decisive for the whole of Europe, merely because it involved members of the opposing alliances.

The leaders of the Hapsburg Empire regarded the issue as critical from the beginning. They felt that the very existence of the Empire was at stake and that self-preservation demanded a final settling of accounts with Serbia. German policy-makers were, almost inevitably, in sympathy with such a course of action. The feeling in Berlin was that 'if Austria failed to do so, if she contented herself with minor amends, she would prove herself to be an ally of no value and Germany would have to look around for other safeguards in Europe'.[15] The problem for the Germans was that, given the nature and structure of the international system, other safeguards and options were not readily available. A firm commitment to support, if not actively encourage, Austria-Hungary in her hard-line stance towards Serbia seemed therefore the only viable alternative. Similarly, on the opposing side the Russian leaders felt compelled to back Serbia. To have reneged on its commitment to the small Balkan nation would have meant abdicating as a great power.[16] In other words, as Schmitt has pointed out, the assassination of the Archduke Franz Ferdinand sparked off a crisis in which 'the whole constellation of European power was at stake'.[17]

The main difference between Sarajevo and the earlier European crises seems to have been in the importance of the issues involved. Any peaceful solution to the 1914 crisis was likely to be extremely far-reaching in its effects; it was also likely to be unsatisfactory to some of the protagonists. It is not surprising therefore, especially when the prevalent attitudes towards war are considered, that the use of force began to seem attractive to the major participants. Consequently, attempts to resolve this crisis peacefully or to prevent it getting out of hand were less vigorous than in earlier confrontations such as that over Morocco in 1911. Although the Central Powers miscalculated the possibility of keeping the conflict 'localised', they were nevertheless always prepared to accept the dangers inherent in its expansion. That they tended to discount these dangers should by now be apparent. There was no perception of a common interest in avoiding war among the antagonists: 'The European states . . . wholly dominated by the will to fight and to win had no realisation of the length of the struggle, the destruction of life and property it was to cause, and the train of evil consequences it was to bring in its wake'.[18] To regard the outbreak of war in 1914, therefore, as a failure or breakdown of deterrence, as A. J. P. Taylor does, is merely a retrospective judgement applying the standards of the present to an age when they were far less applicable.[19] The main purpose of the mass armies possessed by the great powers was to fight rather than deter wars. Yet Taylor is not alone in making this mistake – Geiss too has argued that hostilities began as a result of faulty brinkmanship on the part of the German leaders.[20] Where fear of war is not the prevailing sentiment, however, brinkmanship is impossible. And few people in 1914 regarded the outbreak of war with horror or revulsion.

III   The Transition Period : Chamberlain and Hitler

Nevertheless, the nature, scope and duration of the struggle that followed was to prove a major landmark in transforming many of these attitudes. The change can clearly be seen in the anti-war literature of the interwar years and also in literary fiction dealing with future international conflict. The contrast with the writings on war that appeared prior to 1914 is stark. 'The chief enemy is no longer some foreign power; it is the immense destructiveness of modern weapons. War itself and not the enemy nation is the target for attack'.[21] Such sentiments were shared by many prominent politicians of the period. Stanley Baldwin, for example, described war as 'the most fearful terror and prostitution of man's knowledge that ever was known'.[22] In a similar vein Neville Chamberlain once wrote that war 'wins nothing, cares nothing, ends nothing'. Influenced by thoughts of 'seven million young men who were cut off in their prime, the thirteen million who were maimed and mutilated, and the misery and suffering of the mothers and fathers', he believed that 'in war there are no winners . . . all are losers'.[23]

Unfortunately, the transformation of attitudes had not been universal, and Chamberlain's ideas were not general throughout Europe in the 1930s. The revulsion against war that the horror of the trenches and the struggle on the Western Front had aroused in the Western democracies was not shared by the leaders of Nazi Germany. This gave Hitler a distinct advantage in the crises that resulted from his policies. Indeed, he saw crises almost wholly as situations that provided an *opportunity* for him to further his ambitions and attain his territorial objectives. British and French leaders, on the other hand, put the preservation of peace as their main priority and consequently saw in crises only *dangers* that had to be arrested. The result was disastrous, for, as Kissinger has pointed out, where the majority of states in the international system are concerned above all with preserving peace, then the system itself is likely to be at the mercy of its most ruthless members.[24]

Moreover, the British and French did not regard mass warfare as a rational instrument of policy, especially as many of Hitler's moves seemed to affect only their minor or peripheral interests.[25] Thus, until they finally became aware that Hitler's aims and actions were a threat to their very existence, they were unlikely to take up arms against what they could only regard as lesser provocations. They regarded mass conventional war as the absolute weapon, and fear of using it led to paralysis and indecision. 'The Western democracies, committed to a policy of total violence in international affairs or none at all, could only watch him paralysed, until they took up arms on a scale, and with a crusading purpose which could result only in the destruction of Germany or of themselves, and quite conceivably of both.'[26] Perhaps the best example of this was the reoccupation of the Rhineland in 1936 and the French failure to respond vigorously. Although General Gamelin, the chief of staff, was confident of victory if the French took up arms, he informed his government that because of the German military build-up general mobilisation would be necessary.[27] In the circumstances this seemed too drastic a step, especially as Hitler justified this action, like all his others, as 'reasonable and as inescapably necessary'.[28]

The Rhineland episode also provides a good illustration of Hitler's use of the *fait accompli*, which places all the onus for opening hostilities on the opponent. It was chiefly significant, however, for encouraging the German leader to take even greater risks in the future. Hitler regarded the affair as a test for the democracies, and one in which they had been found wanting. After 1936 he felt able to embark on a more adventurist course, calculating that Britain and France would not intervene against him.[29] But even if the likelihood of such intervention had been greater, Hitler would not necessarily have been deterred. His attitude towards the use of military force was very different from that of most other European statesmen. He regarded war as a continuation rather than a failure of national policy, and consequently felt able to run the risk of open conflict with relative equanimity. Nor were his actions constrained by a fear that hostilities would follow the pattern of the First World War.

> The Fascist image of war was very different to that either of the bourgeois liberal civilians or of the orthodox professional military commanders . . . . It was to be fought by elites: storm-troops, tank commanders, bomber-pilots, heroic and technically expert at the same time. It was to be brief, terrible, and glorious; an adventure to be welcomed rather than a horror to be shunned.[30]

The Munich Crisis provides a vivid example of how this fundamental asymmetry of attitude worked in Hitler's favour, enabling him to exploit the situation both skilfully and profitably. After his meeting with the German leader at Berchtesgaden, Chamberlain realised that Hitler would take the risk of war, and even go to war if necessary, to achieve his ambitions. Thus when he went to Munich the sole objective of the British Prime Minister was to save the peace. The integrity of Czechoslovakia, if not a hindrance, was only of secondary importance and could be sacrificed if necessary. A recent commentator on British foreign policy of the late thirties has suggested that Neville Chamberlain could not adopt a firm bargaining position. The Prime Minister was negotiating from weakness rather than strength and could not afford even a façade of resistance since he was acutely aware that 'if Britain's bluff *was* called, there was a real danger of losing the war which would inevitably follow'.[31]

To argue that Chamberlain's behaviour was dictated by fear of *losing* a war, however, implies a preoccupation with the military balance which is perhaps not warranted. Even if the military balance at the time of Munich had been overwhelmingly in Britain's favour, it is unlikely that Chamberlain would have felt able to 'negotiate from strength'. It is not only military power that counts, but the will to use it. Chamberlain lacked that will. The emotional repugnance towards war which he expressed on a number of occasions seems to suggest a 'simple fundamentalism' of belief: the great divide was between peace and war.[32] It seems unlikely that Chamberlain clearly differentiated between a war that Britain could win and one that she might lose. War was anathema; even the likelihood of victory could not make it palatable. As Taylor has commented, he 'feared war rather than defeat; hence the irrelevance of the calculations about German and Allied strength, the debates whether Germany could have been defeated. Hitler could get his way by *threatening* war without needing to count on victory'.[33]

Supporting this interpretation is the fact that there was intense fear of war throughout Britain at the time of Munich. Wheeler-Bennett sees this as arising out of fear of air bombardment which had been stimulated by works such as Lionel Charlton's *War Over England*, published in 1936: 'There is no doubt that this widespread hatred of the thought of war, which he himself so keenly shared, materially affected Mr. Chamberlain in the formulation and execution of his policy, and also contributed to its failure.'[34] Taylor has gone even further and has argued that for Chamberlain the prime purpose of going to Munich could easily be construed as an attempt to save Britain from air attack.[35] This is substantiated to some extent by the testimony of Basil Liddell-Hart. He claims that Kingsley-Wood, the Secretary of State for Air, estimated that Germany possessed a thousand bombers capable of inflicting at least half a million casualties on Britain in the first three weeks of hostilities. It is quite feasible that these calculations had an important influence on Chamberlain's actions and policy in the crisis.[36]

Hitler exploited this fear to the full. He realised that the British and French concern with the avoidance of war meant that the threat of violence could pay enormous dividends. The Nazi propaganda machine exaggerated the size of the German air force, and as we have seen this proved an effective weapon of intimidation.[37] Hitler skilfully manipulated to his advantage the basic differences in the attitudes towards war of the European states. It was this that put him in a strong position and gave him such an advantage. Consequently, the Munich episode has been appropriately described as 'victory without violence' for Hitler.[38] If crisis management is interpreted as merely 'winning' a crisis, then Munich was undoubtedly a superb example of crisis management on Hitler's part. Where this interpretation falls down is that the Führer was intent on attaining his objectives regardless, and it was almost immaterial to him whether this was to be achieved merely by the threat of force or by its actual use. He did not take precautions to avoid becoming entangled in a war, partly because he felt Chamberlain would surrender anyway, but probably even more because he regarded war as merely an additional weapon in his armoury and one that he was not reluctant to use. Indeed, his willingness to embrace fully the Clausewitzian dictum that 'war is a continuation of policy by other means' added a whole new dimension to the Clausewitzian idea. Hitler's apparent readiness to go to war ensured that the threat of war sufficed for him to achieve his goals.

This was especially the case, as all Chamberlain's efforts were directed towards the peaceful resolution of the crisis. But like Hitler's tactics, this course of action cannot be equated with crisis management either. Appeasement differs from crisis management in that it involves 'peace at any price' or surrender to aggression. It puts peace above all other interests and regards any peaceful solution as preferable to war. Appeasement is the result of unilateral pacifism, whereas crisis management is the result of perceptions on the part of all the antagonists that they have an overriding common interest in making an agreement short of war, while at the same time recognising that there is room to bargain and manoeuvre over the exact terms and nature of that agreement. This common interest was minimal, if not nonexistent, between Chamberlain and Hitler. As we have seen the considerations underlying the behaviour of the two policy-makers differed enormously. Chamberlain was happy with almost any agreement so long as it served to defuse the crisis. For Hitler, the attainment of German objectives was paramount and the means used – diplomacy or military force – almost immaterial. Thus the only possible dialogue was necessary on Hitler's terms.

In what ways does Munich resemble or differ from crises between the great powers in the nuclear age? Is the crucial distinction between those crises that took place before the Second World War and those of the postwar world? The emergence of bipolarity and the development of nuclear weapons has very obviously and dramatically changed the context of major crises. To understand the extent of this change it is necessary to examine the nature of nuclear weapons and to attempt to assess their implications for the role played by military force in international politics.

CHAPTER FOUR

Nuclear Weapons and Crisis Management

I The Use of Force in the Nuclear Age

The advent of nuclear weapons marked the culmination of a long trend in the evolution of warfare during which the means of mass destruction had grown more and more ferociously efficient. At the same time they heralded an unprecedented increase in both the degree of destructive power available and the speed and ease with which it could be delivered. No longer was it necessary to defeat the enemy's military forces before inflicting pain and suffering on his civilian population. The element of attrition in warfare, which had been enormously significant even during the aerial bombing campaign of the Second World War seemed to have been eliminated.[1] As a result of all this, the fear of general war found mainly in the Western democracies before 1939 became far more widespread and more evenly distributed.

This did not happen at once, of course, and it would be wrong to suggest that the atomic bombs dropped on Japan in 1945 presaged immediate and far-reaching changes in attitudes towards war. Nuclear weapons were initially regarded merely as bigger and more effective conventional explosives. Furthermore, their production in the United States remained slow throughout the 1940s, while the Soviet Union did not explode its first atomic device until 1949. It seems most unlikely therefore that the existence of these weapons was an overwhelming factor in the calculations of policy-makers during the early years of the Cold War. This is not to say that it was unimportant, however. Fear of nuclear war may not have been the all-pervasive consideration it was later to become, but there were few illusions in either the

United States or the Soviet Union that a war between them would be anything other than long, arduous and highly destructive. Thus, even before it became apparent that in a nuclear war between the superpowers victory could well be indistinguishable from defeat, they were intent on avoiding hostilities with one another. Indeed, their later reluctance to contemplate the use of nuclear weapons against each other's homelands was no more than 'a continuation, although vastly intensified, of the reluctance to use the older techniques of mass war'.[2] Despite the caveats entered above, therefore, the period since 1945 can reasonably be treated as a whole under the heading 'the nuclear age'.

It is an age characterised predominantly by the vulnerability of modern industrial societies to nuclear attack. The physical destruction and social upheaval likely to result from nuclear war would almost certainly be immense. As Henry Kissinger has argued, the city is 'the distinguishing characteristic of modern civilisation' and 'the repository of a nation's capital and skills'. It is also an expression of a nation's vulnerability. Even if a city managed to survive a nuclear war, the disruption of the specialised activities necessary to its functioning would pose appalling problems. 'A city without electricity, without water supply, without communications is a contradiction in terms – a concrete and steel jungle in which nature does not offer even the barest means of survival.'[3]

The prospect is a terrifying one. But what are its wider implications? What has been the effect of these technological developments on the manner in which states use military power as an instrument of policy? Have nuclear weapons rendered obsolete the Clausewitzian dictum that war is a continuation of policy by different means? More specifically, what has been the impact of nuclear weapons on the behaviour of the superpowers both prior to and during international crises? To what extent do their actions differ from those of the major European governments in the crisis of 1914 or the confrontations of the later 1930s?

The answers to such questions are neither easy nor straightforward. Even at the most general level regarding the effect of nuclear weapons on the conduct of international politics, there is a lack of consensus. Prominent among the wide variety of different interpretations is what has been described as the military obsolescence theory.[1] The essence of this thesis is that the development of weapons of mass destruction has made war obsolete by destroying any reasonable or practical relationship between the means of violence on the one hand and the purposes for which they could be used on the other.[5] It is summed up in the assertion that, far from being a continuation of state policy, resort to war now represents a failure or breakdown of policy.[6]

This interpretation is buttressed further by arguing that, not only have the *military* costs of war become excessive, but the domestic *political* costs may be almost equally prohibitive.[7] For advanced industrialised states, large-scale or long-term hostilities, even if confined to the conventional level, are likely to involve considerable social and economic dislocation, carrying with it the possibility of even more disruptive political upheaval. Indeed, in societies that attach importance to such things as social welfare and widespread educational opportunities, even a minimal allocation of government funds for military purposes may be criticised as an undesirable diversion of resources from more worthwhile purposes. The actual use of force, under any but the most favourable circumstances, would probably require a far greater allocation of human and material resources and is likely to prove highly unpopular as a result. Thus, even if a government is confident that its involvement in war could be kept within carefully defined limits and the use of nuclear weapons scrupulously avoided, the domestic pressures and incentives for abstention from hostilities may prove overwhelming. In addition, it is argued that the range of objectives war is designed to serve has severely contracted.[8] Economic advancement through territorial expansion, for example, has lost much of the attraction it once held, while increased economic interdependence has made resort to military force an inappropriate way to resolve disputes among particular groups of states, such as the members of the European Economic Community.

These arguments are compelling. Nevertheless, they present only part of the picture. It is indisputable that the dangers and problems attendant upon the military instrument of foreign policy are more pronounced than at any time in the past. Yet the impact of this upon international politics has probably been less decisive and less revolutionary than the military obsolescence theory suggests. Indeed, the theory overlooks the possibility that military power may be of continued relevance precisely because it has been adapted to accord with new conditions.

Two changes stand out as particularly significant. The first is that, in many circumstances, the threat of force has become more important than its actual use. As John Garnett has observed:

> One of the changes which has occurred since the Second World War is the increasing sophistication with which military power is exploited without military force being used. This is the age of 'brinkmanship', 'crisis management', 'deterrence', and 'signalling'. All of these phenomena support the thesis that modern military force tends to be threatened and manipulated in peacetime rather than used in war.[9]

The other change is that, where force is used and not merely threatened, it is deliberately held down in a lower key. The widespread recognition that military force has become danger- ously volatile and potentially uncontrollable ensures that many states resort to it only in the face of serious provocation and after the most careful consideration. Faith in victory at an acceptable cost is far less well entrenched than in the past. Con- sequently, in some circumstances that previously might have led to hostilities, force has been replaced by more amicable – or at least, less violent – means of settling disputes. If these other methods are exhausted and force is used then it is consciously 'hobbled' and restrained.[10]

This does not apply under all conditions, of course. The restraints on the use of force are far less prohibitive for smaller powers than for either medium states or the superpowers. Indeed, the problem for small states is not to find a substitute for war but to ensure that they are able to use the force at their disposal without hindrance or interference from the superpowers. As Hedley Bull has so aptly pointed out, the effect of the 'back- ground presence of nuclear weapons' is not to deprive them

> . . . of the possibility of exploiting the military force at their command, only to alter the setting in which they do so – to pose for them such problems as how best to make or threaten war with these risks in mind, how to avoid or postpone intervention by the great powers, how to catch them unawares, present them with a *fait accompli*, ensure that they will be divided or make do in the event they cut off arms supplies.[11]

In other words, so long as international circumstances are pro- pitious, small states can act in what remains essentially a Clausewitzian manner. For the superpowers however it is more complex. Afraid of unrestrained force, they cannot afford to neglect military preparedness. Their concern is with both peace *and* security. Thus it is possible to discern what can be described as a basic duality of purpose underlying the diplomacy and strategy of both the United States and the USSR.

II   The Duality of Purpose

Divided by an intense ideological conflict and bearing widespread responsibilities as leaders of their respective power blocs, Moscow and Washington have global interests that they cannot afford to sacrifice or relinquish. Not only must they protect the vital interests of their own states, but they must also attempt to maintain the security and independence of their allies and clients. Military force is often a necessary tool in fulfilling these obligations. In their clear recognition of this, the attitudes of the superpowers differ considerably from those of Britain and France in the interwar years. Resort to force is still seen as a viable option, and sometimes as the only one available in the search for security or aggrandisement. On the other hand, the use of force in the relationship between the two great nuclear powers or their allies carries with it the enormous and very obvious dangers that have been elaborated. Thus the superpowers have somehow to reconcile the demands of peace with those of the security imperative. Their dilemma is 'how to manage affairs skilfully enough to *avoid* the more terrible weapons and still *uphold* essential interests'.[12] Decision-makers contemplating the use or the threat of force have what for want of better terms can be described as the *positive* or *traditional* aim of securing or promoting national interests and the *negative* and *novel* aim of ensuring that their actions do not precipitate a disastrous nuclear war.

   This helps to explain why the superpower relationship is such a curious mixture of common and conflicting interests. It has appropriately been termed an 'adverse partnership', but could equally well be presented as an example of co-operative conflict.[13] Such descriptions very clearly reflect the common interests of the superpowers in avoiding nuclear disaster. It is this that has moderated what in an earlier era would probably have been an unremitting struggle for complete ideological dominance and total military supremacy. The United States and the Soviet Union have long been involved in *an intense nuclear arms race,* for example, with each trying to pre-empt the other in the development and deployment of new weapons systems. Yet, because of the costs and dangers of a totally unrestrained arms competition, they have introduced tacit and formal measures that help to preserve stability and thereby make it more difficult for either of them to attain a position of nuclear superiority. This is, of course, a greatly oversimplified account of something that involves a complex of strategic, political, technological, economic and organisational factors. Even so, it suggests that, despite their opposed value systems, the superpowers recognise a mutual interest in survival.

Not surprisingly, they also acknowledge many of the major boundaries and divisions in the international system, and in certain areas have reached accommodation on acceptable principles of behaviour. But while each superpower demonstrates at least a minimum respect for the other's sphere of influence, neither is averse to making gains at the opponent's expense. This must not be overlooked. To emphasise the co-operative aspects of the relationship at the expense of the competitive elements – or vice versa – would be a serious mistake. Both the Cold War and *détente* have involved, albeit in different proportions, challenge, coercion and intransigence tempered by prudence, conciliation and accommodation. In fact it is this very mix of motives and objectives that gives the superpower rivalry its distinctiveness and differentiates it from great power conflicts in the past.

The duality of purpose then is a constant theme running throughout the diplomatic and military exchanges of the Soviet Union and the United States, and explaining many apparent paradoxes in their relationship. It helps us to understand both why crises occur and why it is so imperative that they be resolved peacefully. Without nuclear weapons it would be far less important that superpower crises be brought under control before the onset of open hostilities. Were there no conflicting interests or issues in dispute, there would be no need for either side to take actions that are so provocative to the opponent as to create a crisis situation. Thus, although nuclear weapons have made great power crises more frightening than hitherto, they have not succeeded in eliminating them altogether. To understand why, it is necessary to look briefly at the operation of deterrence between the United States and the Soviet Union.

III The Limits of Deterrence and the Occurrence of Crises

The superpowers have not always been in a position of nuclear stalemate with each possessing invulnerable retaliatory forces capable of inflicting unacceptable damage on the opponent even after absolving a first strike attack. This position was probably attained only in the mid-1960s. Yet the United States and the Soviet Union appear to have established a stable deterrence *relationship* much earlier than this. Even when the United States had a monopoly of atomic weapons, for example, the USSR did not lack a potential counter-measure: Western Europe was a useful and important hostage and remained so until the middle of the 1950s, by which time the Soviet Union had developed not only a powerful nuclear capability of its own but also the delivery systems that brought American cities within its reach. Although periodically there has been considerable concern over the delicacy of the resulting 'balance of terror', it seems reasonable to argue that nuclear deterrence has proved enormously, if unspectacularly, successful with each superpower preventing a direct nuclear attack upon its own homeland and the territory of its allies.

Nuclear deterrence, however, does not cover all contingencies, and 'in the late 1950s it was widely believed in the Western world that the very stability of mutual deterrence of unrestrained strategic nuclear warfare would create the conditions in which limited war between the superpowers could be conducted with maximum confidence that the limitations would be preserved'.[14] More specifically, it was feared that the Soviet attainment of an invulnerable retaliatory capacity would enable it to embark on aggressive ventures at lower levels with relative impunity: the threat of nuclear retaliation by the United States would lack credibility where its implementation would be suicidal. In the event, though, such fears appear to have been groundless, as the superpowers have continued to avoid not only unrestrained nuclear war but also limited conventional war. As Hedley Bull has commented: 'the fear of expansion of a conflict to the level of unrestrained nuclear war has in fact deterred them from putting the theory of limited war to the test of a direct encounter'.[15]

Nevertheless, there is still a considerable difference between nuclear deterrence and what Bull has termed 'comprehensive mutual deterrence' in which 'each Power deters the other from any use of force against it' and perhaps even from any other kind of hostile act.[16] Although prudence has dictated against either superpower initiating conventional war in areas vital to the adversary, the fact that nuclear weapons serve primarily to deter their use by the opponent leaves open, even if it does not invite, a wide range of lesser moves or eventualities. In other words, the superpowers retain a certain freedom of action below the point at which fear or nuclear war has immediate and overwhelming impact.[17] There is a level of activity, in fact, at which the risks they incur are not risks of war but risks of confrontation.[18]

Neither superpower has been willing to create and exploit international crises with anything like the same singleminded determination and ruthlessness displayed by Nazi Germany in the 1930s. Yet neither have they followed a policy of crisis avoidance through conciliation – and crisis resolution through surrender – in anything like as systematic, predictable or inflexible a manner as did the governments of Britain and France during the era of appeasement. On occasions, both Soviet and American decision-makers have been prepared to initiate policies carrying a distinct risk of confrontation with the opponent. Where such a course has been embarked upon, however, it seems to have been as a result of sober calculations. Risk-taking of this kind does not imply recklessness. Indeed, the latter quality has intruded very rarely into superpower foreign policies: it has no place alongside their vast nuclear arsenals.

It is difficult to discern the major considerations that influence each superpower's willingness to risk precipitating a crisis with the adversary.[19] Nevertheless, two factors appear to be particularly important. The first is the government's *calculation of its interests*, and its assessment of what it has to gain if its projected actions are successful or what it has to lose by inaction. The greater the value placed on an objective, the more unlikely it is that the state will refrain from policies that put it on a possible collision course with its rival. Consequently, if a crisis does ensue then it is the result of a direct, although not necessarily blatant, challenge as the government takes action in the full knowledge and awareness that it is risking a superpower confrontation. This is a price that it is prepared to pay. In 1948, for example, the desire of the Soviet Union to prevent the creation of an independent West German state prompted it to take actions against West Berlin that inevitably brought it into direct confrontation with the United States.

The second important factor is the government's assessment of the *risks of war* involved in the projected action and the extent to which these are regarded as controllable. It may calculate that even if a confrontation does occur there is little need to worry: serious danger can be avoided and tension reduced merely by easing the pressure, or, if the situation demands it, by retreating. There is perhaps an inverse relationship therefore between the assessment of the probability of disaster should a crisis erupt and the willingness to risk provoking a confrontation in the first place. The more confidence a superpower government has in its ability to defuse a crisis, the less may be its reluctance to become involved in such situations. To revert to the Berlin Crisis of 1948, Stalin may well have believed that he could exert sufficient pressure to force concessions from the West over the German problem without rendering the situation unmanageable. In this instance the two major considerations seem to have been mutually reinforcing. This need not always be so. In some cases the superpowers may have little confidence in their ability to control a crisis situation, but may see little alternative to involvement given the importance of their interests and objectives. The brief superpower crises over the Middle East in 1967 and 1973 are probably the best examples.[20] Conversely, it may be that in 1958 Communist China initiated its campaign of limited and controlled diplomatic and military pressure against the offshore islands of Quemoy and Matsu on the assumption that, if this provoked a firm American response, the decision-makers in Peking merely had to desist from further actions liable to inflame the situation.

As well as arising through deliberate calculation or a determination to take a firm stance on an issue even if this means direct confrontation, superpower crises can also result from a miscalculation of the adversary's resolve. In the latter circumstances the rival's response could take the initiating state by surprise – perhaps putting it at a serious disadvantage as a result. Such would be the case, for example, where an attempt to achieve a *fait accompli* goes awry. The quick, decisive *fait accompli* can pay large dividends so long as it is not challenged, but it may elicit such forceful counter-measures that the government responsible finds itself in an embarrassing and dangerously exposed position. Something like this seems to have occurred in 1962. Although the motives behind the Soviet attempt to instal missiles in Cuba are still not entirely clear, it is fairly certain that an attempt was made to present the United States with a *fait accompli*. In the event, however, the gambit was discovered while construction of the missiles was still in progress and Khrushchev found himself in a confrontation that was probably both unexpected and unwanted.

The implication of all this is that even in the nuclear age the scope for 'sub-crisis manoeuvring' remains considerable, and it is perhaps inevitable that superpower skirmishing of this sort sometimes develops into a full-scale confrontation. When this occurs the prevailing risks become risks of war, and the duality of purpose becomes even more significant.

IV   The Duality of Purpose and Crisis Management

Even when they become involved in a confrontation, the superpowers are not devoid of tactics to protect or advance their interests. Although unadulterated threats to launch a nuclear attack on the opponent and calmly and deliberately begin a nuclear holocaust lack credibility, less outrageous and more effective moves are available. The participants can attempt to 'manipulate the shared risk of war', 'rock the boat' or make 'threats that leave something to chance'.[21] The essence of such actions is that they increase the level of tension or heighten the possibility of events becoming uncontrollable, and thereby bring the prospect of nuclear war much closer. So long as the Soviet Union and the United States regard their objectives as sufficiently important, they will be prepared to create and tolerate such risks. But the superpowers also want to avoid nuclear war and consequently must strive to keep the risks under control. The desire for *positive* gains leads to 'coercive bargaining'. But this is tempered by the *negative* aim of 'disaster avoidance'.[22] As suggested in chapter two, the problem of reconciling these conflicting requirements is central to crisis management. Indeed, it is in this sense that crisis management is a direct reflection of the duality of purpose identified above. The key to success is to start events moving in such a way as to increase the likelihood of disaster without sacrificing too great a degree of control over the situation. Stanley Hoffmann's analogy is most appropriate here. He has stated that, although the superpowers of necessity still play the game of chicken, throughout the game they are extremely careful to keep their feet over the brake pedals.[23] This is in marked contrast to the behaviour of Hitler, who invariably expected his opponent to be the one to swerve aside or stop if a collision was to be avoided.

In other words, at the very time their conflicts become acute, the common interests of the superpowers become most obvious and pervasive. This may well be one of the most novel and distinctive characteristics of contemporary crises, and something that is unique to the nuclear age. Whereas prenuclear crises could be regarded as almost pure competition, in which the interests and motives of the adversaries overlapped to a minor extent if at all, in nuclear crises the motives of each antagonist are likely to be far more mixed. These crises will tend to be typical bargaining situations, which involve

> . . . a curious mixture of co-operation and conflict – co-operation in that both parties with a certain range of possible solutions will be better off with a solution, that is a bargain, than without one, and conflict in that, within the range of possible solutions, the distribution of the total benefit between the two parties depends on the particular solution adopted.[24]

This analysis goes far towards explaining the cross pressures at work on the superpowers in a crisis and helps us to understand rather better the schizophrenic quality of crisis management. As is detailed more fully in part two, the superpowers use threats and make commitments to show resolve, while at the same time striving to keep the crisis under what Charles O. Lerche has described as a 'restrictive ceiling of permissible tension'.[25]

This constitutes a fundamental difference with prenuclear crises. For although ambitious and unscrupulous politicians like Hitler were prepared to attain their objectives without war, they were not averse to going to war if all else failed. Of course, there may have been brief periods when none of the major powers in a crisis felt sufficiently confident of its military superiority to adopt a reckless policy, but these were fortuitous exceptions rather than the rule. More often than not crisis diplomacy aimed merely at creating favourable conditions within which the state could resort to arms with a greater expectation of victory. Thus success in a crisis was certainly not 'incompatible with the recourse to major war. In the nuclear age, such recourse must form the salient feature of a mismanaged crisis'.[26] It is apparent therefore that the basic prerequisite for an attempt at crisis management is the assumption on the part of all the antagonists that they have more to lose than they have to gain by going to war against one another. In other words, they must greatly value peace, or at least be too afraid of large-scale violence to regard war as a rational instrument of policy.

To clarify this further it may be worthwhile to look briefly at the difference between Kennedy's behaviour in the Cuban Missile Crisis and Hitler's at the time of Munich. Although it seems at first sight that both were determined to have their way at any price, there is a lot more to be said than this. In the Munich Crisis, Hitler was unable to find 'an excuse to go to war' because the surrender of his opponents was so total. As one commentator has put it: 'He had had everything he wanted handed to him on a silver salver.'[27] Kennedy, although he put American security before the preservation of peace, did not want to go to war. Feeling that the situation demanded it, he started events moving in that direction, but simultaneously made conscious and vigorous efforts to save the peace. Hitler was concerned almost solely with maximising his gains; Kennedy with achieving his deliberately limited objectives while at the same time concentrating on minimising risks. Hoffmann has put the point very well: 'The superpowers still try to reach objectives beyond survival and security to be sure. However, not only are they obliged to be cautious when they create risks with which they hope to force their adversary to give in to their ambitions, but often they must also give top priority to minimisation of the risks they incur for their own survival.'[28] Minimising risks was very low on Hitler's order of priorities.

This can also be illustrated by making use of Schelling's 'boat-rocking' analogy. Although rocking the boat may be necessary, in the nuclear age the decision-maker responsible for it realises that if the boat capsizes both he and his opponent will drown. As far as possible, therefore, he will try to hedge this tactic round with all sorts of restrictions – although without diluting its effectiveness too far. On the other hand, Hitler seems to have felt that, even if the boat toppled over, his British and French opponents would drown while he would be able to swim to safety. This stemmed largely from the Führer's view of warfare, but it also reflected his belief that the democracies were decadent and incapable of mustering the will necessary for sustained resistance.

In other words, crisis management requires a careful mixture of restraint and firmness by all parties if it is not to degenerate into pure aggressiveness on the one side and appeasement on the other. While it has been argued here that such a mixture is virtually unique to the nuclear age, it is not confined to crisis behaviour alone. Indeed, crisis management is merely one manifestation of the duality of purpose underlying superpower interactions. As such it belongs among the new breed of 'regulatory measures' to control the use of force that have been made necessary by fear of nuclear war.[29] Crisis management, the limitation of war and the control of armaments have much in common. They all reflect the fact that the superpowers have a joint responsibility for the management of conflict, a responsibility that almost transcends their differences, acute though these often are. How they have fulfilled this responsibility even while involved in intense and frightening confrontations is the subject of part two.

PART TWO

Crisis Management: The Practice

CHAPTER FIVE

Decision-Making in Crises

I Introduction

Crisis management has become an indispensable art in the nuclear age. This is not to suggest that it is an easy art to perfect. The obstacles to the effective control of international crises are many and varied. Some stem from the nature of crises and the inter-actions among the protagonists. Others can be found in the decision-making processes within each state. Misperception, insufficient information or simple errors of judgement can all lead to decisions that diminish rather than enhance the prospects for containing and ultimately defusing a crisis. Thus it is necessary to focus on the way decisions are made in crises and to highlight some of the problems that might obstruct or hinder effective and efficient decision-making. The present chapter looks at the procedures whereby such decisions are made and examines those factors that impinge upon the policy-making process. It is not purely descriptive, however, but attempts to relate the *manner* in which decisions are made to the *quality* of the decisions and any subsequent actions. Are the decisions appropriate to the circumstances? Do they reflect both the dangers and the opportunities that are generated by crisis situations? Do they represent a *reasonable response* to the situation rather than the manifestation of internal political needs or the fulfilment of purely personal predilections? In short, to what extent is crisis decision-making a rational process? Can the actions of policy-makers legitimately be interpreted as the outcome of attempts at rational problem-solving?

Important as these questions are, they cannot be answered fully or with a high degree of confidence. The reason for this – the lack of reliable information about crisis decision-making in the Soviet

Union – has already been discussed in chapter one. The major implication is that it is possible to present only half the story of decision-making in superpower crises. Indeed, most of the arguments in the present chapter relate specifically to the United States, and it would be unwise, although in certain instances perhaps not necessarily incorrect, to conclude unequivocally that they apply with equal validity to the Soviet Union. Despite these constraints the issues involved are sufficiently important to merit discussion, even if it is incomplete and inadequate. Consequently, the present chapter attempts to provide a preliminary appraisal and some tentative answers to the questions raised above.

In order to facilitate this a brief digression to explore the nature of rationality may be useful. The notion of rational decision-making or rational choice poses severe problems for the observer of public policy-making. The concept is as formidable as it is important. There are several reasons for this. In the first place, it is an area of analysis where description and prescription merge, often imperceptibly. As one political scientist has commented, 'The nature of concern with rationality displayed in the literature is predominantly normative. That is, its aim has been to prescribe standards that should be used when choosing.'[1] Unfortunately, this prescriptive bias has not always been explicit, with the result that it is sometimes unclear whether particular discussions of rationality are intended as descriptive analyses of what takes place in practice or as attempts to establish standards or procedures that real-world decision-makers should strive to emulate or follow. Secondly, there is considerable disagreement about the meaning of rationality. On the one hand it may be interpreted, very generally, as the application of reason to solving problems. On the other hand it is often given a more specific content as part of an attempt to elaborate the precise procedures involved in rational decision-making. Such differences are reflected in a lack of consensus about the requirements that have to be fulfilled if decision-making is to be judged rational. In some analyses they are far more stringent than in others. Thus it is appropriate to review some of the ideas and arguments that have been presented in the literature on rationality.

Not surprisingly, models of rational decision-making diverge considerably in both form and content. At the most abstract level is the model of 'comprehensive rationality' in which the decision-making process is interpreted in terms of four major stages, all of which are seen as part of an intellectual problem-solving activity. The first stage is the identification of a problem by policy-makers who possess an explicit hierarchy of values upon which the problem impinges. Secondly, there is a search for all the alternative courses of action available to decision-makers in this situation. In the third stage, the consequences or implications of each possible alternative are thoroughly examined in an attempt to assess which option holds out the best prospect of maximising values. The fourth and final stage is the choice itself: the decision-makers adopt that alternative which promises the best ratio of possible gains to losses in terms of their values.

As an idealised model of decision-making, the notion of 'comprehensive rationality' has the advantages of clarity and precision. Yet it also suffers from overwhelming defects, the most important of which is its lack of realism. 'Comprehensive rationality' is so obviously unattainable that even its utility as a prescriptive model must be called into question. It ignores the inherent limitations upon policy-makers who have neither the mental and physical capacities, nor the time and information necessary to explore the whole universe of possible alternatives. Consequently, some analysts have attempted to replace it with the much more modest notion of 'limited' or 'bounded rationality'.[2] The basic model here is little different in essentials from that of 'comprehensive rationality'. At the same time it is far more realistic, and recognises that the 'search for alternatives is neither systematic nor exhaustive'.[3] Rather than attempting to discover and evaluate all possible alternatives in order to maximise their values, policy-makers are usually content merely to 'satisfice'. That is, they tend to choose the first alternative that appears to meet their needs.[4] In addition, the model acknowledges that the ability of policy-makers to assess the potential consequences of the available options is imperfect, so that any assessment will necessarily be incomplete. It could hardly be otherwise so long as decisions are made by fallible officials whose knowledge is partial, whose judgement is sometimes suspect and whose foresight may range from the moderate to the non-existent.

Although the notion of limited rationality appears to provide an adequate description of much decision-making, it has been criticised on the grounds that it oversimplifies the means–end relationship; the sequential model in which decision-makers first clarify their values and objectives and then search for alternatives can be misleading. Indeed, policy-makers do not always have a neat, well-established hierarchy of values. Often they want to promote several values simultaneously or to achieve objectives that may be potentially incompatible with one another. In the choice of alternatives, therefore, it is crucial to know 'how much of one value is worth sacrificing for some of another value'.[5] And this is discovered only when the alternatives are set side by side. 'Policy-alternatives combine objectives or values in different ways.'[6] Thus, it becomes a matter of comparing them at the margin and choosing incremental additions of certain values at the expense of incremental losses of other values.

The 'limited rationality' model and the 'incremental' model of decision-making are not so far apart as is sometimes suggested. Both involve careful consideration of one's objectives and the means necessary to fulfil them. Although the relationship between ends and means is more complex in the incremental model, the procedure outlined is merely an alternative way of making a rational appraisal on the basis of which to choose. It is suggested here that if decisions are based on a careful calculation of possible consequences and if the choices of policy-makers are consistent with their own value preferences – irrespective of whether these values are arranged hierarchically or in more complex combinations – it is possible to speak of rational decision-making. In other words, this is a modest concept of rationality which fully acknowledges not only the limitations that are intrinsic to policy-makers, but also externally imposed constraints such as insufficient, ambiguous or misleading information. As a result of these impediments, policy-makers do not always succeed in fulfilling their objectives or enhancing their values. The important thing, however, is that they try to do so. Rationality lies in the endeavour, not the result. It does not depend on outcomes. So long as a projected action accords with policy-makers' values and is based on a logical appraisal of the situation, it can legitimately be described as rational. Chance developments or unforeseen obstacles may ensure that the action fails in its purpose, but they do nothing to detract from its basic rationality. Merely because policy-makers are not omniscient does not mean they are not rational.

The present concern is primarily with foreign policy decision-making. In relation to this, it is helpful to construct what can be described as a model of 'strategic rationality'. As well as incorporating the very modest notion of rational behaviour outlined above, the model rests upon several assumptions about foreign policy that must be made explicit. The first assumption is that foreign policy is guided by a 'controlling intelligence', that there exists a unitary or monolithic decision-making body, capable of making explicit its major values and objectives and pursuing them in a diligent and systematic manner.[7] The second, and closely related, assumption is that the constituent members of this decision-making body are statesmen and officials endowed with a strong sense of responsibility and concerned predominantly with protecting and advancing the interests of their state in a competitive and highly dangerous environment. In other words, they are custodians of the state's security and always act with this uppermost in mind. The prime task of the foreign policy-maker is 'that of designing strategies for competing effectively in the complex and sometimes deadly game of inter-nation politics'.[8] Consequently, there is a kind of 'chess game' quality about the exercise. The third assumption is that, before embarking upon a particular strategy in this 'chess game', policy-makers consider very carefully the probable responses of other states: they then act in the way that, according to their estimate, is most likely to advance the position and interests of the state *vis-à-vis* its opponents. In short, the choice is made 'on the basis of a sober calculation of potential gains and losses, and probabilities of enemy actions'.[9] The fourth assumption concerns the primacy of foreign policy over domestic politics. The implication is that, if the responsible decision-makers feel that a particular move is necessary or a certain response required, they do not allow themselves to be deflected from the preferred alternative by extraneous pressures. Political expediency takes second place to what is strategically desirable, as statesmen act in accord with reasoned and logical calculation rather than non-rational domestic pressures. They refuse to pursue policies contrary to their own rational judgement even though such policies might serve to strengthen their domestic position or placate public criticism.[10]

This model of 'strategic rationality' merely reveals the foundations on which many analyses of foreign policy and international politics are based. As a description of what take place in practice, however, it is totally inadequate. Although it makes no excessive or outrageous claims about rationality *per se*, its assumptions about the foreign policy-making process may be very suspect. Indeed, the notion of foreign policy as the outcome of a well-insulated process of rational calculation and logical assessment has been subjected to severe and sometimes vitriolic criticism.[11] It has been challenged by several commentators who argue that the attempt to explain decisions and actions in rational, non-political terms obscures far more than it reveals. The critics claim that any notion of a monolithic or unitary decision-making body is mythical, that foreign policy emerges from a process that is often murky and subject to a wide variety of political pressures and influences that are hidden or submerged. There is no single actor but a multitude of actors comprising large hierarchical organisations, each with its own culture, missions and interests, and individual officials, with their own bureaucratic or political positions to defend and career prospects to protect. Individuals and organisations may be highly parochial and concerned with their own self-interest rather than the security or wellbeing of the state. Consequently, there is no single set of value preferences that can be translated into the 'national interest' or national objectives. Foreign policy, far from being the manifestation of the national interest, is the compromise, and often compromised, product of political bargaining among different groups and individuals with different interests, values, and objectives. It

> . . . is not necessarily 'policy' in the rational sense of embodying the decisions made and actions followed by *a controlling intelligence focusing primarily upon our foreign policy problems.* Instead it is the 'outcome' of the political process, the government actions resulting from all the arguments, the building of coalitions and counter coalitions, and the decisions by high officials and compromises among them. Often it may be a policy that no participant fully favours when 'different groups pulling in different directions yield a resultant distinct from what anyone intended'.[12]

According to this analysis, what matters is not the validity or appropriateness of a proposed alternative, but whether its supporters are strong enough to push it through and obtain, if not a consensus strongly in its favour, at least acquiescence in its implementation. Thus, what is feasible politically often takes precedence over what is desirable in terms of strategic rationality. Policy-makers are inward-looking as much as outward-looking, with the result that their decisions and actions, far from being attempts to solve problems on their merits, are often a response to domestic political pressures. The implications of all this for the relevance of the strategic rationality model need little elaboration. There is no room in the model for the intrusion of political factors. Furthermore, 'since the rationality model cannot deal with inconsistent goal structures, and since such structures are not uncommon, the model is limited in explaining much organizational decision-making'.[13]

These arguments carry considerable weight and caution very clearly against the use of the strategic rationality model as the sole basis for a descriptive analysis of foreign policy-making. At the same time, they should not be accepted without qualification. To ignore the 'politics of policy-making'[14] would be foolish. It would be equally artificial and short-sighted, however, to overlook the calculating or deliberative element that is rarely totally absent from policy-making. There may be an important middle ground between those who interpret foreign policy solely in terms of strategic rationality and those who appear to deny the existence of a rational element in favour of explanations that emphasise domestic political needs or bureaucratic bargaining as the prime determinants of policy. Both types of explanation are couched in absolutes, whereas actual decision-making tends to be a mixture of rational, logical inferences on the one hand, and non-rational pressures and influences on the other.

It seems feasible, therefore, to suggest that in reality there are varying degrees of rationality: it is not a matter of all or nothing, but of more or less. Indeed, the concept of strategic rationality is an extremely useful device for evaluating the policy-making process. The kind of decision-making implied by the strategic rationality model is best seen as an ideal or an absolute standard from which there is inevitably some deviation in reality. What matters is the extent of that deviation. The degree of rationality attained will obviously vary from one situation to another according to circumstances. Consequently, the crucial question is whether or not conditions that exist during international crises are conducive to rational decision-making. Does the fact that a situation is characterised as a crisis enhance or diminish the prospects for approximating the ideal? It is this question which must now be answered.

II   The Decision-making Process in International Crises

In an earlier chapter, it was suggested that a crisis exists for decision-makers when a high threat is perceived, when they have been caught unawares, and when they have only a short time in which to agree upon an appropriate response. Each of these characteristics has important implications for the way policy is made. The element of surprise, for example, makes it less likely that the situation will automatically elicit a routine, pre-programmed response. The need for speed limits the number of people who have an opportunity to participate in the policy-making process. The seriousness of the threat ensures that the decision cannot be made at the lower levels of the bureaucratic hierarchy. All three features of the situation conspire to secure the involvement of a relatively small number of top officials and politicians. Indeed, perhaps the most striking feature of decision-making during superpower confrontations is that it takes place at the highest levels of government. As Alastair Buchan has observed, during a crisis the handling of decisions is centralised and elevated within the policy-making establishment.[15] This is in marked contrast to routine decision-making. Foreign policy often emanates from a long, tortuous and tedious process in which a large number of officials and organisations participate. In crises, however, the decision-making body, in the United States at least, is compact and easily identifiable. This emerges clearly from analyses of the decisions to intervene in Korea in 1950 and to 'quarantine' Cuba in 1962: 'The decision-making units that examined the possible courses of action were remarkably similar in nature. In both cases, the primary decisional unit was a small *ad hoc* group rather than the formal organizational machinery normally used to conduct foreign policy.'[16]

Such groups consist largely, although not exclusively, of those people occupying 'command post positions' in areas relating to national security. The chief executive is surrounded by a small, select circle of advisers most appropriately described as an élite within an élite.[17] In other words, participation in decision-making is very narrowly based. There are several reasons for this. The most obvious, as alluded to above, is that the opportunities for widespread discussions are limited: lack of time means that an unusually small number of people are consulted about the merits and dangers of particular options. Perhaps more important is that

. . . when goals are threatened, policy-makers often feel a need for secrecy during the deliberative stage which can best be achieved by limiting the number of individuals involved. The high stakes associated with major threats generate a concern for careful co-ordination and surveillance of actions taken during the crisis. Policy-makers often feel they can best perform these tasks if direction stems from and feedback returns to a small coherent group.[18]

What are the advantages and disadvantages of such procedures? Do the benefits invariably outweigh the dangers?

One of the advantages of this mode of decision-making is that information is fed up the chain of responsibility much more quickly and efficiently than normal. In June 1950, for example, merely four hours elapsed between the United States Ambassador in Seoul drafting his first report on the North Korean attack and President Truman being appraised of the hostilities.[19] As a result of the need for speed the distortions that sometimes occur when information is passed slowly and leisurely through the bureaucratic hierarchy are minimised, if not eliminated. Organisational biases or blockages of intelligence are difficulties with which foreign policy-makers must often contend.[20] They are less formidable in crises because information is dealt with more informally and does not run the gamut of the bureaucracy in quite the same way. The normal channels are short-circuited.[21]

In addition, the uncertainty that accompanies crises may prove functional rather than debilitating. Not only does it stimulate a search for more information, but it ensures that existing information is thoroughly and critically assessed. Indeed, the available data are usually subjected to the most detailed scrutiny in an attempt to uncover every subtlety and nuance of the adversary's position. Although the information is partial and incomplete, therefore, maximum benefit is likely to be gained from it.[22] In short, the task of processing and evaluating intelligence may be carried out more efficiently during crises than in non-crisis situations.

All this is not to suggest that the decision-making procedures are perfect. A possible disadvantage with bypassing the regular channels of communication and decision-making is that the expertise and potentially valuable contributions of particular individuals may be obscured or ignored. This need not happen, of course, and in certain circumstances high-level and well-informed members of the bureaucracy who do not actually participate in the decision-making body as such may be called upon to help prepare recommendations or analyses for the group's consideration. Even when it does occur, however, it may be compensated for by the resulting speed and flexibility. Furthermore, the larger the number of officials who are formally consulted, the greater the opportunity for political bargaining and bureaucratic manoeuvring. Not only could such activities prove dangerously time-consuming, but they might also result in the dilution or distortion of eminently suitable action proposals. This suggests another important advantage of these *ad hoc* groups: they facilitate a more dispassionate and disinterested analysis of the external problem than is usual because they involve 'institutional leaders without their institutions'.[23] The decision-makers obviously have their positions to maintain and are unlikely to advocate options that harm their own personal interests or those of their organisations. Nevertheless, they can, at least temporarily, escape the formalities of organisational leadership and free themselves from the more parochial organisational constraints. As one participant in the United States decision-making in the Cuban Crisis put it: 'We are fifteen individuals on our own, representing the President and not different departments.'[24] The sense of awe and responsibility that is probably an inevitable concomitant of international crises may well be the major inducement for such detachment.

> Those who are expected to be responsible for the consequences of their decisions will be more inhibited in admitting criteria that are not supposed to be relevant. Insofar as responsibility is felt, there will be greater calculation of the effects of decisions, and they will be more likely to be made in terms of the events themselves than in terms of extrinsic nonlogical factors.[25]

This feeling of responsibility is almost certain to be shared by the decision-making group as a whole, particularly in a crisis where the potential costs of miscalculation or a rash move are patently obvious to all its members.

Consequently, it can be argued that the essentially political nature of much foreign policy-making is moderated, if not totally eliminated, during crises. Activities normally accepted as legitimate are regarded as an abdication of the policy-maker's responsibility as custodian of the 'national interest', and the situation is more likely to be dealt with on its merits than in terms of how particular alternatives would benefit certain groups, agencies or individuals within the government. Furthermore, what one astute commentator has called the 'strain towards agreement' is most prevalent during times of crisis.[26] While the major options must be explored and assessed fully, the need for speedy action sets limits to the degree of dissent and intransigence that can be tolerated. The penalties for a failure to reach a consensus and act accordingly are stark.

> Thus it may be, paradoxically, that the model of means-end rationality will be more closely approximated in an emergency when the time for careful deliberation is limited. Though fewer alternatives will be considered, the values invoked during the decision period will tend to be fewer and more consistent, and the decision will less likely be the result of bargaining within a coalition.[27]

Another important feature of the *ad hoc* group is that it is formed specifically to deal with the immediate crisis: once the crisis has been resolved, the group ceases to function as such and there is a reversion to more formal and routine arrangements. That they are short-term expedients rather than permanently institutionalised features of the policy-making apparatus may itself be an advantage, however. The very formation of the group signifies the existence of a serious and urgent problem. The members of the group concentrate almost exclusively on that problem. Although at first sight this might seem a trite observation, it is crucial to an understanding of crisis decision-making. A major defect even in the modest rationality model outlined above is its presumption that policy-makers devote sufficient time, energy and attention to the problem that they are able to explore all its facets in detail before arriving at what appears to be the best available solution. The reality is very different. Foreign policy-makers are frequently faced with a multitude of problems that must be dealt with simultaneously. Officials are often harassed and pressured by events to such an extent that they can analyse many issues only on a superficial level. In a crisis, however, there is an unusual degree of singlemindedness. Matters unconnected with the crisis are either left unattended or handled by subordinates, as top officials and in some cases their most trusted advisers focus solely on meeting the immediate challenge.[28] Crises, like hanging, concentrate the mind wonderfully.

Yet another advantage of these small *ad hoc* decisional units is that the relationship among policy-makers is informal and on a predominantly face-to-face basis. Indeed, there may be an optimum size and composition of the group. There are probably both upper and lower limits to the number of participants who can be involved directly if the group is to function effectively. These limits are difficult to pinpoint exactly. One analyst has argued that 'decision-making groups should be sufficiently large and diverse in outlook to ensure that the available information is subjected to various probing from multiple perspectives not merely from the view of the prevailing conventional wisdom'.[29] At the same time, such a group should not be so large that it becomes unwieldy and loses its cohesion. If the number of members rises above twenty it is perhaps inevitable that the group's proceedings become excessively formalised and rigid, unless of course a division occurs within the group itself between the members with important and distinctive contributions to make and those who play only a subsidiary or minor role. Should such a division occur, some of the officials will be left on the fringes of debate and discussion while others, participating vigorously, form what for all intents and purposes is a small inner or core group. Indeed, the opportunity for the full involvement of each individual is likely to diminish as the size of the group increases.[30]

There are also dangers if policy-makers go too far in the opposite direction. Although 'inequality of participation' might be avoided, other, no less serious, problems arise if the group is too small and restrictive in membership. A decision-making unit of less than ten members perhaps most readily falls into the trap of reinforcing the leader's own prejudices and preferences instead of providing independent evaluations of the situation. If the group consists solely of hand-picked men who invariably bow to the wishes of the chief executive, the type of critical assessment that alone can lead to balanced appraisals and carefully thought out policy recommendations is unlikely to be forthcoming. Furthermore, the smaller the group, the greater the exclusion of expertise, competence and experience. What then is the optimum size of the decision-making group? Past behaviour appears to support the thesis that problem-solving is facilitated by a group of between twelve and fifteen policymakers. The US decision-making group in October 1962 fell within these limits, and although it has been suggested that a group of five or six key officials is more typical, that Cuba provides a 'counter-example' only because Kennedy deliberately enlarged the size of the group beyond normal, this argument ignores the evidence from the Korean decision of June 1950.[31] During the week in which the commitment of American ground forces to South Korea was established, six major meetings occurred between President Truman and his advisers. The most important decisions emerged from groups that consisted of twelve, fourteen or fifteen participants.[32]

Having said this, there is nothing sacrosanct or magical about these numbers. The size of group is not the sole, or even the most important, determinant of whether or not a decision is appropriate to the circumstances. Decisions that, in retrospect, are generally accepted as realistic and far-sighted have been made by smaller groups on several occasions. In 1948, for example, when President Truman responded to the Soviet blockade of Berlin with an airlift of essential supplies, four to seven people were involved at crucial stages in the decision-making process.[33] Conversely, policies that have been patently inappropriate, misguided and doomed to failure have sometimes emerged from larger groups. The disastrous Bay of Pigs invasion in 1961, although not the result of a crisis decision, emanated from a high level group of about sixteen officials.[34]

Such qualifications notwithstanding, it appears that a decision-making unit of about twelve to fifteen members has real virtues and significant advantages over both larger and smaller units. Although small enough to facilitate a consensus on the values to be defended or the objectives to be obtained, it is large enough to provide the 'multiple perspectives', creative ideas and critical analysis that are an indispensable prerequisite for adoption of sound crisis management techniques.

The foregoing discussion suggests that crisis decision-making has a number of distinct advantages over ordinary or routine foreign policy-making, and in several vital aspects is far more likely to approximate the model of strategic rationality outlined above. The analysis also suggests that the effects of surprise, short time and high threat tend to be functional rather than disruptive. One of the implications is that the traditionally acclaimed disabilities and deficiencies of the United States democracy in foreign affairs diminish considerably even if they do not disappear entirely during superpower confrontations. Conventional analyses that highlight the shortcomings of the American political system in the making of foreign policy may have little relevance to the way this system functions in crisis situations. Efficiency is obtained by a kind of 'democratic Caesarism', as decision-making is concentrated in the hands of a narrow circle of executive officials, free from the impediments of either an assertive legislature or an aroused and emotional public opinion – largely because there is usually insufficient time for opposition to coalesce. As one analyst has commented, 'there is no time for dissension to develop. The public poses few problems for the President who acts deftly or even clumsily, in a short and sharp encounter'.[35] Indeed, the government's actions in a crisis generally win tacit approval, and occasionally even enthusiastic support, from the population. What criticism there is tends to be muted, and even if it is well-publicised it can be ignored by decision-makers, who are acknowledged to be better informed than their critics and consequently much more aware of the particular needs and demands of the situation. It seems probable that a government's freedom from domestic pressures is greatest during intense but relatively short international confrontations. Thus, 'President Kennedy, facing threats to Berlin, sent additional troops to Europe and in the summer of 1961 called up 150,000 reservists, an act usually thought to be politically dangerous. The political costs on balance were nil.'[36]

By highlighting the positive aspects of crisis decision-making, the analysis presented so far has painted a very comforting, reassuring picture. But is this picture too one-sided? Is such complacency really warranted, or is it based on a selective and contrived interpretation of what is invariably a more difficult and dangerous process than suggested above? It may be, for example, that the characteristics of crisis situations have negative as well as positive effects and create such pronounced feelings of anxiety and stress among policy-makers that their ability to make rational judgements is severely impaired. Furthermore, the argument that 'politics' is excluded from crisis decision-making can quite legitimately be challenged. There is possibly an insidious intrusion of politics in ways that, although barely detectable to the outside observer, have a profound impact upon the range of alternatives that is considered as well as influencing the choice of the particular option to be implemented. A number of arguments along these lines have been put forward and must be taken into account if the status of crisis decision-making is to be assessed properly.

III The Impact of Stress

The presence of a high threat, the element of surprise and – perhaps most important – the limited time available for decision-making combine with the rise in tension that is an inevitable concomitant of adversary crises to ensure that the members of the decision-making units in the participating states are subject to considerable stress.

What is the effect of such crisis-induced stress? Is it invariably harmful? Does it necessarily undermine the ability of policy-makers to make sound judgements or choose appropriate and realistic policies? It is extremely difficult to provide unequivocal answers to these questions. There are several reasons for this. In the first place the notion of stress is a primitive one, incapable of being measured except in a very crude way. There are formidable problems, for example, in trying to discover whether one set of decision-makers is subjected to a greater or lesser degree of stress than another. Not only are there likely to be significant variations from one crisis to another, but even in the same crisis policy-makers in the opposing states might confront rather different levels of anxiety during different phases of the encounter. Secondly, this is an area where lack of observation is particularly crucial. So long as the discussions are shrouded in secrecy, the opportunities for assessing how decision-makers are affected by – and how they cope with – conditions of stress are strictly limited.

Neither of these problems is entirely insurmountable, however. At a minimum it should be possible to differentiate between decision-making when the stress on those involved is low or non-existent, when it is at moderate levels and when it is at very high or intense levels.[37] Furthermore, the evidence from psychology, laboratory experiments and simulation analyses provides broad indications of the possible effects of stress, while the memoirs of statesmen and officials are littered with comments that offer at least some insight into their behaviour in critical situations, and enable the reader to discern whether or not these effects materialised in specific instances.[38] Thus it is possible to make at least *tentative* assessments of the impact of stress on crisis decision-making.

Much of the impact of stress appears to depend on the level at which it is incurred. Where it is very low, routine reactions are likely to remain the rule as the incentives for creative thinking and innovation will be minimal. It has been argued, therefore, that 'a moderate level of anxiety can be beneficial' since it elicits creativity and thereby aids and encourages problem-solving.[39] If it increases in intensity beyond moderate levels, however, it will tend to have deleterious and disruptive effects, particularly where the problems faced by decision-makers are highly complex. And as one authority has put it,

> Foreign policy issues are nearly always marked by complexity, ambiguity, and the absence of stability; they usually demand responses which are judged by qualitative rather than quantitative criteria. It is precisely these qualitative aspects of performance that are most likely to suffer under high stress.[40]

A crucial aspect of decision-making is the search for, and subsequent assessment of, alternative courses of action. Yet this is also the aspect that is perhaps most vulnerable to the effects of stress in general and to time pressures in particular. The implications of the major alternatives are less likely to be thoroughly assessed if an immediate response is required. The ability to analyse, predict and evaluate the likely consequences of particular actions will therefore be severely impaired. Whether this necessarily overshadows the advantages of short decision time highlighted above is debatable. A number of participants in the group that formulated the response to the Soviet installation of missiles in Cuba have suggested that, had there been less time available, a less judicious and restrained policy than the blockade would have emerged.[41] The implication is that, just as there might be an optimum size for the decision-making group, there could be an optimum length of time for the deliberations themselves: sufficiently long for cool assessments of the situation and calculated consideration of alternatives to be made but not so long that the concentration of policy-makers lapses or the decision-making group is subjected to the distorting influences of bureaucratic or domestic politics.

This highlights an aspect of the problem that deserves greater attention than it has hitherto received, for the impact of stress depends on *duration* as well as *intensity*. Meeting an immediate challenge quickly can present serious problems. But a crisis usually consists of a complicated sequence of actions and reactions, moves and counter-moves. Thus policy-makers may be faced not with a single challenge but with a series of consecutive challenges that arise within the same overall crisis and offer little time for respite and recovery. One difficult and potentially dangerous decision has to be followed by another in response to a rapidly changing situation. There may be little opportunity for anxieties to disappear before they are rekindled and perhaps heightened by further developments in the crisis. The cumulative effects of sustained exposure to stress are likely to be considerable, partly because it has a physiological as well as a psychological dimension.[42] One of the most readily observed manifestations of stress is tiredness, which is essentially a physiological phenomenon. Although individual levels of tolerance to stress differ considerably, if a crisis is prolonged, even the least susceptible members of the decision-making group will suffer from its effects.

Constant feelings of anxiety, coupled with the lack of sleep, could undermine policy-makers' attempts to ensure that their decisions are as rational as possible, and taken only after a calculated assessment of the potential costs and risks of the various options. Although such drastic effects appear to have been avoided in the superpower confrontations that have occurred since 1945, there is ample evidence that, in the Cuban Missile Crisis at least, decision-makers in both Moscow and Washington were subject to intense pressures that almost certainly would have taken their toll had the crisis gone on longer. The Americans agonised through thirteen days, whereas the Soviet leaders faced a challenge to their plans and objectives for merely half as long, since it was only on Monday, 22 October, a week after the missiles had been discovered, that Kennedy announced the quarantine. Even so there are several indications that decision-makers in the Kremlin were not immune to crisis-induced stress. William Knox, an American businessman in Moscow, was summoned to meet Khrushchev on 24 October. He later described the Soviet leader as 'in a state of near-exhaustion' and 'like a man who had not slept all night'.[43] This is a picture that is borne out by Khrushchev himself with his candid admission that the 'anxiety' of the Soviet leadership was 'intense'.[44] Equally revealing is Khrushchev's reference to Anatoly Dobrynin's report of Robert Kennedy's visit to the Soviet Ambassador later in the week. Apparently, 'Robert Kennedy looked exhausted. One could see from his eyes that he had not slept for days. He himself said that he had not been home for six days and nights.'[45] Nor was the Attorney-General the only member of the American decision-making group – later labelled the Ex. Comm. – under severe strain. Accounts of the meetings of the group towards the end of the second week indicate that tempers were becoming increasingly frayed, and that both the quality and the style of the discussions were deteriorating. Indeed, the President himself is said to have felt that 'pressure and fatigue might have broken the group's steady demeanour in another twenty-four or forty-eight hours'.[46]

This suggests that, at the fairly intense levels of stress that are an inevitable accompaniment of a direct confrontation between the superpowers, there is probably an upper time limit within which decision-makers can operate efficiently. Beyond this limit they cease to function effectively: cool detached officials who are able to calculate the logical implications of each move will be replaced by tired, emotional men liable to make rash, unwise and perhaps irrevocable choices. Actions and policies that would normally be eschewed may be advocated by decision-makers whose critical and analytical abilities have degenerated temporarily as a result of sustained exposure to stress. Fortunately, this time limit has not yet been reached in a superpower crisis, although it was perhaps not far away in October 1962.

Against this it can be argued that other crises, such as that over Berlin in 1961, have actually lasted longer than the Cuban episode. It must be remembered, however, that tensions between the superpowers became inflamed only sporadically over Berlin, and then for very brief periods. When barriers dividing the city were erected on 13 August there was an immediate and natural increase in tension. As it became obvious that the Western powers were prepared to tolerate this move with little more than diplomatic gestures and verbal reprisals, tension subsided and did not increase significantly again until the short-lived tank confrontation at 'Checkpoint Charlie' on 27 October. Thus policy-makers were not subjected to sustained exposure to acute stress: it was intense only intermittently.

What then can be said about the overall impact of crisis-induced stress? If it is *intense enough* for *long enough* it is likely to be a severe handicap, far outweighing the many assets of crisis decision-making. High stress and long duration could prove fatal. Other combinations however are more manageable and less damaging. Indeed, it is misleading to suggest that stress always undermines efficiency. In so far as stress is provoked by concern about the possible consequences of one's action, it can be sobering, and could invite cautious rather than reckless behaviour. Furthermore, the vulnerability of officials should not be exaggerated. Most policy-makers have gone through a long, tough apprenticeship before reaching the higher positions, and are unlikely to succumb easily to the worst effects of stress. Their natural resilience, acquired through years of experience in dealing with difficult and dangerous situations, also ensures that in crises where they are affected adversely they recover quickly. If the periods of acute tension are not too prolonged, therefore, or the pace of events too hectic, policy-makers can be expected either to retain their composure or, if it is lost, to regain it without delay.

In addition, there are a number of ways in which policy-makers can attempt to moderate the levels of stress on both themselves and their adversaries. Khrushchev's idea of going to the Bolshoi Theatre with other members of the Politburo at the height of the Cuban Crisis, for example, was a good one, not so much because it reassured and calmed the Soviet people as is claimed in his memoirs, but because it probably calmed the Soviet leaders themselves, providing an indispensable opportunity for them to relax, at least momentarily.[47] The degree of stress to which the opponent is subjected is also partly controllable. By deliberately slowing down the momentum of events through the avoidance of ultimata, or steps that demand an immediate response, policy-makers can ease the time pressures on their adversary, thereby making rash moves or ill-considered actions less likely.[48] This technique facilitates the adoption and continuation of a more rational and deliberative approach by the adversary. Although stress is a dangerous ingredient in crisis situations, therefore, it need not be as fearsome in its implications as is sometimes suggested. It can undermine the rational element in decision-making; but it need not do so.

IV 'Victims of Groupthink'

A danger that under certain circumstances may be related very closely to the existence of stress is what has been called 'groupthink'.[49] A persuasive argument has been put forward that crucial shortcomings and imperfections of group decision-making can have a disruptive influence, seriously damaging the quality of the policy that emerges. Although it was suggested above that one of the advantages of a small group was its cohesiveness, this carries with it certain dangers. It can be a drawback as well as a benefit. 'The more cohesive the group . . . the greater is the inclination of the members to reject a non-conformist.'[50] Furthermore, because the members place a high value on remaining part of the group, they may silence their own doubts and reservations over proposed policies if there is an apparent consensus in favour of them. This can lead to 'instances of mindless conformity and collective misjudgement of serious risks which are collectively laughed off in a clubby atmosphere of relaxed conviviality'.[51] Indeed, one result of this self-suppression of both anxieties and criticisms is 'a tendency for the collective judgements arising out of group discussion to shift towards riskier courses of action than the individual members would otherwise be prepared to take'.[52] Not only will there be a disconcerting rise in the propensity for risk-taking, but there will also be a greater likelihood of miscalculation or bad judgements resulting from the 'deterioration of mental efficiency, reality testing and moral judgement' that is an almost inevitable consequence of in-group pressures.[53]

In short, groupthink is 'a mode of thinking that people engage in when they are deeply involved in a cohesive in-group, when the members' strivings for unanimity override their motivation to realistically appraise alternative courses of action'.[54] It is also something that at first sight appears particularly relevant to crisis situations, partly because it is in a crisis that the small group is best insulated from outside pressures, but also because the existence of stress tends to 'generate a strong need for affiliation', thus inviting the policy-makers to provide mutual reassurance and support for each other.[55] This can be achieved only through the kind of self-suppression mentioned above.

Because groupthink is a *possibility* in crisis decision-making, however, makes it neither inevitable nor highly probable. There are certain features of crises, apart from the existence of stress, that militate against the pressures for groupthink. The key aspect of crisis decision-making appears to be the sense of felt danger and responsibility. Where this is high, as it almost inevitably is during superpower confrontations, then the strivings for unanimity, important though they are, will hardly be sufficient to override or outweigh the incentives to evaluate the alternatives in a thorough and realistic fashion. The motivation of those involved is crucial. The main danger of groupthink appears to arise when the members of the decision-making unit exude great self-confidence and firmly believe that the policy they adopt is almost bound to succeed. The Bay of Pigs invasion and the escalation of the Vietnam War under President Johnson are both classic examples of over-confidence in one's own plans and under-estimation of the capabilities and resourcefulness of the enemy.[56] With the superpowers locked in a direct confrontation, however, there is a marked tendency for decision-makers in the United States – and almost certainly in the Soviet Union too – to adopt a very different attitude, with the result that caution rather than recklessness marks their behaviour. Before the Bay of Pigs invasion many of Kennedy's top advisers assumed that Castro had little domestic support and that the Cuban exiles would face only scant opposition; in Vietnam it was assumed that the Communists would be unable to counter the US escalation and that bombing would inevitably destroy the morale of the North Vietnamese. In the event all these assumptions proved badly mistaken: yet prior to it either they went unchallenged or the challenges were ignored.

That such dogmatic assumptions were unexamined was possible largely because the risks and costs of their being wrong were not immediately and overwhelmingly apparent. In a superpower crisis, however, the risks and potential costs of acting on wrong assumptions loom extremely large in policy-makers' calculations. Acute awareness of the dangers is perhaps the best antidote to the pressures for groupthink. There is no room for complacency and an indulgent self-confidence in a situation where one false move could push the superpowers into open hostilities.

Thus it is perhaps less than surprising that Irving Janis, the author of the groupthink hypothesis, has held up the decision to establish a quarantine around Cuba as a case of 'vigilant appraisal', the 'antithesis of groupthink'.[57] This decision was made through a process in which a fairly wide range of alternatives was canvassed, the possible costs of each option, including the one finally chosen, were assessed carefully and critically, available information and expertise were used skilfully, and the possibility of failure was explicitly taken into account. At certain stages the group divided into two in order to thrash out the alternatives more forcefully, and throughout the proceedings Robert Kennedy and Theodore Sorensen acted as 'intellectual watchdogs', vigorously probing all the recommendations that were made in order to highlight both their advantages and their weaknesses.[58] These were extremely useful aids to decision-making, although they proved painful and uncomfortable to the participants. They were gone through only at the expense of the 'clubby atmosphere of relaxed conviviality' as the group members underwent the 'unpleasant experience of hearing their pet ideas pulled to pieces, and the acute distress of being reminded that their collective judgements could be wrong'.[59]

Whether such decision-making procedures are representative of other crises is debatable. The evidence is mixed, with some crises exhibiting a strange mixture of 'vigilant appraisal' on the one hand and tendencies towards groupthink on the other. The Korean decision is a good example of this curious combination that does not fit neatly into a particular category. There are several indications that policy-makers may have succumbed to some of the temptations of groupthink. The President's initial interpretation of the North Korean attack as a challenge to the United Nations and the 'collective security' system was readily accepted by other members of the decision-making unit. So too were the parallels he drew between the communist move and the fascist aggressions of the 1930s. Such analogies proved a powerful factor in the discussions, and although the commitment of ground forces came only after a week of careful calculation it was the logical consequence of the 'emotional quality of the dedication to no appeasement'.[60] The lessons of the past were regarded as crucial; the implications for the present as obvious. No one in the group attempted to question the validity of the analysis or suggest that such analogies were crude and over-simplified. As one analyst has commented:

> Truman and his advisers should have recognized the important role that historical evidence played in their reasoning. They should also have recognized that they were fixing on only one piece of history – and that a piece which had as yet been subjected to little detached examination. Had they noticed the characteristics of their thinking and tried to employ history more reflectively, the records of their deliberations might at least show that they had seriously analyzed alternatives before electing to spend life and sow destruction. This they did not do.[61]

The failure to appraise the alternatives thoroughly and vigorously may be explained in part by the mechanics of groupthink. Too much should not be made of this however. Even in the Cuban Missile Crisis there was a general acquiescence in President Kennedy's initial assessment of the situation. His interpretation of the Soviet move as drastic enough to overturn the political, if not the military, balance of power encountered no sustained disagreement.[62] It is also important to avoid the trap of enshrining the deliberations of October 1962 with a mystique that is not deserved. There may be other, equally valid, ways of making decisions. Indeed, some of the differences in the decision-making procedures in June 1950 can be accounted for by the distinctive presidential style of Harry Truman. Whereas President Kennedy was content to remain in the background for much of the time, Truman, together with his Secretary of State Dean Acheson, adopted a more positive leadership role.[63] 'This is not to say that the President inhibited the free expression of views; he did not. In fact, he called for them.'[64] But rather than attempting to promote a creative identification of alternatives by the group members themselves, President Truman asked for comments on an action programme presented by Acheson on the basis of staff work completed on a co-operative basis and at the highest levels in the Departments of State and Defense. It is hardly surprising therefore that a 'group consensus around a single action proposal' quickly emerged.[65] This does not mean that there were no differences of opinion, or that debate was not frank and open. Indeed, Truman suggests that, although basic agreement was reached on the US objective at the first meeting of the decision-making group, there was a pronounced difference over what this would require in terms of US military assistance to South Korea. Some of the military advisers felt that air support might be sufficient to turn the tide of battle, whereas others argued that only a firm commitment of American ground forces could save the rapidly deteriorating situation. Another contentious issue arose later in the week, when Chiang Kai-Shek offered to contribute 33,000 Nationalist Chinese troops to the struggle against the North Koreans. Initially inclined to accept this offer, Truman abandoned the idea when some of his advisers objected to it, and pointed out its attendant dangers.[66] Thus the picture of group discussions in which all dissenting ideas are withheld and doubts suppressed hardly squares with the operation of Truman's decision-making body. Although groupthink might have had some effect, it was certainly not overwhelming in its impact.

This conclusion is borne out by the manner in which the decision-makers strived to obtain adequate information. They were certainly not complacent about the amount of available information. Details of the emerging situation in Korea itself were sparse; details of the Soviet position and policy were even more fragmentary. Not surprisingly, therefore, orders were given that strenuous efforts should be made to acquire a fuller picture both of developments in Korea and of Soviet activities elsewhere.[67] Only in that way would it be possible to discover if the Korean hostilities were part of a larger pattern of Soviet advancement, information that was crucial for the attempt to ascertain Soviet intentions. This concern with possible Soviet behaviour indicates that the decision-making unit was cautious rather than reckless. There was nothing resembling the over-confidence that characterised the later interventions in Cuba and Vietnam. Nor were policy-makers oblivious to the long-term domestic costs of military involvement in Korea. Although there was immediate and overwhelming support for Truman's firm stance, the President and his advisers were aware that this might not be sustained as the human and financial costs of the commitment began to rise.[68] The decision to intervene was made in full awareness of the dangers and potential difficulties, and the worst excesses of groupthink were avoided.

Groupthink intruded even less into the 1948 decision to resist the Soviet blockade of Berlin with an airlift of essential supplies to the city. Alternative courses of action were discussed and dissected more vigorously than in the Korean case two years later. At first there was even disagreement over whether or not the US should attempt to remain in Berlin, with Secretary of the Army Kenneth Royall expressing concern that a firm commitment to the city might lead to a situation where the United States would have to fight its way in.[69] Although Royall was overruled by Truman, further disagreement arose over the wisdom of the air lift itself. Finally, Truman demonstrated his willingness to 'take the necessary action in the teeth of the conflicting and, indeed, the contrary opinions of his principal advisers'.[70] If the President was not swayed by the hesitancy of some of his advisers, neither was he prepared to accept the demands of others for a land convoy to break the blockade. The overall picture, however, is again one of frank and open discussion in which anxieties and doubts were honestly and sometimes brutally expressed.

It should be apparent by now that, although the precise style and manner of decision-making may differ from one set of policy-makers to another, critical scrutiny of the challenge and careful evaluation of alternative ways of meeting it are features of superpower crises. The motivation to avoid the comfortable platitudes and mutual reassurances of groupthink is highest when the result could be not merely a foreign policy fiasco, but war with the opposing superpower. Thus it seems that neither stress nor groupthink necessarily erode the ability of decision-makers to form rational judgements on which actions in crises can be based.

V Politics and Decision-making in International Crises

But what of the political elements in decision-making? Is not any analysis of policy-making less than adequate if it fails to acknowledge the intrusion of domestic political considerations into official calculations? Does the above analysis present an interpretation of crisis decision-making that is artificial, apolitical and almost 'antiseptic' in its approach? Can it really be the case, for example, that 'during the brief period of decision-making in June 1950, there was no time, and no need, for politics in the conventional sense'? [71] Merely because a decision was confined within the executive branch and sheltered from immediate public and parliamentary scrutiny does not mean that its authors were immune to political pressures or oblivious to political needs. The fact that policy-makers face an international crisis does not automatically ensure that they cease to be domestic politicians. They still have to operate against a backdrop of domestic politics which may expose them, indirectly, to severe pressures or subject them to significant constraints. How important are such pressures and constraints? Can they cause policy to deviate from the rational?

It is acknowledged that the onslaught of the 'political' explanation is by far the most challenging, and potentially the most damaging, to the present argument that crisis decision-making approximates closely to the model of strategic rationality. There are two major theses that must be examined since both imply that Roger Hilsman's claim that 'policy-making is politics' is as relevant to crisis situations as to non-crises. The first is that the way policy-makers interpret and respond to 'threatening' or 'challenging' international developments is influenced enormously by domestic political needs. The second is that crisis decision-making cannot be understood apart from the political dynamics of small group decision-making. Both propositions have been framed most strongly in relation to John Kennedy's behaviour and policies during the Cuban Missile Crisis. Particular attention is focused on this crisis, therefore, and an attempt made to demonstrate that the choice of the 'quarantine' or blockade option can be explained most satisfactorily in terms of rational calculation for crisis management purposes. Although the 'political' perspectives provide added insights, they are less crucial to our understanding than their proponents claim.

One aspect of the first argument is the extent to which political considerations help determine those situations that policy-makers define as crises. An extreme variation of the same thesis suggests that, on occasions, policy-makers deliberately and unnecessarily create or provoke an international crisis in order to rally domestic support and silence internal dissent. When American nuclear forces were put on alert during the Middle East War of October 1973, for example, the opinion was widespread that this had more to do with the threat to the Nixon Administration resulting from Watergate than with the Soviet threat to Israel.[72] It is argued below that the alert was, in fact, appropriate to the circumstances. Nevertheless, the possibility cannot be dismissed that an international crisis can have a practical and immediate utility for a government facing strong domestic opposition and criticism. Whether these short-term political considerations are sufficient to lead a government into deliberately initiating a crisis as opposed to overemphasising the dangers of any confrontation that does occur, however, is doubtful.

There is another, and more important, variation of this type of argument which cannot be dismissed so easily. It has been expressed extremely well by Thomas Halper in his claim that

. . . Presidents define situations as 'crises' if they are perceived as constituting serious and immediate threats to national or presidential appearances of strength, competency, or resolve, even if these situations do not pose substantial dangers to national security and are seen as not posing such dangers.[73]

The Soviet installation of missiles in Cuba obviously did challenge such appearances, in part because Kennedy had made several speeches stating that the presence of 'offensive' missiles on the island would not be tolerated by the United States. Moreover, it is indisputable that a failure to oppose Khrushchev's move would have provoked serious political problems for Kennedy. As Halper puts it, 'A defeat in Cuba might have cracked the brittle surface of Kennedy's public image and self-esteem, no small matter for a man as concerned with public opinion as he was,'[74] It was a question of effectiveness as well as image. Kennedy's prestige was in danger of being severely tarnished within his own administration and the Congress as well as with the public. If this had happened he would have been a less effective President, unable to maintain the loyalty of his subordinates and almost certain to encounter strong opposition on a variety of issues and problems having nothing to do with Cuba. Thus a policy of inaction would have been to 'invite a second "Bay of Pigs", thereby sealing the fate of his administration: a short chapter in the history books entitled "Crucified over Cuba" '.[75] Salvation could be achieved only through a firm stance resulting in the removal of the missiles. The President and his advisers were fully conscious of the political pressures for action. Although there was no explicit discussion of the domestic aspects of the crisis during the Ex. Comm. deliberations, all the participants were aware of the political implications of failure.[76] As John Kenneth Galbraith has noted, once the missiles were there, 'the political needs of the Kennedy Administration urged it to take almost any risk to get them out'.[77]

Prominent among these political needs were the impending mid-term congressional elections. Not surprisingly, several commentators have suggested that Kennedy's actions were dictated primarily by the desire to avoid a Republican landslide victory in the November polls. At the time *The Tribune* put the point very strongly: 'It may be that Kennedy is risking blowing the world to hell in order to sweep a few Democrats into office.'[78] A less passionate and more reasoned version of the same theme has been put forward by I. F. Stone. He has argued that, after staking his reputation on keeping Soviet missiles out of Cuba, for the President to have gone into the elections with the missiles intact would have been disastrous for the Democratic Party and, by implication, for him as its leader.[79] Such a view has become increasingly popular as the Missile Crisis has receded in time. One recent analysis has reiterated and developed the theme at length:

> Why was there a crisis in the first place? The answer is found in part in one of the unacknowledged necessities in the conduct of American international affairs – domestic political considerations. The Kennedy Administration's sense of its own precarious electoral position . . . argued for an immediate and forceful response, no matter what the strategic reality was of having Russian missiles near American borders.[80]

As a result some of the possible options, such as doing nothing, going to the UN or taking only diplomatic action to get the missiles removed, were completely dismissed at the outset.

The picture is in some respects very persuasive. It is easy to go too far in this direction, however, and overlook the compelling demands of the international situation faced by Kennedy. A swift and energetic response was regarded as essential, primarily because of the drastic nature of the Soviet action and its possible international repercussions. Even if the domestic inducements and pressures for action had been non-existent, Kennedy could hardly have allowed Khrushchev's move to go unchallenged. To have done so would have been a blatant abdication of his responsibility as chief custodian of the interests and wellbeing of the United States. As one analyst has commented, the statesman or policy-maker '. . . is virtually compelled by his role to view his primary responsibility as that of advancing the interests of his own nation-state in competition with . . . other nation-states'.[81] To revert to the strategic rationality model, the firm American stance can be understood in terms of the chessgame analogy. The competition between the superpowers had dominated the international system since 1945. It had also reached a fairly intense stage in the early 1960s with Khrushchev seemingly embarked on a renewed offensive against the West. The pressure on Berlin, the announcement of Soviet support for 'wars of national liberation' and Khrushchev's brutal treatment of Kennedy at the Vienna Summit meeting all suggested that the Soviet leader had scant respect for Eisenhower's successor. In a contest in which a willingness to take risks and honour commitments was of the essence, this augured ill for the United States.

Indeed, the Soviet installation of missiles in Cuba seemed to be a flagrant and direct challenge to the Kennedy Administration. Not only was Khrushchev trespassing in an area that had long been the exclusive preserve of the United States, but he also appeared oblivious to public warnings about the type of weapons that would be tolerated in Cuba. If Kennedy had failed to respond, therefore, his prestige would have been seriously damaged in the eyes of both friends and enemies. Acquiescence in Khrushchev's move would not only have sown doubts in the minds of allies about US promises and commitments, but would also have been an invitation to the Soviet Union to undertake further probes. Furthermore, if the missiles had remained in Cuba, Khrushchev's bargaining position would have been significantly enhanced for a renewed offensive against Berlin. It was considerations such as these that Kennedy had in mind when he commented that the missiles would overturn the political balance of power if not the military balance.

Even if all the arguments about the missiles adding to the vulnerability of the US homeland and posing an immediate and

direct threat to national security are given little credence, therefore, the logic of a strong response is almost unassailable, the
dangers of a weak one clearly apparent. Security was not defined
in purely military terms. Kennedy was aware of something that
those who attribute his behaviour to domestic political considerations seem to ignore, namely the identification of the president
with the state itself. If the president is regarded as weak, then
the United States itself may be seen as incapable of forceful
action in international affairs. In a conflict like the Cold War,
where will is probably of greater import than military strength,
it is essential that vacillation and indecision be avoided. Thus, as
Alexander George has pointed out, 'not merely his personal
prestige and his political future, but also the prestige and interest
of the United States were at stake'.[82] Consequently, Kennedy's
actions can be interpreted as a rational response to a perceived
threat to United States' interests and security rather than a policy
motivated by considerations of political expediency or personal
gain. In the last analysis, however, it is impossible to prove con-
clusively that domestic factors were only secondary. 'It is idle
to attempt to sort out and weigh separately, as some critics have
tried to do, these two dimensions of the President's motivation',
since they complemented and reinforced each other.[83] What was
good for the international statesman was also good for the
domestic politician.

The same is true of the Korean decision. If Truman had
allowed the North Korean invasion of 1950 to go unchecked, this
would have been added to the fall of China as 'proof' of the
Administration's 'softness' on communism and provided the
critics with further grounds for attack. Although there is little
evidence that this was a vital factor in the President's calculations, it might have reinforced his preference for a strong line,
particularly after his initial firmness won overwhelming and
immediate public support.[84] In the 1948 Berlin Crisis, however,
domestic and international pressures worked in opposite direc-
tions. Robert Murphy, General Clay's political adviser in Berlin,
has argued that, when discussions over how to respond to the
Blockade were taking place in the White House, 'several extraneous factors were influencing the momentous decisions'.[85] But,
as he himself admits, although Truman was far behind Dewey in
the election polls, and it was felt that action that might be con-

sidered reckless by the voters could only lead to a further decline in his popularity, the President was still far more willing than his advisers to take risks. Calculating the effects of inaction, the President saw an independent West Berlin as being crucial to the maintenance of America's position in Western Europe. Aware that the situation demanded a vigorous response, Truman acted accordingly. In this instance, therefore, compelling international needs overrode the domestic constraints on policy.

The conclusion is that, although domestic politics should not be overlooked in any worthwhile analysis of crisis decision-making, it is misleading to attribute to them the dominant influence that some recent observers have claimed. Political considerations are not irrelevant, but they are a far less salient or prominent element in policy-makers' calculations than is the international situation. In Cuba, Korea and Berlin, United States policies can best be understood as *reasonable* or *natural reactions* to threatening international situations. The threats were all the more menacing because of the bipolar division of the international system. As John Spanier has noted:

> Bipolarity leaves the principal adversaries feeling such a high degree of insecurity that they are virtually 'compelled' to react against one another's external threats. The reason is that in such a distribution of power the balance is constantly at stake. Each superpower, fearing that its adversary will achieve hegemony, will be extremely sensitive to the slightest shifts of power.[86]

Although this argument exaggerates the sensitivity of the superpowers to each other's actions, it nevertheless provides considerable insight into why some situations are interpreted as crises. This does not mean that domestic factors are superfluous to explanations of American policies; but it does suggest that, in each of the cases examined, decision-makers had ample justification for defining the situation as a crisis and for taking resolute actions irrespective of domestic circumstances. As Stanley Hoffmann has written, 'more often than not a crisis is to the policy-makers not an event of debateable relevance to the US interests which they *choose* to treat as an emergency, but an event believed, rightly or wrongly, to be of indisputable importance, creating a *compelling necessity* for action.'[87]

But what of the exact form of that action? Can it also be interpreted as a *natural* or *typical* response, little influenced by the personalities of those involved in formulating it? Against this, it has been argued that personal relations in the decision-making unit exert considerable influence on the shape of the policies adopted, that 'choices are based on the relative political influence of those who favour certain ones, not on an abstract calculus in which the best choice is deduced from the facts of the situation'.[88] This hypothesis has been put forward with particular force in relation to the choice of the blockade option by the United States in 1962. Graham Allison, in a work highlighting hitherto neglected dimensions of policy formulation, has suggested that the choice of the blockade over the air strike cannot be understood apart from the politics of small group decision-making. 'What prevented the air strike was a fortuitous coincidence of a number of factors – the absence of any one of which might have permitted that option to prevail.'[89] These included inaccurate information suggesting that a 'surgical' air strike to eliminate the missiles could not succeed, Robert Kennedy's argument about the immorality of an air strike against a small nation, McNamara's emphasis on the need to 'maintain options', and often-overlooked personality factors. It is suggested that the President came down firmly on the side of the blockade proponents because they were personally more congenial to him than the air strike advocates. 'The advisers in whom the President had the greatest confidence' – McNamara, Robert Kennedy and Theodore Sorensen – were the major opponents of the air strike. On the other hand, 'the coalition that had formed behind the President's initial preference gave him reason to pause. *Who* supported their air strike – the chiefs of staff, McCone, Rusk, Nitze, and Acheson – counted as much as *how* they supported it.' They were 'not the President's natural allies'.[90]

In other words, the choice of a blockade was influenced by a strange mixture of careful calculation, mis-information and personal preferences. Although it is difficult to disentangle the relative importance of each of these influences, the rational and calculated aspects of the choice should not be minimised. Indeed, it is easy to overestimate the importance of both the personality factors and the inaccurate information. That the latter was far from decisive is suggested by Robert Kennedy's account of a meeting between the President and the Commander-in-Chief of the Tactical Air Command *after* it had been decided to implement a blockade. Kennedy claims that there was a 'small linger-ing doubt' in the President's mind about the wisdom of this choice but that it disappeared when he learned that even a major sur-prise attack could not be certain of destroying all the missile sites.[91] While it is true that equally pessimistic assessments of a 'surgical' air strike had influenced the earlier deliberations, the fact that the President's doubts were only 'small' hardly suggests that more optimistic – and in fact more accurate – information would have swayed the decision. Nor were the 'lingering doubts' really surprising. With a decision of such magnitude it was almost inevitable that the President would have some reservations over whatever course of action was finally adopted.

There is also a danger in attributing too much weight to the politics of personalities. By emphasising who the advocates were rather than what they advocated, it is possible to lose sight of the arguments themselves. Care should be taken, therefore, not to downgrade the fact that the rationale for the blockade was ulti-mately more compelling than that for the air strike – irrespective of who the proponents for each alternative were. This emerges very clearly from an examination of the President's problem. Essentially, his task was to find an alternative that would reconcile two potentially conflicting objectives. He had to manage the crisis skilfully enough to get the missiles in Cuba removed, with-out thereby precipitating a nuclear war. What were interpreted as vital national interests had to be preserved, but not at the cost of mutual annihilation. The difficulty was that the United States could hope to obtain this first objective only through moves that carried substantial risks of escalation. Yet for the second to be achieved the risks had to be minimised and the escalation process kept firmly under control. The various alternatives, therefore, had to be assessed in terms of their contribution to *both* these objec-tives. At the extremes were options that kept risks low but held out little prospect of removing the missiles and those that were more likely to remove the missiles but involved an inordinate risk of war with the Soviet Union. The rational policy in these circum-stances, however, was one that offered a reasonable prospect of achieving both objectives simultaneously and thereby reconciling as far as possible the divergent values and objectives of the Presi-dent. It was not a case of fulfilling one objective at the expense of the other, but of finding that course of action which held most promise of satisfying both.

When the problem is expressed in these terms, the logic of choosing the blockade over the air strike clearly emerges. The 'quarantine' offered a better prospect that the crisis could be managed in such a way that the missiles would be removed and the uppermost levels of conflict avoided. The air strike, while more relevant to the problem of the missiles already in Cuba than was the blockade, carried a far higher risk of escalation. For this reason it was rejected. This is not to say that there were no disadvantages to the blockade. Indeed, it may have erred on the side of the cautious.[92] But it was better to err in this direction than the opposite, particularly as it was only the preliminary move. As McNamara so forcefully argued, the blockade did not rule out an intensification of pressure, including possible resort to an air strike, if it did not itself suffice to make Khrushchev withdraw the missiles. In choosing it, Kennedy 'accepted the risk of war; but he did not behave recklessly to increase its probability'.[93] Thus the blockade can be seen as the *natural* or *typical* reaction, given the need to moderate the demands of 'coercive diplomacy' with those of 'disaster avoidance'. Of all the options, it best fitted the requirements of crisis management, and although not ideal it lacked the dangers, deficiencies and disabilities of the other possible alternatives. It can best be understood, therefore, as 'the distillation of a collective intellectual effort of a high order'[94] rather than the product of an essentially political process.

This is not to say that decision-making in a crisis will invariably be rational and non-political : the participants are unlikely to be totally oblivious to the needs of domestic politics or immune to the effects of stress and the temptations of groupthink. Furthermore, it is not inconceivable that in the Soviet Union political infighting among the leadership is not only more intense than in the United States, but continues unabated through superpower confrontations.[95] Nevertheless, the American experience does suggest, albeit tentatively, that such factors tend to diminish in importance during these crises. If this is so, then analyses that emphasise the rationality of Soviet decision-making may be particularly appropriate to crisis situations. Indeed, it may be that, in the Soviet Union as well as the United States, crisis decision-making does not deviate too markedly from the model of strategic rationality; leaders clarify their values to a greater extent than usual, assess the possible alternatives more thoroughly and calculate more explicitly the potential costs and risks of their actions. Perhaps the main reason for this is the awareness of being 'in a dangerous, unpredictable situation, from which could easily erupt a war which neither side wants'.[96] As a result, decision-makers realise they have a particularly crucial task to perform. How they perform it is the subject of subsequent chapters.

CHAPTER SIX

Maintaining Control
Over Events

I Introduction

The desire to control or defuse a superpower confrontation may be a necessary condition for its peaceful resolution, but it is hardly a sufficient condition. A crisis situation can get out of hand and lead to war despite strenuous efforts by the participants to avoid such an outcome. Even if decision-makers successfully resist the pressures discussed in the previous chapter, there remain two major sources of danger. The first is that crisis bargaining will go awry – with disastrous results; the second, which is equally disturbing, is that the participants inadvertently will lose control over events. The problem is that both possibilities may be endemic in crisis situations. Bargaining and manoeuvres, threats and counter-threats are a central feature of international crises. The decision-makers have certain objectives for the attainment of which they are prepared not only to tolerate but also to create risks of war. In addition there are risks, dangers and uncertainties that are neither deliberately created nor entirely controlled by the protagonists: these have been identified by several commentators as the *autonomous* risks of crisis since they are almost intrinsic to such situations.[1]

Glenn Snyder has suggested that the major problem in bargaining, which involves 'controlled behaviour based on reasoned calculation', is possible miscalculation. 'The parties calculate, but for a variety of reasons . . . they calculate badly.'[2] The opponent's actions may be misperceived or, if perceived correctly, may be wrongly evaluated. There is also a danger of being over-confident that the adversary will back down, of assuming that his commitment is weaker than one's own. This can lead to a far riskier and more provocative course of action than an accurate assessment of the opponent's resolve would have warranted. As a result the participants unintentionally become committed to incompatible objectives. This is even more likely if there is a failure to appreciate the extent of the adversary's interests, an inability to assess the weight he puts on the issue in dispute. Thus, coercive bargaining tactics and the manipulation of risks are perilous undertakings that can all too easily go wrong.

Miscalculation is *not* the only problem though. Some bargaining moves are particularly dangerous not because they may be based on faulty calculations, but because they diminish the controllability of the situation. Indeed, the inherent uncertainties of a crisis can be exploited for bargaining purposes by making 'threats that leave something to chance' and raising the possibility that events might unintentionally get out of control.[3] The distinction between the two types of risk, therefore, is far from absolute: there is considerable overlap between bargaining and control problems. Consequently, it is hardly surprising that the same considerations that lead to measures to counter the autonomous risks also infuse the bargaining process and influence which tactics are adopted and which rejected as too volatile. Concern with freedom of action, for example, necessitates vigorous attempts to monitor and control the behaviour of both subordinates and allies to ensure that the government does not get locked inadvertently into a position where its freedom of choice is severely restricted.[4] It also militates against those bargaining moves that depend for their effectiveness on relinquishing such freedom. Similarly, great care is taken to ensure that violence does not break out accidentally, while violent bargaining moves also tend to be avoided as potentially uncontrollable.

In other words, efforts to maintain control of the situation and attempts to reduce the risks of crisis bargaining complement and strengthen one another. Just as the dangers in a crisis are inextricably linked and mutually reinforcing, so are the techniques of crisis management mutually supporting. The desire to maintain control of events, in fact, helps to establish the parameters within which bargaining occurs and to define the limits of permissible behaviour. For analytical purposes however the autonomous risks and the bargaining risks to some extent can be dealt with separately, and the main concern in the present chapter is with the former. The range of potential dangers is identified more fully, after which the 'techniques' or modes of behaviour that have been developed and refined by the superpowers in order to counter, reduce or overcome such dangers are explored at length.

The intractable nature of crisis situations has already been mentioned in connection with the possibility of events getting out of hand and developing a logic or momentum of their own. It is conceivable that events may pass outside the scope of conscious choice and decision, with the result that, despite all the efforts of the participants, their interaction ends in an unwanted and potentially disastrous outbreak of hostilities. In other words, a crisis can lead to a war that no one really desired, planned for or expected. To develop Stanley Hoffmann's analogy: although the superpowers may keep their feet over the brake pedals when they play chicken in the nuclear age, this does not eliminate the possibility of mechanical failure and consequent disaster. The way in which such failures might occur must now be examined.

II The Problem of Loss of Control

Some of the most alarming and eloquent passages of Robert Kennedy's account of the Cuban Missile Crisis concern the possibility of a loss of control over events, a development which it was felt could precipitate a nuclear holocaust between the superpowers.[5] His fears that the United States and the Soviet Union might somehow stumble into war have been echoed and amplified by many participants in this and other crises. But what precisely are they afraid of? What are the ways in which events can get out of control?

The first way in which the participants might lose control of events is through the outbreak of violence. It is generally felt that, if a crisis spills over into a process of violent interaction between the superpowers, then they are likely to be swept along by a 'logic of events' powerless to resist, let alone reverse direction. A kind of action-reaction process sets in which is not susceptible to the will and direction of the protagonists themselves. 'The idea here seems to be that once violence breaks out a whole new set of forces takes over, a new pattern of interaction with an inner "logic" of its own which tends to develop to its fullest extent more or less autonomously.'[6] Once the superpowers are engaged in violence as opposed to coercive bargaining and diplomatic manoeuvres, military necessity could replace political calculation as the key to action, with the result that both sides almost inexorably commit more and more of their resources to avoiding defeat. The commitment of each state's prestige and resources in fact could become so overwhelming that neither superpower would be prepared to tolerate even a limited setback, and would react to any intensification of effort by the opponent with an even greater increase in its own efforts. In other words, because violence is inherently uncontrollable, its outbreak could precipitate an ever-deepening conflict from which both sides find it impossible to extricate themselves. Once started the process may be irreversible, with the result that the protagonists eventually find themselves involved in large-scale hostilities. This danger was recognised one hundred and fifty years ago by Carl von Clausewitz who wrote: 'as one side dictates the law to the other, there arises a sort of reciprocal action, which logically must lead to an extreme'.[7] This process could begin in one of three ways. It could be sparked off by an inadvertent outbreak of violence such as a riot or an unauthorised use of military force. It could begin with a calculated gamble involving a deliberate resort to violence by one of the participants. Finally, it might be the result of emotional or irrational actions by policy-makers in one or other of the states involved.

Emotional or irrational decisions, however, seem far more likely *after* violence has broken out than before and could prove critical factors in maintaining the upward spiral of hostilities. The process is likely to be a cumulative one, since the higher the level of violence, the greater the degree of stress to which policy-makers would be subjected and the more difficult it would be for them to regain their equanimity. Anger, frustration, pride, suspicion or a plain desire for revenge might provoke actions that careful consideration or rational calculation would have urged the decision-makers to avoid. Emotional intrusions could blind them to opportunities for containing or dampening down the level of violence. In one sense, therefore, the initiation of nuclear war need be little more than a 'crime of passion'. Thus, the second way in which events become uncontrollable is through a series of irrational actions which compound one wrong move upon another in a race towards extinction. 'The statesman "loses control" here in the sense that he stops calculating rationally; his emotions replace reason; he can only be provoked not coerced.'[8] In such circumstances the worst possible construction would be put on the actions of the adversary: his moves towards accommodation would be treated with disdain and suspicion and his resolute actions interpreted as highly provocative and further evidence of aggressive intent. As a result disaster might be impossible to avoid.

Closely related to these first two dangers is the possibility that a government's freedom of action may diminish considerably during the course of an international crisis. The situation could easily get out of hand as policy-makers on one or both sides find their actions restricted, their freedom of choice severely curtailed. Yet it has been suggested that this is an inevitable feature of crisis decision-making: the number of alternatives available to the participants gradually but ineluctably narrows.[9] Thus governments may find themselves unwilling captives of past decisions, taken without full knowledge or awareness of the probable consequences. They may see no alternative other than to continue along the prescribed course despite the excessive risks involved. An overwhelming belief that the state is too deeply enmeshed in the conflict to disentangle itself unilaterally without an intolerable loss of prestige and a disastrous diminution of its credibility is one possible manifestation of this problem. Another is a situation where the government comes to regard its opponent's demands as so unreasonable that a further intensification of the struggle seems to be the only feasible option. Indeed, it has been argued that 'the danger of war is never greater than when the nation's leaders define the situation as one in which the options are reduced to a war or humiliation with a crippling loss of "face" '.[10] Such compulsions are likely to be even more intense if they are related to time pressures: policy-makers may perceive the necessity to take particular actions not because they are especially beneficial, but because to refrain would allow the opponent to obtain advantages liable to prove decisive if hostilities occur.[11]

Freedom of choice, however, is not solely a matter of perceptions. Under certain circumstances only a few alternatives may actually be available. One of Graham Allison's most important contributions to our understanding of crisis behaviour is the awareness he has provoked of how policy-makers may be severely curtailed in their choice of options by what the organisations that they nominally head and control are equipped, prepared and trained to undertake. As he has written, 'Existing organizational routines for employing present physical capabilities constitute the range of effective choice open to government leaders confronted with any problem.'[12] Yet crisis management demands flexibility, a willingness to innovate, creative adaptation to novel circumstances and a delicacy of touch – all qualities that large-scale bureaucratic organisations lack. Nor do formal hierarchical agencies eagerly respond to demands to develop these qualities. Each organisation has its own particular ethos, rationale and modes of behaviour that have developed through tradition and long experience. By the time a government is in the midst of a crisis, therefore, it may be too late: organisations that work according to carefully prepared scripts are almost invariably unwilling and unable to ad lib. Thus, unanticipated options may be difficult if not impossible to implement at short notice.

The restriction of alternatives in this way could prove a serious enough problem for officials. It would be even worse if they are burdened with prelaid plans that not only threaten to rob them of all flexibility, but are patently inappropriate to the specific tasks at hand. The implementation of such plans could have incalculable consequences for the decision-makers' ability to control the situation. Nevertheless, they may be strongly advocated by those who have nurtured and developed them. Enthusiastic proponents of prelaid plans are unlikely to see their attendant drawbacks until it is too late.

Even if the small inner core of crisis decision-makers does not allow pre-existing plans to dictate policy, they may encounter other organisational obstacles equally damaging to their aspirations to control events and maintain freedom of action. There is perhaps an inevitable gap between those who decide policy and those who implement it. Consequently, there may also be a gap between the wishes of the former and the deeds of the latter. As Allison has put it,

> Activity according to standard operating procedures and programmes does not constitute far-sighted flexible adaptation to "the issue" . . . . Detail and nuance of actions by organizations are determined chiefly by organizational routines, not government leaders' directions.[13]

If the commands of top officials are clear, explicit and detailed, 'authority leakage' and the distortion of policy-makers' intentions that sometimes occurs when subordinates are given considerable discretionary powers in the interpretation or execution of orders may be avoided.[14] Even so, the organisations implementing policy could prove unresponsive to the precise needs of diplomatic management during crises. Wanting a surgeon's scalpel, policy-makers may find themselves with a butcher's knife.

The problem is likely to be particularly acute if military forces are in close proximity to those of the opponent. Trained specifically for warfare, military forces are not an ideal instrument in situations demanding an enormous degree of caution and restraint. Although it is highly improbable that hostilities would be initiated without explicit orders, a clash between opposing forces resulting from the actions of an over-zealous military commander cannot be discounted entirely. Thus, policy-makers could find themselves losing control over a crisis because of the actions of subordinates. This may be even more of a problem when geographical distance is added to the organisational distance between those who formulate and those who execute policy. Considerable differences of perspective and judgement may arise between decision-makers in the capitals and officials directly caught up by events in the immediate locality of the crisis.[15] The latter, highly conscious of local needs, and the demands of military effectiveness could prove unsympathetic to the cautious attitudes prevailing at the higher levels, and may demand greater discretion and the freedom to carry out what they regard as necessary actions. Any attempt by high-level decision-makers to extend their direction and control into territory traditionally the sole preserve of military competence and expertise or the exclusive domain of the men on the spot could provoke resentment and might even encounter considerable resistance.

Equally intractable problems could arise in relations with allies. States closely allied to the superpowers and conscious primarily of their own needs, interests and objectives could demand a level of support that the superpowers find intolerable. Yet if their alliance obligations and commitments are to have any meaning they may regard it as incumbent upon themselves to provide such support – although only with hesitation and reluctance. Situations where the clients of the United States and the Soviet Union are engaged in open hostilities against each other could be particularly dangerous. If the outcome appeared likely to be disastrous for one of the smaller states, the pressure on its superpower ally to intervene would be considerable. Indeed, the government might feel compelled to provide direct assistance, and thereby become far more deeply entangled than originally intended. Whether the other superpower could afford to see its ally crushed without a similar military intervention seems doubtful. Thus both governments might find their freedom of choice diminished by the precipitate actions of allies, and have little alternative other than to accept a level of risk that under most circumstances they would regard as intolerable. The result could be that the superpowers become locked in to a collision course not through conscious choice and careful calculation of advantage and disadvantage, but because of their limited control over their clients.

Such dangers are inextricably bound up with each other. The actions of military commanders, for example, could lead to a violent incident sparking off an escalation process that is then fuelled by emotional or irrational decision-making, and from which decision-makers feel unable to withdraw. Alternatively, a resort to violence by one side might elicit an even more violent response from the opponent primarily because the capacity for a limited and flexible use of force is not built into its repertoire of options. To attempt to separate these difficulties from one another in a wholly rigorous manner and treat them as distinct and discrete problems, each calling for its own particular and unique solution, would be a highly artificial approach doomed to failure. The peaceful resolution of crises requires carefully concerted measures. Co-ordination is vital. Not surprisingly, therefore, some of the 'techniques' adopted by the superpowers have served several purposes simultaneously. This emerges clearly in the following analysis, which also demonstrates how, in practice, recognition of the problems and dangers outlined above has led to efforts to overcome them.

III The Avoidance of Deliberate Violence

Perhaps the first and most important way in which control of events considerations manifest themselves is through the superpowers' unwillingness to resort to deliberate violence. Although both Russia and the United States have been prepared to use coercive bargaining methods to gain advantage, they have concurrently been extremely reluctant to employ overt violence. Indeed, the distinction between coercion and violence has formed the most salient threshold in superpower crises.[16] Both governments on the whole have studiously avoided crossing this threshold, which consequently has had far more relevance and importance than the better publicised distinction between conventional and nuclear hostilities. Not content with avoiding nuclear warfare against each other, the United States and the Soviet Union have been scrupulous to avoid *any* type of open and violent conflict: the *threat* of violence has been permissible, its actual *use* against each other's forces virtually outlawed. In fact, it is little exaggeration to suggest that the coercion-violence threshold has been almost religiously observed.

The initiation ceremony began with the Berlin Blockade of 1948, and it is significant that even in the first major crisis of the Cold War the superpowers attempted to keep their differences within bounds. The Kremlin, so it appears, determined that its action over Berlin should not end in war. Consequently, only non-violent pressure was exerted against the Western position. Soviet propaganda was aggressive in tone, but Soviet policy was cautious in action.[17] Although nuclear deterrence was not the all-pervading factor it has since become, the antagonists were intent on avoiding open hostilities and on maintaining peace. War weariness was still a rampant force in both countries: the Soviet Union was too absorbed in repairing the devastation of the Second World War to embark on further military adventures, while the United States had demobilised a large part of its forces and was acutely aware of the weakness of its military position in Europe.[18] In retrospect, it is clear that the crisis took place on a subdued note. Each side was immensely careful to avoid any action that might invite a violent response from the opponent. The Soviet blockade was built up gradually, and conciliatory justifications were provided at each stage. By placing the onus on 'technical difficulties', the Soviets left themselves with a way of retreat if needed. The gradual buildup was also a probing process designed to test Western determination.[19] Since Western reactions were relatively mild, Stalin probably felt confident that the land blockade would not provoke the kind of violent military response likely to lead to war. It can be argued therefore that, although the Russians have been more willing to take risks over Berlin than over any other point of conflict with the West, the most striking feature of their behaviour is the way they have tried to keep these risks controllable. Despite an overwhelming local military preponderance the Soviet Union has not resorted to violence to make its will prevail.[20]

The United States has been equally prudent. This is reflected in the response to the Soviet blockade of 1948. Despite the exhortations of General Clay in Washington and Aneurin Bevan in London, neither the United States nor Britain would sanction an armed convoy in an attempt to break the blockade. Clay's argument was based on the manner in which the Russians had carefully avoided actions likely to elicit a forceful response. Although he did not deny the 'possibility of trouble', he claimed that 'the chance of such a convoy being met by force with subsequent developments of hostilities was small' because of the Soviet determination to avoid war.[21] President Truman was not convinced. Having decided that the United States could not relinquish its position in Berlin, he rejected armed road convoys as too risky, opting instead for an airlift.[22] While this was a response that displayed Western firmness and an unwillingness to retreat under pressure, it was not an irreversible step and was less likely than the convoy to cause an armed clash.

Such advantages notwithstanding, a number of former diplomats closely involved with the Berlin problem have been extremely critical of Truman's decision. Robert Murphy, General Clay's political adviser in Berlin in 1948, has described the airlift as a 'deceptive victory' and claimed that, in retrospect, he should have resigned over the Administration's failure to challenge the blockade.[23] Writing in the early 1960s, he stated: 'Few observers seemed to realize that our decision to depend exclusively upon the airlift was a surrender of our hard-won rights in Berlin, a surrender which has plagued us ever since.'[24] Consequently, a land convoy, by protecting Western access rights and avoiding such a surrender, would have been a more appropriate response. Similar views have been echoed more recently by another 'old Berliner' in his description of the airlift as 'a cowardly evasion'.[25]

Such criticisms are hardly justified. Although Truman may

have overestimated the risks of directly challenging the blockade, a tank convoy would undoubtedly have been a dangerous gamble at best and one that could have resulted in both Soviet and American soldiers being killed – with unpredictable consequences. Having firmly established the blockade, could the Soviet Union really be expected to allow it to go by default at the first direct challenge? If not, then the West would have had to resort to violence to render its challenge effective. This was something that President Truman was reluctant to contemplate, perhaps because it would have been an enormous departure from the type of campaign being conducted by the adversary. Although the distinction between coercion and violence may not have been explicitly and formally acknowledged at this stage in the Cold War, it was already proving of great practical significance.

It could be argued, of course, that Truman was playing into Stalin's hands and allowing the Soviet Union to dictate the terms on which the crisis was conducted, terms that naturally were to Soviet advantage.[26] But this interpretation overlooks that the concessions were not all one way: Moscow demonstrated a comparable reluctance to adopt violent alternatives and made no serious attempt to interfere with the airlift. An earlier incident in April 1948 – before the crisis began in earnest – had shown that the Western Allies were prepared to take strong actions to deal with Soviet interference in the air. This probably cautioned Moscow against anything more than minor harassment.[27] Indeed, 'to disrupt the airlift, which soon acquired its own momentum, Stalin would have had to resort to shooting down planes in the air corridors, that is, to military measures parallelling those Washington had rejected'.[28]

In a curious perhaps unintended way, therefore, the actions of each of the participants were cumulative in imposing restraint. By finding a non-violent reaction to a non-violent Soviet move, Truman had very skilfully pushed the onus for opening hostilities back on to Stalin. Yet by the cautious way he had implemented the blockade in the first place, the Soviet leader had signified both his intention and his desire to avoid violence. For him to have changed the 'rules' halfway through would have injected a novel and extraordinarily dangerous element of unpredictability into the situation. Furthermore, to the extent that he was exploiting President Truman's desire to avoid violent exchanges and the

American unwillingness to initiate hostilities, any action taken by Stalin in this direction could only prove self-defeating. Not only would it invite retaliation against Soviet planes, but it might also make the tank convoy appear a far less drastic step to the policy-makers in Washington. Once one of the superpowers crossed the threshold it would have been much easier for the other to follow it: the fact that each desisted from so doing added to the incentives of the opponent to observe similar restraint.

The extent to which these calculations figured consciously in the minds of the opposing policy-makers is difficult to establish. Nevertheless, it can be argued that the Berlin Crisis of 1948 established a precedent with considerable relevance for the behaviour of decision-makers in subsequent confrontations. The similarities between the handling of the Berlin Crisis and the confrontation in Cuba fourteen years later are remarkable. Truman's rejection of the armed convoy in favour of the airlift, for example, finds a distinct parallel in Kennedy's rejection of the invasion and air strike options as the initial methods of removing the Soviet missiles from Cuba. Both options would almost inevitably have killed some of the 22,000 Russian soldiers in Cuba, and Ambassador Llewellyn Thompson warned that Khrushchev would probably react impulsively to this.[29] Although it is sometimes argued that the Soviet soldiers and technicians in Cuba were expendable, killing them would have been a direct affront to Khrushchev's pride and prestige. In such circumstances an emotional or angry response could not be discounted. Furthermore, it would have changed the rules of the game significantly, perhaps prompting a violent Soviet move against West Berlin. Since the city was extremely vulnerable to Warsaw Pact conventional forces, the Communist leaders could have taken the opportunity to go much further than in 1961 and rid themselves of what had been a chronic irritation since the inception of the Cold War. This is not to suggest that the Russians were eager to do this, particularly as the Berlin Wall had solved many of East Germany's problems. Nevertheless, it may be important that Moscow was not given a pretext for such a move. By avoiding resort to violence in the Caribbean, the United States perhaps helped to ensure that the *status quo* in Europe was not challenged.

The need to avoid violence is further emphasised by the

emotional manner in which President Kennedy reacted to the shooting down of a U–2 over Cuba. Initially, he regarded the incident as a development that put the superpowers in 'an entirely new ball game' and as a result he almost sanctioned an attack on one of the surface-to-air missile sites.[30] After more sober reflection, however, the President decided to wait and see if a continuation of the blockade, combined with preparations for increasingly forceful actions and more forthright diplomatic communications to the Kremlin, would achieve the desired results. Without these second thoughts a violent and potentially explosive series of interactions might have been precipitated. Indeed, the initial reaction to the death of *one* American pilot suggests that Ambassador Thompson was correct: had a substantial number of Soviet personnel been killed or injured, emotion could well have succeeded reason as the basis of decision-making in the Kremlin, perhaps leading to a rash, hasty and ill-considered response.

The shooting down of the U–2 in the first place was, of course, a crossing of the line between coercion and violence. But it was a less drastic flaunting of this convention than almost any other violent action, largely because of the famous incident in 1960 in which a U–2 flown over the Soviet Union had been brought down and Gary Powers, the pilot, captured. Although Krushchev's disclosure of this had disrupted the Paris Summit Conference, there was no question of Western retaliation. Having created a precedent with impunity, Soviet policy-makers may have regarded such an action as an accepted, and acceptable, part of Cold War tactics: planes engaged in espionage activities and deliberately violating the national air space of an adversary were not immune from attack – crisis or no crisis. If the destruction of the U–2 over Cuba on 24 October 1962 resulted from a conscious decision in the Kremlin, therefore, the Soviet leaders may have calculated that their move was endowed with a certain degree of legitimacy by past experience and consequently could be undertaken without serious risk of escalation.[31] It was certainly not a violation of the coercion–violence threshold that was anything like as far-reaching in its effects as some of the options contemplated by the United States would have been. Even so it was an action that nearly had dire repercussions. Although it was a relatively minor transgression of previously observed conventions, it almost provoked a series of moves that would have rendered those conventions totally devoid of meaning. This is perhaps the best indication of both their importance and their fragility.

In other aspects of the crisis the superpowers were even more circumspect. American decision-makers tried to avoid a clash at sea by their careful conduct of the blockade. Although Soviet submarines were harassed and forced to the surface, Kennedy tried to keep to a minimum the possibility of sinking a Soviet ship and thereby presenting Khrushchev with the same kind of direct challenge that would have been involved in an invasion or air strike. By allowing the *Bucharest*, a Soviet oil tanker, through the blockade and selecting the *Marucla*, 'an American-built liberty ship, Panamanian owned, registered from Lebanon, and bound for Cuba under a Soviet Charter', as the first ship to be stopped and boarded, the United States minimised the likelihood of hostilities at sea.[32] The Soviet Union also contributed to this by making no serious attempt to run the blockade. In fact, Khrushchev's decision not to challenge the 'quarantine' closely resembles Stalin's decision in 1948 not to interfere with the Berlin airlift. The onus for taking actions liable to precipitate violence had in both cases been passed back to the Russians: like Stalin, Khrushchev was faced with the dilemma of whether or not to make a move that would almost certainly result in violence. In 1962, though, it was not so much a case of the Soviet Union having to fire the first shot, but of Soviet leaders being faced with the stark alternatives of either provoking or averting an armed clash. As in 1948, the latter course was chosen as Moscow reciprocated and magnified Washington's desire to avoid hostilities.

The distinction between coercion and violence, therefore, is an important aid to crisis management and central to the control of events. Its rigorous observance stems from the feeling that even a localised clash between the armed forces of the two superpowers could spark off a train of events leading to disaster. The prevailing image seems to be very much in accordance with Schelling's view that violence is a hot-headed activity in which actions and commitments can develop a momentum of their own.[33] So deep a hold has this Clausewitzian image of violence obtained that the extreme caution of the superpowers in their direct confrontations has been reproduced in situations where their close allies have been at war. During these latter conflicts the superpowers have generally stood on the sidelines and, although prepared to make bellicose statements and vigorous gestures of support for their clients, have been equally if less obviously active in urging caution and restraint upon them. Most important, they have been unwilling to run on the field and join the mêlée – particularly where it was felt that the opposing superpower might do the same. Attempts to influence events indirectly have not been without their dangers or their frustrations, but the superpowers have regarded this as eminently preferable to being sucked into a violent clash with each other.

The importance attached to non-intervention in such situations is illustrated by an incident during the Arab–Israeli War of 1967. When the Arabs claimed that they had 'real proof of interference' by American and British carrier aircraft on the side of Israel, the United States took great pains to demonstrate that the charges were unfounded. Secretary of State Rusk publicly stated: 'We know that they and some of their friends know where our carriers are.'[34] The same point was emphasised by President Johnson in private communications over the 'hot line' with Kosygin.[35] The United States made clear that it was adopting a stance of non-intervention and that a fabricated charge of this kind should not be used as a pretext for direct interference by the Soviet Union. Although both Washington and Moscow had interests that they were not prepared to sacrifice and commitments they were not prepared to relinquish, they were anxious not to go beyond indirect military aid and diplomatic manoeuvre. To have done so would have invited a deepening and inextricable involvement, perhaps resulting in Soviet and American forces engaged in direct combat.

Nevertheless, there were some threats of military intervention. Early on 10 June, the day the war finally ended, Kosygin used the hot line to inform the United States that, because of Israeli violations of Security Council cease-fire resolutions, an 'independent decision' by Moscow might be necessary. 'He foresaw the risk of a "grave catastrophe" and stated that unless Israel unconditionally halted operations within the next few hours the Soviet Union would take "necessary actions, including military".'[36] This message was almost certainly prompted by Soviet concern about a possible Israeli drive to the Syrian capital Damascus, and was designed to ensure that the United States forced the Israelis into more scrupulous observance of the cease-fire.[37] President Johnson replied that he had already demanded that Israel 'make the ceasefire completely effective and had received assurance that this would be done'.[38] He also ordered the Sixth Fleet to speed up its movement towards the Syrian coast, knowing that this would be carefully monitored by Soviet intelligence and interpreted as a warning against unilateral intervention.[39]

Even without the firm American response, however, the Soviet Union would probably have made further moves only with great reluctance and after considerable hesitation. Paradoxically, the threat to intervene was designed specifically to ensure that intervention would be unnecessary. This interpretation appears to be borne out by Soviet actions:

> Movements of Soviet ships in the Mediterranean were circumspect throughout the crisis. On the day the fighting began, Russian vessels not engaged in the shadowing [of the US Sixth Fleet] remained in their anchorages near the eastern shores of Crete and Cyprus. By their very deeds the Soviets indicated that they were not going to become involved even though their large investment in military equipment for the Arabs was being demolished.[40]

The behaviour of the two superpowers, although superficially different, was actually very similar during the Yom Kippur War of 1973. The reluctance to intervene militarily prevailed intact, even when the Soviet Union became so concerned about the fate of Egypt, in the light of Israeli advances immediately prior to and after the initial cease-fire of 22 October, that its verbal protests were supplemented by visible preparations for direct military intervention. What appeared as vigorous preparation for military action was probably intended as a substitute for it. In order to ensure Israeli restraint the Soviet Union threatened Jerusalem with the 'most serious consequences', while favourably acknowledging President Sadat's request for superpower intervention to enforce the cease-fire. Furthermore, Soviet air force alerts and troop concentrations suggested that if there was no joint superpower peace-keeping force then Moscow would intervene unilaterally.[41] But these preparations, together with diplomatic messages to the United States that have been described as 'brutal' and 'leaving little to the imagination', were probably designed to ensure that Nixon and Kissinger also used their influence to restrain Israel – and thereby eliminated the need for Soviet actions.[42] The United States responded by increasing its efforts to bring about strict observance of the cease-fire. At the same time, American Secretary of State Kissinger emphasised the risks and costs of direct military involvement. As he stated, 'It would be a disaster, if the Middle East, already so torn by local rivalries, would now become . . . a legitimised theatre for the competition of the military forces of the great nuclear powers.'[43] Although the Soviet leaders were far less candid about the dangers of superpower forces being in close proximity in an inherently volatile and potentially unstable situation, they were probably as relieved as United States decision-makers when such actions became unnecessary. This is not to argue that the Soviet Union would not have intervened, merely that, had it done so, it would have been an act of desperation taken only as a last resort. Even when the superpowers have been one step back from hostilities, therefore, they have been reluctant to use overt violence against a government receiving the *full* support of the opponent. Threats and material assistance are permissible: violent intervention is not.

It could be argued that direct American involvement in the Korean War, despite the close relationship believed to exist between the Soviet Union and North Korea, provides a major exception to this 'rule' of non-intervention. The speed and decisiveness of the United States response to the North Korean attack strongly supports this argument. The high degree of caution displayed by American policy *vis-à-vis* the Soviet Union, however, should not be overlooked. Assistance to South Korea was initially confined to air and naval forces and was accompanied by a note to Moscow requesting assurance 'that the Union of Soviet Socialist Republics disavows responsibility for this unprovoked and unwarranted attack, and that it will use its influence with the North Korean authorities to withdraw their invading forces immediately'.[44] Among other things, the note provided an excellent opportunity for the Soviet Union to dissociate itself from the war. It was exploited with consummate skill. Although the Soviet reply laid the responsibility for hostilities on South Korea, it also emphasised that the USSR had withdrawn its troops from Korea earlier than the United States 'and thereby confirmed its traditional principle of non-interference in the internal affairs of other states. And now as well the Soviet government adheres to the principle of the impermissibility of interference by foreign powers in the internal affairs of Korea.'[45] The statement was not entirely unambiguous, but appeared to indicate that the Soviet Union was unwilling to become directly involved, and thereby opened the way for a substantial commitment of American ground forces. Thus, although there was a resort to large-scale violence by one of the superpowers, its adversary had tacitly consented to this and indicated that there were limits to the support *it* was prepared to give *its* client. Despite the American intervention, therefore, the superpowers observed a fundamental tenet of crisis management by avoiding open hostilities against *each other*.

Throughout the war too the United States policy-makers were intent upon avoiding actions likely to provoke a Soviet intervention. This desire was manifested in a number of ways. Perhaps most important were targeting restrictions on bombing. Although President Truman sanctioned air attacks on North Korea early in the war, United States aircraft were ordered to stay well clear of the border with the Soviet Union. Similarly, when the President and the Joint Chiefs of Staff in Washington authorised General MacArthur to conduct operations north of the 38th parallel, their instructions were very specific:

> Your military objective is the destruction of the North Korean Armed Forces. In attaining this objective you are authorized to conduct military operations, including amphibious and airborne landings or ground operations north of the 38th parallel in Korea, provided that at the time of such operations there has been no entry into North Korea by major Soviet or Chinese Communist Forces, no announcement of intended entry, nor a threat to carry out operations military in North Korea. Under no circumstances, however, will your forces cross the Manchurian or USSR borders of Korea and, as a matter of policy, no non-Korean Ground Forces will be used in the north-east provinces bordering the Soviet Union or in the area along the Manchurian border. Furthermore, support of your operations north or south of the 38th parallel will not include Air or Naval action against Manchuria or against USSR territory.[46]

In fact, such restrictions were not fully observed and bombing raids were carried out five miles from the Soviet border. On one occasion American planes actually attacked an airfield a hundred kilometres inside the Soviet Union. The United States, however, was not slow to indicate that the attack was unintended. In a public apology before the United Nations, it stated that 'the pilots had been specifically briefed not to violate the Manchurian or Soviet border. The attack was the result of navigation error and poor judgement in that it was made without positive identification of the target'. The government indicated its intention of taking disciplinary action against those involved, and not only expressed 'its regret that American forces, should have been involved in the violation of the Soviet frontier' but offered to compensate the Soviet Union for the damage that had been inflicted.[47] In spite of such incidents, therefore, the Soviet Union and the United States averted direct military hostilities.

Communist China and the United States were not able to do the same; and, as a result of a series of miscalculations and communication failures, Peking entered the war. Both governments learned a great deal from the experience, however, and in the 1958 Quemoy Crisis were much more cautious, scrupulously observing the distinction between coercion and violence. What had been a major factor in the control of Soviet–American crises was reproduced in what was primarily a Sino-American confrontation. In its verbal statements throughout the 1950s, Peking had deliberately and very carefully cultivated a reputation for recklessness. Yet its actual behaviour in this crisis was anything but reckless. Both the Chinese People's Republic and the United States were anxious to avoid an eruption of hostilities. Thus, although there were violent exchanges, these were restricted to Communist and Nationalist forces and did not involve the United States. The intense artillery bombardment of Quemoy by the Communists initiating the crisis was met not with military force but with an unequivocal demonstration of military power by the United States:

> The Seventh Fleet was ordered to sail for the Taiwan area . . . and US armed forces in the area were put on alert. Additional ships were assigned to the Formosa Strait patrol force and the Seventh Fleet was ordered to 'show itself by supersonic fighter sweeps through the Formosa Straits'.[48]

Such actions were firm without being unnecessarily provocative, and both sides tacitly acknowledged that there was a considerable difference between moves of this kind and the use of violence against one another's forces. This emerges clearly from the cautious manner in which the United States helped to resupply

Quemoy, as well as from Communist China's cautious response. At first, US naval forces escorted the Nationalist convoys only at night and were careful to stay outside the range of the Chinese artillery. Even when they graduated to daylight operations similar precautions were taken: 'United States escorts continued not to approach closer than three miles to the offshore islands. The United States sought to avoid acts that could be construed as combat operations and to lessen the material risk of coming under the fire of shore batteries, . . . The Chinese reciprocated by carefully avoiding attacking US vessels.'[49] In addition, the decision-makers in Washington clearly and publicly rejected Chiang's request for retaliatory strikes against the Chinese mainland.[50] It is also significant that Communist China did not employ its large bomber force against either Quemoy itself or American forces in the area.[51]

Thus a high degree of restraint was exhibited by both Washington and Peking. But although the violent activities – such as the struggle for local air supremacy – were confined to the Chinese Communists and Nationalists, they introduced a disturbing and dangerous element, making it possible, if not probable, that a large-scale Sino–American conflict could be sparked off by an accidental or unintended outbreak of hostilities. Conscious decisions by the major participants to avoid violent actions against each other's forces might not have been sufficient, and there was considerable concern lest an unintended outbreak of violence lead to rapid escalation. Such anxieties were not peculiar to this crisis, of course, and have been an even more pronounced feature of Soviet–American confrontations since 1945. Violent interactions could be enormously damaging to attempts to maintain control over events, irrespective of the way they begin. As well as the adoption of alternatives that do not cross the threshold between coercion and violence, therefore, successful crisis management requires efforts to prevent the inadvertent or accidental outbreak of violence.[52]

IV The Prevention of Inadvertent Violence

On occasions, inadvertent or unauthorised violence has been seen as *the* major problem. In the Berlin Crisis of 1948, for example,

President Truman felt that 'a more immediate danger' than the Russians deliberately initiating hostilities was the possibility that a 'trigger happy Russian pilot or hot-headed communist tank commander might create an incident that could ignite the powder keg'.[53] Equally dangerous was the possibility that riots in the city might get out of control and spill over into fighting between opposing troops. This came very close to happening when guards at the Soviet War Memorial in the British sector of the city fired into a crowd of Western demonstrators who had lowered the Russian flag and were attempting to burn it. Several people were injured, at least two were killed and the situation turned ugly. Fortunately, it was prevented from deteriorating further by the British Provost Marshal, who swiftly ordered the Russians to cease firing, and by British Military Police, who dispersed the crowd and restored order.[54]

Civilian demonstrations of this type have been a particular hazard in Berlin where the passions of the populace in both the Eastern and Western sectors have often run extremely high. In 1961, therefore, the Communist forces were careful to guard against possible protest in East Berlin over the division of the city. Their troop dispositions seem to have been as concerned with cowing any signs of popular resistance as with meeting Western counter-actions to remove the blockade. Indeed, it may be that there was great anxiety on both counts. One analyst has even concluded that 'Fear of a violent uprising on the part of the East Berliners, as well as apprehension of possible Western efforts to remove the barbed wire by force, were undoubtedly strong among the Communist leadership.'[55] Many aspects of the operation can perhaps be understood as attempts to ensure that these fears did not materialise. Precautions were taken in order to avoid any repetition of the 1953 uprising and to reduce the likelihood of a strong Western counter-move. By sealing the borders in the early hours of a Sunday morning, the likelihood of public confusion and immediate violent protests was significantly lessened; by ensuring that the operation was 'a model of concealment, deception, and surprise', the likelihood of a firm Western reaction was considerably diminished.[56] Furthermore, the troops actually working on the barriers, while appearing heavily armed, had not been issued with ammunition. It had been confined to the officers, presumably with the intention of minimising the danger of incidents.[57]

One reason for the cautious and tardy response to the erection of the barriers was that the Western authorities were equally alive to the danger of hostilities being started by an incident within Berlin and wanted to avoid any actions liable to inflame further an already enraged population.[58] Even when the immediate tension surrounding the erection of the wall subsided, caution remained the keynote of American policy. Some displays of firmness were made however. Among them was the despatch of General Clay to Berlin as President Kennedy's special representative. Clay quickly realised that both the morale of the West Berliners and the prestige of the NATO allies had been seriously undermined and saw his first priority as being to bolster them up. In order to do this he took a series of measures, each of which was relatively minor in itself, but which together added up to a significant demonstration of Western resolve.[59] Clay's helicopter flights to Steinstuecken – a small Western enclave in the East – were designed explicitly to achieve this. After the initial threats and protests of the East Germans had subsided, the flights virtually became accepted as routine. Western military patrols along the *autobahn* were also resumed without serious incident. It soon became clear, however, that General Clay's actions disturbed decision-makers in Washington almost as much as they did those in Moscow. Realising this, the Soviets took full advantage. Although on Clay's insistence the *autobahn* patrols had continued for over a week, Soviet officials protested against them in the hope that he would be overruled. They were not disappointed – Clay was ordered to desist from these activities. United States troops were also withdrawn from the Wall for fear that shootings of refugees by East German police would lead to a major incident.

Some critics have suggested that such caution was excessive. One former official in West Berlin who sympathised fully with General Clay's policy has asserted that 'as in 1948, the risks seemed to multiply the further one moved from the scene of action'.[60] Another has complained that the views of the men on the spot were disregarded even though they clearly reflected an awareness of local needs and conditions.[61] Yet it is hardly surprising that Washington was not prepared to sanction moves that carried substantial and apparently unwarranted risks. Although there was a necessity for strong measures to prevent a further erosion of the Western position and to reaffirm the US commitment, this had to be balanced against the desire to avoid any inadvertent outbreak of violence. Thus the criticisms are perhaps less than fair to the Administration. The dangers were real and the American government highly conscious of them. It was concerned that, with tensions so high, an incident might spark off lightning escalation in the middle of Europe. This was particularly so during the tank confrontation at Checkpoint Charlie, which has been described as a 'dangerous period, when incautious actions could have led to shooting at any moment'.[62] It is hardly surprising therefore that throughout much of the crisis President Kennedy was so involved in detailed issues that he became known as the 'Berlin desk officer' in the White House.[63] Central direction and control were indispensable.

Similar anxieties were generated in the Cuban Missile Crisis, with the result that once again top officials became preoccupied with the implementation of policy as well as its formulation. When the quarantine had been established, the dangers still seemed enormous. As one member of the decision-making group put it, 'The greatest danger of war as we saw it then was that we would sink a Russian ship trying to run the blockade. If that happened it seemed highly doubtful Khrushchev would hold still without further action.'[64] Secretary of Defense McNamara attempted to impress this on senior naval officials, particularly Admiral George Anderson, the Chief of Naval Operations, who bitterly resented what he regarded as unwarranted political interference. McNamara emphasised that the object of the blockade was to communicate US determination and resolve to Khrushchev, while at the same time avoiding any actions that might humiliate him in the spotlight of world attention. If it was necessary to stop a Soviet ship, the utmost care had to be taken in order to avoid sinking the vessel and killing Russians. 'By the conventional rules blockade was an act of war . . . . But this was a military action with a political objective. Khrushchev must somehow be persuaded to pull back, rather than be goaded into retaliation.'[65] Firm political direction, therefore, was to extend to areas that had hitherto been regarded as beyond the 'jurisdiction' of civilian officials. Provocative actions and unintended violence had to be avoided, even if this meant trampling all over, let alone trespassing upon, the traditional preserves and prerogatives of the military. McNamara wanted to ensure that the blockade was executed in the manner desired by the President, and he concerned himself with minute details of the naval operation in an attempt to accomplish this task. Underlying this close personal direction of the blockade was Kennedy's

> . . . determination not to let needless incidents or reckless subordinates escalate so dangerous and delicate a crisis beyond control. He had learned at the Bay of Pigs that the momentum of events and enthusiasts could take issues of peace and war out of his own hands. Naval communications permitted this operation . . . to be run directly out of his office and the Pentagon.[66]

Despite these precautions, the degree of control was far from total. Indeed, at several stages in the crisis the members of the Ex. Comm. felt that they were no longer fully in command of the situation, that events were slipping out of their grasp. Robert Kennedy has described his own emotions as the group waited for news of the Soviet ships approaching the quarantine. They are, essentially, feelings of helplessness: 'One thousand miles away in the vast expanse of the Atlantic Ocean the final decisions were going to be made in the next few minutes. President Kennedy had initiated the course of events, but he no longer had control of them.'[67] Not only did these anxieties reflect an inevitable uncertainty about Soviet intentions, they were also symptomatic of the fact that, despite the explicit instructions on how to run the blockade, the US Navy might somehow provoke a clash at sea. A disturbing possibility was that the blockade could be implemented successfully *only* through the use of large-scale violence. Attempts to stop or temporarily disable Soviet ships could so easily lead to more drastic actions. It was a delicate position, the outcome of which depended ultimately on the judgement and expertise of those running the blockade. Such concerns may also have played a part in the Soviet decision not to challenge the quarantine. As it turned out, therefore, the anxieties of American decision-makers proved excessive, although far from unnecessary.

Incidents of the kind feared are perhaps most likely when the superpower relationship is juxtaposed with on-going hostilities between their respective allies. In the Arab–Israeli War of 1967, for example, a United States communications ship, the *Liberty*, was attacked by Israeli gunboats and planes while stationed off the coast of Syria. Washington was informed of the incident but at first knew little of the details. As President Johnson stated, 'For seventy tense minutes we had no idea who was responsible.'[68] Since Soviet intentions were still unclear there was inevitably some speculation that Moscow was to blame and that the action heralded a Soviet intervention on the side of Egypt and Syria. Secretary McNamara subsequently admitted, in fact, that he 'thought the *Liberty* had been attacked by Soviet forces'.[69] Until further and more reliable information was received, though, there was no precipitate order to retaliate. Fortunately the decision-makers were cautious in their response and aware that their information was insufficient to make an accurate appraisal. The President ordered carrier planes to the scene in order to look for survivors and to investigate the incident. Johnson was also concerned with minimising the danger of this action being mis-understood by either the Arab states or the Soviet Union and used the hot line to inform Kosygin of the mission of the Ameri-can planes. He also assured him that the United States had no intention of becoming involved in the war. As soon as it became known that the attack had been launched by the Israelis, this too was communicated to Moscow.[70] The dangers of misinter-pretation of what was, in effect, a very tentative and cautious move were thereby reduced. Equally significant, of course, was the behaviour of the American naval commanders in the Medi-terranean, who acted in a careful and responsible manner and avoided any rash or unnecessarily provocative moves. Secretary of Defense McNamara was obviously relieved by this, and some time after the incident candidly expressed his feelings when he said 'Thank goodness, our carrier commanders did not launch immediately against the Soviet ships who were operating in the Mediterranean.'[71] The incident, therefore, remained an isolated although tragic one. In so far as the danger stemmed primarily from the possibility of events provoking rash decisions, an aware-ness of the problem did much to alleviate it.

In all these crises violent exchanges between the forces of the two superpowers have been avoided. Although this owes some-thing to luck as well as to good judgement, it suggests a cautious optimism about the ability of statesmen to cope with international crises. It should not lead to complacency, however, as even the most strenuous attempts to maintain control have not been wholly effective. This is illustrated by what has been described as the 'Strangelove Incident' when, at the height of the Cuban Missile Crisis, a U-2 on a routine patrol apparently went off course, violated Soviet air space and was chased by Soviet fighters.[72] In the event the Soviet leaders avoided a rash response but it is not inconceivable that with tension so high they could have interpreted the flight as a reconnaissance mission prior to an American nuclear attack – with far-reaching consequences. The incident suggests that a potential loss of control is inherent in any crisis and that all statesmen can do is attempt to keep it to a minimum. In addition to the avoidance of violence, however, this requires an awareness of the need to maintain freedom of choice and action.

V Maintaining Freedom of Action

If international crises are to be resolved peacefully the participants must ensure that they retain their freedom of action. Once again the United States 'quarantine' of Cuba in October 1962 provides an appropriate illustration of how to accomplish this task. Indeed, it is in connexion with this aspect of crisis management that the wisdom of the blockade most clearly emerges. As was suggested in the previous chapter, the 'quarantine', despite its drawbacks, had advantages that other options lacked. It was not a move that threatened to push decision-makers, unwillingly and unwittingly, into the kind of automatic action–reaction sequence liable to disrupt all attempts at control. Nor was it likely to speed up the pace of events to a pitch where the level of stress upon the decision-makers would be intolerable. As Robert McNamara, argued, the blockade 'was limited pressure, which could be increased as the circumstances warranted. Further, it was dramatic and forceful pressure, which would be understood yet, most importantly, still leave us in control of events.'[73]

This is not to suggest that American freedom of action was not diminished by the establishment of the blockade: obviously it was, since the move was designed in part to place the onus for escalation back on Khrushchev. The point is, however, that the

blockade did not involve any action with irreversible consequences. Once the wholly diplomatic alternatives had been rejected, the quarantine was the option with most flexibility. It did
nothing to preclude the simultaneous use of diplomatic channels
either to emphasise further the American determination or to
offer possible concessions in return for the removal of the
missiles. Rather than ceasing to function, diplomacy was made
to work overtime: whereas the air strike would have made it
irrelevant, the blockade gave it an added urgency. As Arthur
Schlesinger put it, 'Here was a middle course between inaction
and battle, a course which exploited our superiority in local conventional power and would permit subsequent movement either
towards war or towards peace.'[74]

Not only did the blockade have advantages for the United
States, but it also left the Soviet leadership with a certain amount
of leeway and flexibility. It meant that Khrushchev as well as
Kennedy was able to retain some freedom of action. He was
given time to consider the Soviet position carefully and not be
pushed into a 'spasm response'. There was nothing about the
blockade that provoked an automatic and violent counter-move.
It was an action strictly defined in scope and restricted in purpose. Khrushchev's understanding of this probably reduced any
incentives for a provocative response. Indeed, the Soviet leader
avoided any actions that threatened to reduce *his* freedom of
choice or deprive him of the ability to retreat if necessary. So
long as Kennedy did not act precipitately and take any action
that posed a direct threat to Soviet security, therefore,
Khrushchev probably felt able to end the confrontation merely by
ceasing work on the missiles and agreeing to their withdrawal.
This is not to suggest that the Soviets had complete control over
the situation, but that they could reduce the level of tension at
almost any time they desired. Throughout the crisis they were
careful never to relinquish this ability. The United States was
equally reluctant to take any action that might undermine it. As
George Ball pointed out shortly afterwards, the crisis illustrated
both the wisdom and the 'necessity of the measured response'.[75]

The behaviour of the superpowers in the Missile Crisis was in
marked contrast to the policies and actions of the major European states in the July Crisis of 1914. In 1962 the organisations
entrusted with the implementation of decisions were, with some

minor exceptions, the servants of the statesmen involved; in 1914 they were the masters of policy. The 'measured response' was in most cases just not an available option during the Sarajevo Crisis as the choices and actions of governments were severely limited, if not completely dictated, by organisational plans and procedures. Unfortunately, the constraints were not always clear to the participants themselves, many of whom acted under the illusion that they possessed maximum flexibility and freedom of choice. This was particularly the case in Russia, with Sazonov, the Foreign Minister, believing he could wield threats in a selective and discriminate manner that enabled him to maintain full control over the situation. His appalling ignorance of military affairs was scarcely disturbed by Janushkevich, the Russian Chief of Staff, who did nothing to disabuse him of the idea that partial mobilisation was a feasible and readily reversible step. Indeed, the knowledge and understanding of the Chief of Staff was probably only marginally greater than that of Sazonov. He had held his post for only five months and does not seem to have been fully familiar with the Russian mobilisation plans or aware of their implications. It is perhaps little exaggeration to suggest that Janushkevich was virtually incapable of giving Sazonov sound advice, having achieved his position not out of merit or expertise but through 'the personal favour of the Tsar'.[76]

Thus the Foreign Minister went ahead with the partial mobilisation procedures acting on the assumption that 'he could at will regulate their application and scope'.[77] In fact, there were a number of problems with this option that made it a far more drastic and fateful step than Sazonov initially thought. The first problem was that the plans for partial mobilisation had not been worked out fully because Russian mobilisation procedures were undergoing a process of reformulation. Thus it was an option in which the military had little faith.[78] Secondly, even partial mobilisation was a large step, involving the widespread call-up of reservists. It was certainly not the delicate and discriminate pressure that Sazonov apparently intended. The third difficulty with the 'partial mobilisation' alternative followed directly from the second. Because it was such a far-reaching move, it worried the Germans as much as Austria–Hungary. It was almost impossible to frighten the Austrians and make them adopt a more moderate policy towards Serbia without making the Germans feel almost equally threatened. A final flaw was that the implementation of partial mobilisation would hinder rather than aid the speed and efficiency of total mobilisation, should it become necessary. In the event of war with Austria–Hungary, therefore, the Russians would have been in an exposed position, dangerously vulnerable to a possible German intervention in support of its ally. Consequently, there was considerable pressure for a full mobilisation. Among the most vociferous critics of the lesser move was the Russian Quartermaster General, Danilov, who argued that: 'Any partial mobilisation was . . . nothing more than an improvisation. As such it could only introduce germs of hesitation and disorder in a domain in which everything ought to be based on the most accurate calculations made in advance.'[79] Thus Sazonov discovered too late that the choice really facing him had been one of all or nothing. But by this time the choice had diminished even further: there could be no reversal of the preparations without causing organisational chaos. Thus, the partial measures were quickly replaced by the order for total mobilisation. Sazonov's early misunderstanding and the actions based upon it were to have disastrous implications, for it was the Russian military preparations that sparked off the train of mobilisations that took events out of control of the dip'omats and led almost inexorably towards war.

Not only did these military plans and preparations rob the Russian government of its freedom of choice: they had an equally profound and far-reaching impact upon German policymakers. The effort of the Russian mobilisation was felt most dramatically in Berlin, where the military plans were equally rigid. The reasons for this are to be found in prevailing military technology and strategic doctrines. In 1914 speed was of the essence. It was a firmly entrenched article of faith among the military leaders that the best way to ensure disaster was to be left behind in the mobilisation race prior to hostilities. The protagonists feared that 'whichever power completed its mobilization would strike first and might even win the war before the other side was ready'.[80] This fear was a vital factor in the July Crisis. It completely undermined the assumptions of the civilian leaders that diplomacy would continue unhindered as the military plans went into effect. Once mobilisation began, a new set of calculations and forces was injected into the crisis, making a diplomatic solution increasingly remote.

Diplomacy was being reduced to silence. The General staffs were not concerned with averting war but with winning victory. And to come out victorious they must attempt to forestall the enemy. Every hour gained was of moment for their chance of victory.[81]

As a result, a move which in Russian eyes was directed primarily against Austria and seen only as a precautionary action against Germany was regarded in Berlin as highly provocative. The policy-makers in 1914 faced the 'security dilemma' in a particularly acute and dangerous form. Moves taken by one state to bolster its security or strengthen its diplomatic position were invariably interpreted by opponents as offensive in character. The emphasis on speed made the Germans in particular feel that to allow the Russian mobilisation to go unchallenged would be to court disaster. The fear of defeat loomed larger than the fear of war in official calculations, and diplomatic conciliation was brutally sacrificed on the altar of military preparedness.

This was all the more tragic because German military planning was at least as inflexible as that of Russia. At the heart of German military thinking was the Schlieffen Plan, a strategy designed to cope with the unique problem of hostilities on two fronts – against Russia in the East and France in the West. The plan projected an initial holding campaign against Russia, together with what was intended to be a bold and decisive flanking movement through Belgium into France. It was anticipated that a rapid victory in the West would enable Germany to switch its attention to the East and devote its efforts to defeating the Russians. Even more than the military strategies of the other major powers, the Schlieffen Plan depended for its success on speed, so much so that for Germany mobilisation and war may have been almost synonymous. Certainly, a posture directed primarily against France was inappropriate for a confrontation with Russia, despite the alliance between the two powers. Yet there was little alternative in July 1914. Albertini is extremely critical of German military planners because of this:

> It should have been the General Staff's duty to provide for several alternatives, and prepare the relevant plans for mobilization and concentration, so that the political authorities would be free in whatever international crisis to choose the solution most in accordance with the interests of the Reich.[82]

Thus, it appears that decision-makers found themselves the prisoners of military plans made with little allowance for the political and diplomatic context in which the need to use them might arise. Towards the end of the crisis it was briefly suggested that German forces be directed primarily against Russia rather than France. The suggestion encountered enormous resistance from Helmuth von Moltke, Chief of the General Staff, who argued that such an option was not technically feasible. It appears however that this was not strictly true. Deploying the bulk of German forces against Russia would obviously have run counter to the main thrust of the formal and elaborate military planning that had taken place prior to 1914. But Moltke's fears of confusion and dislocation were grossly excessive since, until 1913, annual revisions had been made of a secondary plan for deploying forces East rather than West. If this alternative was 'technically possible', it was certainly not 'temperamentally possible' for Moltke to sanction an abrupt reversal at the last minute.[83] What little flexibility had been left by rigid military planning was eliminated by rigid military thinking.

German policy-makers, like their Russian counterparts, gave little consideration to the need to maintain freedom of action, with the result that their alternatives were reduced to one. Throughout the crisis, therefore, prelaid plans were probably the major determinants of action, robbing the diplomats of all flexibility. In mobilising, the various states were not only restricting their own freedom of choice but were also pushing their opponents into a corner where they felt they had no choice but to act similarly. Thus there was a kind of action–reaction sequence that led almost automatically from the Russian 'partial mobilisation' to the German violation of Belgian neutrality. As one analyst has observed:

> . . . . their plans precluded the use of military power for any purpose other than attack. Actions that might be used merely in prudent self-defence, for diplomatic bargaining, or to demonstrate determination were identical with those that would be taken as the prelude to an all-out attack. And, once set in motion, it was virtually impossible to stop mobilization without creating such vast confusion as to leave oneself militarily vulnerable.[84]

What are the implications of the July Crisis? Does it provide any 'lessons' for contemporary crisis management? The answer to this second question is 'yes', although not without certain qualifications. Most important, there was not the same incentive to avoid war in 1914 as there is today, and to suggest that policy-makers in the respective capitals were all dragged unwillingly into war would be a serious distortion. They *were* pulled into war by their military plans, but did not try very hard to prevent this. The various misunderstandings and mistakes alluded to above had considerable influence. Of this there can be little doubt. If the desire to maintain peace had been uppermost, however, the worst misunderstandings might have been avoided or quickly corrected, and their damaging effects thereby averted. Such caveats not-withstanding, the mobilisation procedures of the great powers in 1914 highlight a number of dangers to freedom of action during superpower confrontations. They also suggest possible ways in which these dangers could be dealt with.

Serious problems can arise from a lack of flexibility in a state's military capabilities. Where there is no apparent capacity for selective, discriminate options as opposed to large-scale and drastic actions, a government is likely to be severely handicapped in its crisis behaviour, and lacking in alternatives. The choice, therefore, should not be an all-or-nothing one: there must be a wide range of intermediate options that can be used for bargaining purposes without proving disruptive of attempts to keep control. If they are to be effective, such options have to be built into a state's military organisation and capabilities. Lacking this, the decision-makers will face severe difficulties. Even so they should not blandly assume that prelaid and carefully elaborated plans are the only possible basis for action, and must be prepared to explore other alternatives. In this task, however, they some-times encounter considerable antipathy if not open opposition from military planners who, aware of the dangers of disruption, are justifiably hostile towards improvisation or last-minute altera-tions of plan. Thus, it is important that decision-makers probe and question military estimates and recommendations in order to evaluate their possible implications for diplomacy and to highlight any biases or omissions in the presentation of alternatives. Indeed, in certain circumstances it will probably be necessary to overcome the natural reluctance of military organisations to implement policies that are not preplanned and formally sanctioned options in their repertoire.

The Berlin Crisis of 1948 not only illustrates some of these problems, but also demonstrates how strong and imaginative political leadership can prove decisive in overcoming them. Although a government's choices *are* restricted by existing organisational options, policy-makers are not compelled to accept organisational estimates of the feasible. Similarly, an agency's reluctance to undertake a particular task need not be an absolute prohibition. Estimates can be challenged, reluctance overcome. The Berlin airlift, for example, was certainly not a preplanned and meticulously prepared option: decided upon fairly spontaneously, it was implemented at relatively short notice. Nor was it free of opposition. In the preceding discussions the Air Force Chief of Staff, General Vandenberg, strongly objected to the commitment of a large proportion of United States air power to one specific task. He was particularly concerned lest the Berlin airlift so disrupt the Military Air Transport Service that it would be impossible for America to meet an emergency elsewhere in the world.[85] Although the parallels should not be overdrawn, this kind of objection emerges as reminiscent of the arguments put forward by some of the military leaders in 1914. In 1948, however, purely military considerations were not allowed to dictate policy and the President's preference prevailed.

Truman's determination to ensure that the airlift was properly implemented overrode all objections and difficulties – including the fact that it was not an alternative that figured prominently on the menu of choices presented by the Air Force. To some extent the President was aided by General Clay's 'mini' airlift that had been initiated three days earlier, on 25 June, as a virtually immediate response to the Soviet blockade.[86] But this was very different from a full-scale programme of aid to the besieged city that would have to include fuel supplies as well as food. Indeed, there was considerable uncertainty about the prospects for the airlift and it is extremely doubtful whether, at the outset, either Soviet or Western decision-makers fully realised its potential. The practical problems were enormous and included the construction of an extra airfield in Berlin in order to handle the unprecedented increase in air traffic. As such problems were overcome the airlift increased enormously in both momentum and efficiency.

Thus an imaginative and wholly unexpected response to the

Soviet blockade proved successful even though improvised at short notice. The 1948 crisis suggests, in fact, that the organisational constraints upon policy-makers are not always overwhelming. Obviously, if the United States had possessed no planes, then the airlift would not have been a viable alternative. But the knowledge that neither Air Force planes nor Air Force plans were geared to this particular task was not sufficient to deflect policy-makers from adopting a course of action they deemed necessary and appropriate. And it was, indeed, most appropriate. In contrast to 1914 a military option was found that communicated the determination of one of the protagonists without threatening the security or challenging the prestige of its adversary. The Berlin Crisis shows that the desire for flexibility on the part of policy-makers need not be thwarted by the organisations under their command. There are limits to the extent to which government institutions can defy the wishes of their leaders. This was demonstrated further – although in a much more trivial way – during the Middle East War of 1967. The incident is a minor but interesting one, concerning the first use of the hot line by the superpowers in a crisis. As President Johnson relates:

> . . . when McNamara heard Moscow was calling on the hot line, he instructed his communication people to pipe it into the White House. To his amazement, they advised him that it could not be done, that the hot line ended at the Pentagon. McNamara said sharply that with all the money we had invested in military communications there must be some way to send Moscow's message directly to the White House Situation Room, and they had better figure it out. They quickly found a way.[87]

The implication of all this is that, although decision-makers are dependent upon their subordinates for information, advice and implementation of policies, they are not wholly their prisoners. Even if there is no immediate provision for a particular option this does not necessarily exclude it as a feasible alternative, although it does perhaps make it more difficult to implement. If organisations are explicitly ordered to undertake a particular course of action, they will almost certainly acquiesce, albeit reluctantly. The power of subordinates to 'sit still' is less formidable during crisis situations than at any other time, largely because high-ranking officials are so clearly and unequivocally involved in the policy process. This is not to say the will of the men at the top is an automatic guarantee of action, merely that organisations may be more adaptable than is sometimes claimed. Prelaid plans and carefully prepared alternatives will be more elaborately detailed than those that have to be developed quickly in the midst of a crisis, but the latter will be far more appropriate to the circumstances, and this, after all, is the crucial consideration. Indeed, in past superpower crises existing contingency plans – in the United States at least – have been cast aside in favour of alternatives that were more expedient and better tailored to the demands of the moment. This was certainly the case in October 1962 when, as was discussed above, creative analysis generated a particular option that appeared more satisfactory than any of the existing military plans.[88]

Even if decision-makers are successful in imposing their preferences, the precise manner in which the chosen option is implemented may be more difficult to influence. Standard operating procedures of military establishments in particular may prove impossible to alter, with the result that a government's ability to control the situation is seriously eroded. It has been argued, in fact, that the quarantine of Cuba illustrates how presidential orders can be sabotaged by the rigid manner in which military operations are conducted. Most accounts of the crisis suggest that, on the advice of David Ormsby-Gore, the British Ambassador to Washington, the quarantine line was brought nearer Cuba than originally intended. The desire of the naval authorities to keep their ships out of range of the MIG fighters in Cuba was overshadowed by the desire to give Khrushchev more time to make the hard choices with which he was confronted, and thereby reduce the likelihood of a rash response.[89]

Graham Allison has claimed however that, although the logic of Ormsby-Gore's argument was very compelling to the President, and quickly accepted by him, it had little effect on the actual deployment of American ships: they stayed where they were. In support of this thesis he cites the fact that the *Marucla*, the first ship to be boarded, encountered the blockade '500 miles out from Cuba's eastern tip, along the Navy's original line'.[90] This, together with the arrival of a Soviet tanker in Havana on 26 October, leads Allison to emphasise the possibility 'that the Navy's resistance to the President's orders . . . forced the President to allow one or several Soviet ships to pass through the blockade after it was officially operative'.[91] Against this must be set the testimony of the participants, three features of which stand out as particularly important. The first is Robert Kennedy's statement that the interception line was originally extended eight hundred miles into the Atlantic, but was brought back to five hundred miles.[92] Secondly is the evidence suggesting that the President and his civilian advisers were fully acquainted with the positions of Soviet and American ships. Theodore Sorensen in particular describes how the President was able to watch 'the tracking of each ship on a large board in the White House Situation Room'.[93] Presumably, it would have been apparent if the Navy had not carried out its orders and had failed to bring the blockade nearer Cuba. Thirdly, it was this detailed knowledge of the situation that enabled Kennedy to decide that certain ships – including an East German passenger liner with 1,500 people on board – be allowed through the barrier unhindered. Although this was designed to give the Soviet Union more time, it also represented the President's desire to minimise the risks, by personally selecting an appropriate ship to be stopped and boarded.[94] To interpret the implementation of the blockade as a prime example, either of naval intransigence or of standard operating procedures obstructing presidential objectives, may be misleading. The evidence for it is ambiguous at best and lends itself equally well to other interpretations.

The dangers involved in the blockade were real none the less. In the last analysis, it *was* the Navy that had to impose the blockade, and, despite guidance from the top, dependence on the ability, caution and wisdom of particular naval commanders was inescapable. This type of problem cannot be eliminated. It can be rendered more manageable, however, by the use of modern communication channels that enable direct contact to be maintained between the respective capitals and the scene of the local encounter. Indeed, it is advantageous to all the protagonists to ensure that these communications be maintained intact and without interference. This is an area where the common interests of the adversaries are overwhelming. Traditionally, the opponent's command and control facilities were legitimate targets for attack, as their disruption helped to create confusion and panic in the enemy forces. In a superpower confrontation, however, it is crucial that confusion be avoided and that the military forces of the adversary – as well as one's own – remain responsive to central direction. Thus, it is hardly surprising that in 1962 the United States respected the integrity of Soviet communication links with the ships heading towards Cuba.[95] It was no less essential for Moscow to maintain its freedom of choice and keep control over Russian ships, than it was for Washington to do the same.

Even if the dangers involved in the implementation of policies are contained, the problems are not at an end. An equally important source of anxiety in some crises is the behaviour of allies. Independent-minded governments can prove unsympathetic to superpower efforts to maintain control over the situation. Consequently, both the United States and the Soviet Union have been extremely cautious about the degree of freedom they are willing to allow even close and trusted allies. In the Cuban Crisis, for example, the Soviets made quite clear to the Americans that the missiles were strictly under their control or, as Khrushchev himself put it, 'in the hands of Soviet officials'. The possible gains that could have been made by a certain amount of ambiguity as to whether the 'volatile' Cubans were anywhere near the firing buttons were not felt to be worth the risks involved.[96] 'Castro in charge of nuclear rockets might be convincingly reckless', but to allow Castro to get in this position was incompatible with the Soviet policy of trying to maintain control over events – and over allies.[97] It would have taken some of the crucial decisions out of Moscow's hands, and this could not be tolerated. In fact, the final plans provided for 'four battle groups of special ground troops armed with tactical nuclear weapons to give the missiles close-in protection', and when the crisis erupted 22,000 Russian troops were already on the island.[98] Their purpose was almost certainly to ensure that the missiles remained under strict Soviet control. In the crisis, this probably served to reassure the United States, thereby making a precipitate resort to violence by Washington unnecessary.

In much the same way, the leaders of the Kremlin, for all their pronouncements, were careful not to delegate too much authority to the East Germans in the 1961 crisis over Berlin. When they felt that accommodation was necessary, there was little hesitation about disregarding the Ulbricht regime. This emphasises further that, in international crises, the superpowers are completely averse to giving 'blank cheques' to allies. Furthermore, they scrupulously try to prevent any moves by the latter entangling them in a position from which it is impossible for them to extricate themselves. They are intent on ensuring that even a major ally does nothing to destroy their freedom of choice.

Difficulties arise, however, because some allies are not readily amenable to the precise direction and control of the superpowers. This is particularly the case in the Middle East where, as was implied above, the clients of both superpowers have been anything but docile and pliant. Prior to the June war of 1967, for example, the Soviet Union may have disapproved of the blockade of the Gulf of Aquaba. Yet Nasser went ahead regardless – and provoked an Israeli attack.[99] Similarly, Israel took actions that were disconcerting to the United States:

> In attacking Egypt, Tel Aviv disregarded Washington's advice, and later in the war Israel appeared to try to accomplish its military objectives prior to complying with American requests that it adhere to UN cease-fire resolutions. The delays particularly antagonised the embarrassed Russians.[100]

As was discussed above, the Soviet Union found it necessary to use the hot line several times in order to impress upon Washington the need to bring the conflict to an end as soon as possible. The Kremlin was anxious to avoid military confrontation with the United States, but afraid that Israel might so exploit its military success that the Soviet Union would be compelled to intervene militarily, and thereby bring about the kind of superpower clash it wanted to avert. Indeed, the episode demonstrates yet another aspect of the common interests of the superpowers. It benefits both of them to keep their respective allies under control. In the Middle East the burden of this task has fallen most heavily on the United States because of Israeli military superiority, but would almost certainly be an equally salient problem for the Soviet Union were the military positions reversed. In both 1967 and 1973 the United States eventually succeeded in restraining the Israelis, but only through sustained diplomatic efforts and after tense exchanges with the Soviet Union. The difficulty is that the superpowers are committed to states that not only have an implacable hostility towards one another but are sometimes both independent and headstrong in their behaviour. At least tacit superpower co-operation to moderate their excesses and to keep hostilities within tolerable bounds has therefore been essential.

Other dangers arise where the clients or allies are devious as well as headstrong, and attempt to embroil the superpowers in their conflicts to an unwarranted extent. In the 1958 Quemoy Crisis both Moscow and Washington faced problems of this type. Prior to the crisis, Chiang Kai-Shek stationed a third of his army on the offshore islands, thereby increasing the importance of the islands and making it difficult for America to refuse to defend them. That he succeeded in this objective was demonstrated by the American decision to convoy supplies to the islands in the face of the Communist artillery bombardment. At the same time there was considerable reluctance in Washington to get further involved than necessary, a feeling that perhaps 'Chiang's ambitions went beyond US interests'.[101]

Thus the limits of the American commitment were also firmly established. It was made clear that it was solely a defensive commitment: there would be no American help or encouragement for any attempt by Chiang to return to the mainland. If he was 'unleashed', he would have to act alone. Furthermore, several statements critical of the Nationalists' behaviour were issued by United States officials. The most notable was a speech by Secretary of State John Foster Dulles in which he characterised the emplacements of large garrisons on the islands as 'rather foolish'.[102] On another occasion Under-Secretary of State, Christian Herter, apparently spoke of the 'Nationalists' "pathological devotion" to the islands and described a chain of events beginning with attacks on mainland artillery positions and airfields and ending in war between the US and Russia'.[103] The caution and concern reflected in such utterances was also manifested in American actions. Although the delivery to Quemoy of eight-inch Howitzers capable of firing nuclear shells was well publicised, for example, it did not involve any serious danger and there was never any intention of supplying the Nationalists with atomic weapons. Washington was prepared to underwrite the Nationalist position, but simultaneously ensured that nothing it did gave Chiang an opportunity to exploit its support and entangle it any deeper in an unwanted conflict with Peking or Moscow.

The Soviet predicament was no less worrying. Just as the United States feared that Chiang might be trying to involve it in a war with the Chinese People's Republic, so the Soviet Union may have been afraid that vigorous support for Peking would lead to a confrontation with Washington – and this was something it wished to avoid. The Soviets

> . . . had problems very similar to those of the Americans in dealing with a stubborn and unpredictable ally. In fact, the Soviet policy was practically a mirror image to that of the United States. Moscow also had to find the proper proportions of encouragement and discouragement in dealing with their Chinese comrades.[104]

While there were the mandatory public declarations of support for Peking, therefore, the Soviet Union emphasised in both its words and deeds not only that it regarded the situation with alarm but that there were clearly defined limits to its commitment. It was scrupulous to indicate that, although American aggression against the mainland would elicit a firm Soviet response, there would be no direct military support for a Chinese invasion of the offshore islands or Taiwan. Khrushchev's famous letters to Eisenhower of 7 and 19 September were no exception to this; they threatened Soviet nuclear retaliation only in response to an American nuclear attack on China.[105] The absence of any Soviet military manoeuvres in the area, coupled with an emphasis on the strength of the US Seventh Fleet and the danger of a world war, suggested that Russian support was unlikely to go beyond rather perfunctory verbal gestures. Even the announcement by Peking that it had extended its territorial waters from three to twelve miles did not evoke the unqualified enthusiasm of its ally. 'The Soviets emphasized "respect" for rather than enforcement of the new territorial limit', and thereby absolved themselves of any obligation to respond to US violations of Chinese waters.[106]

Thus both superpowers demonstrated their preoccupation with maintaining freedom of choice and not allowing the actions of allies to provoke a direct confrontation in which both have firm and perhaps irrevocable commitments. The imperative that events be controlled requires keeping allies on a tight leash. It seems unlikely though that the difficulties caused by independent-minded allies can be wholly eliminated. As with the other control problems that have been discussed above, recognition is no guarantee of a solution. Nevertheless, the very acknowledgement of such problems has led to moves designed to ease rather than exacerbate them. As a result, superpower decision-makers have managed to avoid the more damaging possibilities. They have refrained from deliberate violence and have either prevented or contained *inadvertent* violence. Furthermore, they have chosen options unlikely to have irreversible consequences, and have attempted to ensure that neither subordinates nor allies robbed them of their freedom of action. All these activities attest to the superpowers' concern over the dangers of crises. But there are also opportunities for advancement, and these lead to coercive bargaining, the techniques of which are examined in the following chapter.

CHAPTER SEVEN

The Moderation
of Coercive Bargaining

I Introduction

Hitherto the main focus of attention has been the manner in which the superpowers dampen down their confrontations and attempt to minimise the risks inherent in crises. The emphasis on common interest, however, must not be allowed to obscure the conflicting interests that lie at the heart of a crisis and tend to sustain it even while simultaneous attempts are being made to terminate it peacefully. Co-operation is only one facet of crisis management. Equally important are the elements of antagonistic or adversary behaviour. Although the governments of the superpowers want to maintain the peace, this is not an absolute or necessarily overriding value. They also have certain interests and objectives for which they are prepared to adopt coercive bargaining tactics that carry with them a significant risk of war. As John Foster Dulles put it in his famous interview with James Shepley of *Life* magazine in 1956:

> You have to take chances for peace just as you have to take chances in war . . . . The ability to get to the verge without getting into war is the necessary art. If you cannot master it you inevitably get into war. If you try to run away from it, if you are scared to go to the brink you are lost.[1]

The implication of Dulles's statement is that an unwillingness to take risks puts the state at the mercy of those who are less inhibited. Not only does it make challenges more likely and more frequent, it virtually guarantees that during crises themselves the government will concede to the demands of any state that is more adventurous. On the other hand, there are very substantial difficulties and dangers involved in attempts to manipulate the risk of war. Brinkmanship may be a necessary art, it is certainly not an easy art to master, and the penalties for mistakes or miscalculations are stark. Although brinkmanship and escalation are vital to crisis management, they make the equally central task of 'disaster avoidance' both more formidable and more urgent. Thus, paradoxically, coercive bargaining techniques are an aid to crisis management but can also obstruct it. There is constant tension, therefore, between the pressures for adopting such techniques and the pressures for eschewing them as too dangerous. It has been emphasised in the preceding chapters that the desire to obtain a *satisfactory* outcome to the crisis has to be balanced against the need for a *peaceful* outcome when the costs of war are excessive. How this balance has actually been arrived at and the conflicting demands of crisis management reconciled with one another in practice is the subject of the present chapter.

Neither superpower has been willing to refrain from coercion during international crises. Indeed, to have done so would have meant not only abandoning all hope of positive gain, but being content with little alternative other than to appease the opponent. At the same time, an awareness of the dangers of the bargaining process has led the United States, the Soviet Union and even Communist China to hedge it around with all sorts of restrictions and restraints. Indeed, one of the most striking and remarkable features of Cold War confrontations is the way in which tacit, but none the less indispensable, limitations have been established on coercive bargaining. In order to highlight these limitations it may be useful to elaborate what can appropriately be described as a 'model' of unadulterated or unrestrained coercive bargaining. Although some reference is made to the bargaining behaviour of Adolf Hitler in the 1930s, particularly where it appears to offer appropriate and illuminating examples of specific tactics, the 'model' is based primarily on the techniques discussed and dissected at length by analysts such as Herman Kahn, Thomas Schelling, Daniel Ellsberg and Glenn Snyder. There is inevitably something contrived about it. Nevertheless, it reveals very dramatically the potential dangers and disabilities, and also enables us to discern more easily the means whereby the superpowers have kept their crisis bargaining within tolerable bounds in practice.

II Coercive Bargaining : The Model

Bargaining during international crises is, essentially, an attempt by the participants to determine who gets what; to influence the distribution of gains and losses in the final settlement.[2] Indeed, bargaining takes place because the most desirable outcome for one of the protagonists will almost certainly be far less than satisfactory to the opponent, perhaps requiring very substantial sacrifices on his part. Until it is put to the test, the extent to which each party is prepared to accept such sacrifices is uncertain. Consequently, there are enormous incentives for adopting coercive bargaining moves. On the one hand, they may succeed in extracting considerable concessions *from* the adversary. On the other hand, they are necessary to demonstrate *to* the adversary, one's own unwillingness to make the concessions that he, in turn, is demanding. In short, coercion can be used for either offensive or defensive purposes. Those involved, of course, may be influenced by both considerations: a determination to hold on to most of what they have, coupled with a desire for further gains.

Put at its simplest, coercion involves an attempt by one party to influence the behaviour of another party in desired directions by making him fear the consequences of not acting in the way demanded. As many analysts have pointed out, the relationship between those involved is psychological rather than physical. The party being coerced is not physically forced or compelled to do something against his will. He is merely made to believe that to act in the manner specified is in his best interests: by so doing, he at least avoids the costs or sanctions that would be inflicted upon him for a failure to comply. Thomas Schelling has put the point superbly:

> There is a difference between taking what you want and making someone give it to you, between fending off assault and making someone afraid to assault you, between holding what people are trying to take, and making them afraid to take it, between losing what someone can forcibly take and giving it up to avoid risk or damage. It is the difference between defense and deterrence, between brute force and intimidation, between conquest and blackmail, between action and threats.[3]

One of the best known and most thoroughly documented types of coercive tactic is the deterrent threat. If this is successful, the adversary is coerced into inaction, into refraining from certain kinds of behaviour that in many respects may be highly appealing and attractive, by being made to believe that, if he chooses such options, wholly unacceptable costs will be inflicted upon him. But not all coercion is designed to stop an opponent embarking upon a particular course of action. Threats can also be used more positively to make the adversary either give up something, or modify his behaviour in a way more consonant with one's own preferences. Nevertheless, the basic principles remain the same. The effect of the threat on the opponent's cost–gain calculation is crucial. Not only must the potential costs outweigh the gains that stand to be made, but the recipient must also believe that, were he to ignore the threat, he would almost certainly incur the stated penalty. For a threat to be successful it must be credible; if it is interpreted as a bluff it will fail.

There are other available tactics which do not differ from this in essentials. If there are differences, they are of style rather than substance, reflecting the dynamic situation in which the participants find themselves. Threats are issued as part of a rapid and complex interaction process in which each side strives to influence the opponent to move in the desired direction or give up something it values, while simultaneously trying to resist the influence of the opponent. Coercive bargaining moves need not be confined to these relatively simple threats however. The participants can also attempt to manipulate the 'autonomous' risks that were discussed at length in the previous chapter. 'Pressure is exerted on the adversary not by threatening deliberate violence, but by raising the danger that war will occur through autonomous processes beyond the control of either party.'[4] Given the fears of a loss of control that are an inevitable concomitant of contemporary crises, 'threats that leave something to chance' appear to have a great deal working in their favour.[5] The notion of brinkmanship, in fact, is predicated on the efficacy of such threats. It assumes that the governments involved in a confrontation are prepared to exploit the possibility that events might become uncontrollable. As Schelling has so cogently argued:

> . . . brinkmanship is the deliberate creation of a recognizable risk of war, a risk that one does not completely control. It is the tactic of deliberately letting the situation get somewhat out of hand, just because its being out of hand may be intolerable to the other party

and force his accommodation. It means harassing and intimidating an adversary by exposing him to a shared risk.[6]

Deploying military forces near those of the opponent, for example, raises the possibility of an inadvertent clash provoking a rapid and perhaps irreversible escalation. In the previous chapter such possibilities were treated solely as dangers to be avoided, but they are also opportunities that *could* be exploited by policy-makers, particularly those who are either ruthless or desperate. Indeed, such a move could profitably be coupled with a verbal warning to the opponent that, unless he refrains from his present behaviour, a clash between the armed forces of the two sides may be inevitable, not out of conscious choice and decision by the governments themselves but merely because military commanders may be capable of rash and ill-considered actions. Once the stage is set, no further act of will is required by the state that issues the warning. It merely 'points out to the opponent *natural* consequences that are likely to follow from his non-compliance' with the state's demands.[7] The act that raises the possibility of disaster is an act of bargaining. So too is the prediction of disaster. The disaster itself however arises not through the bargaining process, but because of the imperfect control exercised over the situation by the participants.

This appears to avoid the type of problem that can arise when the implementation of a threat is costly *and* requires a deliberate act of will. Where the execution of a threat involves substantial costs to its author as well as the party being threatened, the threat may lack credibility. As a result, the recipient will be far more likely to interpret it as a bluff and continue his chosen path regardless. The 'threat that leaves something to chance' does not suffer from this deficiency in quite the same way because, once the warning has been issued, no further positive action is required. This advantage, however, is more apparent than real. Far from being eliminated, the problems merely take a slightly different form. Instead of being a question of credibility, it becomes a matter of which side has the greatest tolerance for risks. The party that is being threatened or warned may feel that although the opponent has been prepared to create or accept the risk of events becoming uncontrollable, he has done so only on the assumption that the impact of this would be immediate and overwhelming. If this assumption is challenged and the threatened state continues its present behaviour rather than complying at once with the demands made on it, the party responsible for the threat may have to reconsider his own position. His predicament is no less dangerous and disconcerting than that of the government he is attempting to intimidate. The risk of disaster is the same for both of them. Knowing this, the recipient may calculate that the pay-off for standing firm could be considerable. In this case the adversary may find that the dangers he consciously helped to create and hoped to exploit are intolerable, and that, in order to defuse the situation very quickly, he has to back down or make concessions. It is not inconceivable that a 'threat that leaves something to chance' might ultimately frighten the government that made it as much if not more than the opponent. Thus there is a distinct possibility that such threats will prove self-defeating and that the combatant responsible for them may find himself hoisted by his own petard.

The limitations to this type of tactic have been summed up by Stephen Maxwell in his analysis of brinkmanship:

> A contestant can change the risk of a fall by moving towards, or away from the brink, estimating that a degree of risk which it is rational for him to accept will be found irrational by his opponent. In this sense he can *use* the risk. But he cannot load the risk, as a die can be loaded, so that it is greater to the opponent than to himself.[8]

Thus the outcome pivots on which side has most nerve, and is better able to withstand the desire to reduce the risks and return the situation to normal. In such circumstances the uncertainties will be considerable. Although one of the participants may have been prepared to start events moving in such a way that disaster might be the outcome, this does not necessarily indicate that he is prepared to go any further along this road than is his adversary. As Snyder has so aptly put it, 'the risk created is a shared one, and it is not clearly apparent why the other party should be less willing to tolerate the risk than the opponent initiating it'.[9] Thus very serious problems remain. In so far as such threats do nothing to demonstrate unequivocally that A will be prepared to take greater risks than B, then they are unlikely to be a total success. The issue of credibility is not avoided, therefore; it is merely reformulated. Instead of having to convince the opponent that one is prepared to carry out threats even at great cost to oneself if he does not comply with one's demands, it is necessary to convince him that one will accept a level of risk that he is likely to find unbearable.

Consequently, such bargaining may well take the form of a 'competition in risk-taking', a test of nerve, will and skill in which each of the participants tries to influence the determination of the opponent.[10] This can be done by altering the adversary's perception of one's own determination and resolve. Indeed, the aim is to convince the opponent that, for whatever reasons, one's own propensity for creating and tolerating risks is by far the higher. Since neither party wants the contest to end in disaster – and both are acutely aware of this – the skill is somehow to demonstrate to the adversary that he must be the one to turn aside if disaster is to be avoided. The opponent must be made to believe not only that you are unwilling to give way at the present level of conflict, but that you are ready to go even further if necessary. And if the opponent increases the scope or intensity of the conflict, then you must be prepared not only to match this escalation but to go beyond it to a level at which he cries 'enough'. How to demonstrate this willingness is both the key to success and one of the major problems facing the participants.

It is often suggested that the best way of convincing the opponent of one's resolve is by making commitments. Indeed, both the direct threat to inflict costs on the adversary and the 'threat that leaves something to chance' can be substantially reinforced and strengthened by commitments. As Iklé has written, 'If you issue a warning or a threat, you try to alter your opponent's expectations about *his* gains or losses that would result from certain choices he can take; if you make a commitment you try to alter your opponent's expectation about your future conduct.'[11]

You can do this by changing your own incentives so that it becomes enormously costly to fail to carry out a threat or to back down when challenged. You can also do it by reducing or eliminating opportunities to act other than in the manner stated. The opponent's calculation of probable gains and losses, of course, depends crucially on his expectation of your behaviour. The importance of a commitment, therefore, is that it makes it *more difficult or more costly to avoid* either inflicting a level of damage on the adversary that would outweigh any gains he could hope to make (even though such actions might involve acceptance of a high level of pain and damage to oneself) or exposing him to a degree of risk that he would find intolerable (even though this means exposing oneself to the same level of risk). The benefits that can accrue from sacrificing one's freedom of action in this way have been emphasised by Thomas Schelling, who has argued that in bargaining 'the power to constrain an adversary may depend on the power to bind oneself' – particularly as 'freedom may be freedom to capitulate'.[12]

An extreme form of this tactic is the 'irrevocable commitment', which requires that the government deliberately relinquishes its own room for manoeuvre or retreat to such an extent that only the opponent can avoid disaster. Choice and flexibility are replaced by what is virtually an automatic response should the opponent not back down or concede to one's demands. The adversary, however, is left with choices, and it is he who has to decide whether or not to proceed to a collision. At its most brutal, the 'irrevocable commitment' presents the adversary not only with the 'last clear chance' of avoiding disaster but with surrender as the price it must pay to do so. This technique was adopted by Hitler in March 1939 in connection with the German invasion of Czechoslovakia. President Hacha and the Czech Foreign Minister were both summoned to Berlin and, once there, were informed by Hitler that German troops had been given the order to march into Czechoslovakia. The Nazi leaders were emphatic that the decision had been taken and everything was set in motion. Nothing could be done to reverse the process: in five hours the German invasion would begin. If the Czech army resisted, 'the punishment would be automatic, indeed it would be out of Hitler's hands'.[13] Thus President Hacha was presented with the last opportunity to prevent a catastrophe for the Czech nation. When this was coupled with further threats concerning the devastation the German air force would inflict on Czechoslovakia if it came to war, the pressure became very compelling, and peaceful surrender began to look the least unattractive of the two alternatives – war or capitulation. Finally, Hacha grasped the opportunity to save his nation from destruction, telephoned Prague and ordered that there be no resistance to the invading army. In this instance an 'irrevocable commitment' was very skilfully combined with a time limit, so that the threat took the form of an explicit and extremely credible ultimatum.

There are other means of establishing or strengthening commitments which do not cut off quite so irretrievably all possible escape routes. Although the essence of a commitment is that it deliberately limits one's freedom for manoeuvre, this need not always be pushed to its ultimate conclusion. There are degrees of commitment. In some cases merely making the commitment clear and explicit may suffice to convey one's determination – particularly if the commitment is a public one. To renege on a well-publicised commitment or to revoke a formal pledge as soon as it is challenged can do considerable harm to a government's standing in international politics. Not only would it invite further challenges from the immediate opponent, but it might so damage the state's bargaining reputation that other states also become more assertive and less compliant in their dealings with the government. In other words, the state's behaviour in this situation will tend to influence the expectations of others about its future behaviour. This point can be used to impress upon the adversary why one cannot yield.

If the bargaining is conducted in secret and the commitment is not publicised, there may be less concern about the 'lessons' that other states are likely to draw from the outcome. It may be possible none the less to exploit the likelihood that other bargaining situations will occur in the future between the present participants. By claiming that, if you fail to act in this crisis in the manner pledged, the opponent will interpret it as a sign of endemic weakness and be encouraged to make similar extortionate demands in any future confrontation, it may be possible to convince him either that you regard the concessions he is demanding as too costly, or that you will execute the threats you have made unless he complies with your demands. This can be done most satisfactorily by linking the current crisis to other outstanding issues between the two states. The 'coupling' of issues in this way may be a useful tactic and one that pays high dividends.[14] This is not to suggest that all a state's commitments are interdependent, or that policy-makers invariably regard them as such: obviously governments discriminate, to some extent at least, between those interests that are of primary importance and those that they might be prepared to sacrifice. Nevertheless, statesmen may perceive significant advantages in establishing linkages between issues that are actually rather tenuous. So long as such linkages are clearly perceived and understood by the opponent, they may strengthen the credibility of one's threats by making a failure to carry them out more costly.

Another way of establishing risk-taking resolve or the credibility of threats is somehow to convince the opponent that one is not entirely rational. What has been described as the 'rationality-of-irrationality' strategy is, in fact, an explicit recognition of the significant bargaining advantages that can accrue if the adversary believes one is capable of irrational behaviour, of executing threats and tolerating risks even when to do so could be disastrous to oneself. 'It is not a universal advantage in situations of conflict to be inalienably and manifestly rational in decision and motivation . . . . It may be perfectly rational . . . to wish for the power to suspend certain rational capabilities in particular situations.'[15] The important thing, however, is not that one should actually be irrational, but that the opponent is made to believe that this is so. As well as the 'irrevocable commitment' discussed above, there are several ways in which this belief can be implanted in the adversary's calculations.

The first and perhaps most obvious way is by sheer force of character and the deliberate cultivation of an image of irrationality. Although it is far from easy for a statesman to convince others that he is not entirely rational and therefore oblivious to the risks and costs of actions, it can be done, as was demonstrated so skilfully by Hitler in the 1930s. Although the asymmetries of attitude towards war made it far easier for Hitler to exploit his opponent's fears than it is in the nuclear age, the way he did this was none the less remarkable. The diplomatic brutality of his meeting with President Hacha has already been described. Schuschnigg, the Austrian Chancellor, suffered a very similar experience when he met Hitler at Berchtesgaden in February 1938. In the first place Schuschnigg was exposed to a long and bitter tirade about Austrian policy. Then, when the Chancellor appeared to balk at some of Hitler's demands, he was ordered out, and one of the German generals, who had very pointedly been presented to Schuschnigg at lunch, was called in for discussions with Hitler.[16] This was all part of a carefully thought out intimidation process, as were Hitler's rages, during which

> His face became mottled and swollen with fury, he screamed at the top of his voice, spitting out a stream of abuse, waving his arms

wildly and drumming on the table or the wall with his fists. As suddenly as he had begun he would stop, smooth down his hair, straighten his collar, and resume a more normal voice.[17]

There was almost certainly a large element of calculation in these performances, and it is little exaggeration to talk of Hitler's 'skilful and deliberate exploitation of his own temperament'.[18] For foreign diplomats and policy-makers to be harangued and bullied in this way was, of course, a totally alien experience for them, and all the more effective as a result.

This interpretation of Hitler as deliberately creating an image of irrationality is strengthened by Albert Speer's account of the German leader's comments on the new chancellery, opened in Berlin in January 1939:

> Hitler especially liked the long tramp that state guests and diplomats would now have to take before they reached the reception hall . . . he was not worried about the polished marble floor: 'That's exactly right, diplomats should have practice in moving on a slippery surface'.[19]

Speer adds that Hitler was particularly pleased with his study, especially by the 'inlay on his desk representing a sword half drawn from its sheath. "Good, good . . . When the diplomats sitting in front of me at this desk see that, they'll shiver and shake".'[20]

Nor was it merely when he granted personal audiences that Hitler excelled in such tactics. His behaviour in crises was so effective largely because it was not too pronounced a departure from his behaviour prior to them. His inflammatory public speeches, for example, were designed to instil a sense of fear in other European states. Thus, not long before the partition of Czechoslovakia in 1938, Hitler used the Nuremberg party rally to put on 'an exceptionally effective performance . . . . Playing the enraged leader of his nation, and supported by the frenzied applause of his followers, he tried to convince the contingent of foreign observers that he would not shrink from war'. As Speer concludes, it was 'intimidation on a grand scale'.[21] It was also extremely effective. The very fact that Chamberlain tried to defuse the Czech situation and avoid European war by flying to Germany to see the man who, 'half-mad', controlled 'the fate of hundreds of millions' is indicative of this.[22] The image that Chamberlain had of Hitler put the British Prime Minister at an immediate disadvantage in the negotiations that followed. The Führer's meticulous and systematic cultivation of the idea that he was an irrational, unpredictable and militaristic leader paid enormous returns in the later 1930s and showed just how effective the 'rationality-of-irrationality' strategy can be when fully and skilfully expoited.

In order to create an image of irrationality, decision-makers can also make use of the fact that governments are large bureaucratic organisations in which reckless subordinates may act in a way that top officials regard as irresponsible, but can do little to prevent. By appearing to give these subordinates greater discretion, it may be possible to convince the opponent that you are willing to accept enormous risks in order to obtain your objective. A similar image might be created by apparently linking yourself to allies who are obviously far less cautious and less averse to a collision than yourself. If they are able to commit you to a dangerous position that you find unwelcome but would be unable to withdraw from, the desired effect on the opponent might again be obtained.

At first sight these tactics appear similar to 'threats that leave something to chance', and they are in fact very closely related. The differences, however, are crucial. The 'rationality-of-irrationality' strategy, like the commitment, is designed to endow these threats with greater force and enable the problems discussed above to be overcome. Although both Maxwell and Snyder rightly point out that the risks cannot be loaded so that they are greater for one party than the other, one's apparent awareness of, and sensitivity to, these risks is potentially a much more malleable element in the equation. If the opponent can be made to believe you are almost totally oblivious to the risks and costs of war, success is virtually assured. His perception of your 'irrationality' will make him realise that it is he who has to back down. As Thomas Schelling has argued, 'Sometimes we can get a little credit for not having everything quite under control, and for being a little impulsive or unreliable.'[23]

Another way of demonstrating one's risk-taking resolve is to take dramatic and forceful actions that involve a profound escalation of the crisis. Such moves are in some ways just a variation of the bargaining ploys already discussed, but they are of sufficient importance to be worthy of separate analysis.

Deliberate escalation contains elements of the 'rationality-of-irrationality' tactic as it is intended to convince the opponent that one is innately reckless. It also has much in common with commitments. Indeed, escalatory moves generally involve a substantially increased allocation of the state's resources and prestige to the conflict and thereby make it more difficult for the state to withdraw unless it has made positive, and perhaps even spectacular, gains.

Finally, escalation closely resembles 'threats that leave something to chance': as well as implying that one is prepared deliberately to intensify the conflict if necessary, most actions of this type also heighten the possibility that further escalation will occur inadvertently as events get out of hand. Escalation tactics depend in large part for their success on shock value, on the impressions of doubt, confusion and fear they are able to create in the opponent's mind. Thus the dramatic crossing of thresholds, the flouting of conventions or the violation of limits that have hitherto been observed are likely to prove particularly effective moves. Crossing the line between coercion and violence, for example, would demonstrate very clearly to the opponent that one's threats cannot be lightly disregarded or one's risk-taking propensity underestimated. By playing on the adversary's fear of violence and demonstrating by one's own actions far less fear, it may be possible psychologically to pulverise the opponent.

The type of escalation move most commonly discussed is the straightforward increase in either the actual or the potential level of violence. This is not the only possibility, however. Perhaps equally feasible is what can be described as an *escalation of issues*, whereby the scope and extent of the crisis are deliberately widened. If a state finds itself at an overwhelming disadvantage in terms of the conventional power balance in the immediate locality of a crisis, it may decide to exert pressure against the adversary in other areas where the relative military capabilities incline far more in its favour. This is not a form of retaliation but of counter-pressure, of horizontal escalation as opposed to vertical escalation. The second point of confrontation is chosen not because it has any intrinsic relationship to the first, but merely because the opponent is far more vulnerable there. Although this is a rather different form of escalation from that usually considered, it is still an important way in which a state can demonstrate its resolve and its unwillingness to be bettered in a crisis.

It is also highly dangerous. Indeed, nearly all the techniques described above involve serious difficulties. They are far from infallible and if followed in a pure and unadulterated form would have provided a perfect recipe for superpower confrontations to lead to mutual extinction.

III Coercive Bargaining : The Dangers

The main dangers involved in coercive bargaining arise from the fact that it *is* a highly competitive process. Each of the participants may decide to adopt these tactics, either singly or in combination, in an attempt to make the other back down. But each one knows not only that the opponent is attempting to frighten him into submission, but also that the opponent does not want the bargaining process to end in war. Consequently, there may be a tendency to regard the adversary's moves with a certain contempt, a failure to treat them with the seriousness they deserve. Each move, instead of making the enemy government capitulate, may elicit an even more vigorous response.

This danger emerges very clearly from a thorough analysis of escalation tactics. It has frequently been argued that the notion of escalation lies at the heart of sound crisis management. William Kintner and David Schwarz, for example, have suggested that, on occasion, escalation may be the only means of effectively resolving a conflict situation. Some awareness of its dangers may be implicit in their statement that 'the aim of crisis management is to escalate to the most favourable position but at the same time to the least possible extent'.[24] Such caveats notwithstanding, they do not appear to regard escalatory tactics as an immense threat to peace. Yet escalation is in many respects an inherently dangerous and volatile instrument. While it may make the adversary more accommodating and thereby facilitate the attainment of satisfactory terms on which to resolve the crisis, this is far from a foregone result. It is at least equally plausible that it will add insurmountable difficulties to the task of 'disaster avoidance'.

Much depends, of course, on whether there is a unilateral or bilateral use of escalation tactics. Serious complications arise when each of the protagonists is willing to match any escalation by the opponent with an equivalent or greater move of its own. In such circumstances, it may be impossible to contain the conflict on the lower rungs of the escalation ladder. As Herman Kahn has noted, the problem is that either side could 'win' by increasing its efforts, so long as the opponent does not do the same:

> Neither side is willing to back down precisely because it believes or hopes it can achieve its objective without war. It may be willing to run some risk of war to achieve its objective, but it feels that the other side will back down or compromise before the risk becomes very large.[25]

If this feeling is mistaken and the other side does not back down or compromise at one level, the opposing policy-makers may feel that they merely have to escalate a little more in order to create the desired result. Just as, in the First World War, the generals appear to have felt that with a little more effort or slightly different tactics the military stalemate on the Western Front could be broken, so the decision-makers in an international crisis may feel that with a little more effort the psychological stalemate could be broken and the adversary made to capitulate. The danger is of consistently underestimating the opponent's will to resist and consequently overestimating one's own ability to 'persuade' him to comply with one's demands. If the expectations of the adversary's behaviour are wrong, the consequence may be a kind of *creeping* or *incremental* escalation process in which both sides gradually become 'wedded to incompatible policies, each in the belief that the opponent is bluffing or can be forced to give way'.[26] Indeed, they may have been confirmed in those beliefs by the very fact that the process was incremental, and that the adversary did not make any large-scale moves or take any drastic actions. Finally, they may reach a point where each state's commitment of prestige and resources becomes so great that it calculates that it cannot afford to back down. The expectation that the adversary will capitulate is replaced by the decision that the adversary must capitulate.

A closely related possibility is that a similar series of consecutive miscalculations will take the escalation process to a point where calculation becomes irrelevant. Although it may be the case, as some have argued, that the escalation ladder is very long and has stopping places where it is possible to get off and reverse direction, it is no less conceivable that the spiral of action and reaction between the protagonists could reach a stage at which the process becomes irreversible and almost totally out of control.[27] To some extent, as was indicated in the previous chapter, this is what happened in the Sarajevo Crisis. Russia's attempt to put pressure on Austria provoked Germany into a corresponding escalation that, for a variety of reasons, precipitated war. What was in fact most surprising about the whole mobilisation sequence during the crisis was the speed with which it occurred. There was also a kind of automatic quality about it. Indeed, it illustrates vividly that somewhere on the escalation ladder there may be what Bruce Russett has termed a 'point of no escape' after which it becomes impossible to avoid the outbreak of war.[28]

This point could be described equally well as the stage of *critical escalation*, beyond which all hope of deliberate and massive restraint becomes utopian. In superpower crises it may lie at the threshold between coercion and violence, the crossing of which takes policy-makers into new, uncharted and hitherto forbidden territory. Although some limitations may still be imposed on the conflict after violence has broken out between the forces of the two superpowers, there can be little confidence in their effectiveness. Further restraints are likely to be fragile at best. On the other hand, the stage of critical escalation may lie below rather than above the coercion–violence threshold. It has to be remembered that in 1914 substantial levels of violence did not occur until after the formal declarations of war were issued. Probably there is no uniformity here. The point of critical escalation may differ considerably from one crisis to the next. It is the consequent uncertainty that helps to make escalation a particularly dangerous bargaining ploy.

Furthermore, in adopting escalation tactics policy-makers face a serious dilemma. In order to maintain control over the situation, they want to escalate to the least possible extent and act in as delicate and discriminate a manner as possible. Yet this can lead to the kind of creeping escalation in which neither side manages to gain a decisive advantage. Dramatic escalation moves, therefore, might appear an attractive option, particularly as they are more likely to convince the opponent of the seriousness of one's intent. Acting in a disruptive manner, and deliberately and blatantly crossing thresholds – particularly that between coercion and violence – might succeed in frightening the opponent into submission. There is no guarantee of this, though. Far from securing compliance, such drastic actions may serve to elicit an emotional and violent response, not least because the opponent feels that a deliberate attempt is being made to humiliate him. Thus, both incremental escalation and the more flamboyant moves carry with them certain dangers. Whereas the former may involve a sequence of small miscalculations, each of which is relatively minor in itself, the latter may rest upon one or two gross miscalculations about the effect on the adversary. Both can take the interaction process far beyond the stage of critical escalation; the latter type of move merely does it more quickly.

The difficulties that beset 'rationality-of-irrationality' tactics are not very different. Many of them arise from the fact that each of the participants is acutely aware that if it placidly and uncritically accepts the opponent's 'irrationality' at face value, considerable gains will be made by the other party. Thus there may be a tendency to treat hints of 'irrationality' in the opponent's behaviour with a certain incredulity, to regard them as being made solely for effect. For these tactics to impress the opponent, therefore, it will be necessary *actually* and *visibly* to delegate authority to those who *are* less responsible in their actions and less statesmanlike in their behaviour. But this requirement contrasts markedly with the necessity for decision-makers to ensure that they are not robbed of their freedom of action by either subordinates or allies. If it is possible to appear irrational without actually being so, all well and good; but when it becomes necessary to take actions that really do contain elements of irrationality, decision-makers might well balk at the prospects – particularly in view of the opponent's natural scepticism. Should they go ahead anyway, and the opponent not be convinced, the prospect of the crisis getting out of hand will have been enormously increased without any corresponding gains being made.

The problem with commitments is rather similar, since they demand that states relinquish the initiative and deliberately surrender their freedom of action. Furthermore, like escalation tactics, they depend for their success on a unilateral use. The success of a commitment tactic is dependent almost totally on the opponent not adopting a similar technique. Once one side has become irrevocably committed to a collision course, the avoidance of disaster depends on the other having retained its freedom of choice. If each party believes that the opponent has considerable leeway and can back out of the conflict, when in fact this is not so, the mistake can result in both making commitments they would have avoided had their assessments of the other's position been more accurate. The misperceptions themselves may be caused by a breakdown in communication between the two sides. In this case there is a failure to see that the opponent is committed. Alongside the danger of misperception, however, must be set that of miscalculation. In this case the opponent's commitment is perceived, it is just not taken seriously. The other party calculates *wrongly* that it is not a meaningful commitment. If one side establishes its commitment well before the other, there is a chance that these errors of perception or calculation can be rectified. The possibility cannot be ruled out though of there being a simultaneous establishment of irrevocable commitments.

By analysing the problems attendant upon escalation, 'rationality-of-irrationality' tactics and commitments, the dangers and difficulties of 'threats that leave something to chance' are also dealt with, albeit in a roundabout manner. In so far as these other techniques are designed to support or strengthen threats, their dangers, deficiencies and drawbacks are almost certain to be reflected in the threats themselves rendering them less effective and more dangerous than if the supporting techniques were foolproof. Seriously underestimating the credibility of the opponent's threats may be made less likely by the adoption of one or more of the tactics described. Uncertainty about the opponent's risk-taking propensity may be diminished in a similar manner. But the first of these possibilities can never be entirely ruled out, and as for the second, there is perhaps an irreducible minimum of uncertainty, a permanent residue of doubt that cannot be eliminated. The practical implications of all this must now be examined.

IV Coercive Bargaining : The Practice

It could be contended that this analysis exaggerates the danger of coercive bargaining, and as a result is unnecessarily pessimistic and alarmist. Taking this argument further, it might be asserted that, in confrontations such as that over Cuba, not only were coercive bargaining tactics used with considerable success by the United States but the disastrous consequences alluded to above failed to materialise. It is important to remember, however, that although coercion worked well for the United States it did so because of special conditions existing in the Cuban Missile Crisis. These are unlikely to be reproduced in all circumstances. So much depends on the context within which coercive bargaining tactics are adopted. The outcomes of superpower confrontations are determined not merely, and perhaps not even primarily, by the respective manipulative skills of the adversaries but by what can be described as contextual, structural or situational factors. Whether or not a crisis is resolved peacefully, as well as the precise terms on which it is ended, depend in large part on its basic structure and the setting within which bargaining moves are made. This is something that analyses of coercive bargaining have sometimes ignored. 'Threats that leave something to chance' and the techniques that reinforce them are sometimes discussed as if the parties to the conflict operate in a vacuum, as a result of which bargaining skill is *all*. This is patently not the case in superpower confrontations.

Furthermore, the superpowers have not only recognised the dangers of coercive bargaining but have taken steps to combat and to reduce them. The desire for credibility has been balanced by caution, the need to demonstrate resolve tempered by prudence and fear. Thus, the difference between the coercive bargaining process as presented in the preceding pages and the bargaining that has actually taken place in superpower crises is enormous. It is the difference between a conflict ungoverned by rules, regulations or restraints, and one in which the participants have recognised a common interest in establishing or observing certain tacit guidelines. It is the difference between an undisciplined game in which 'anything goes' and one played according to set rules or codes of conduct that are no less significant because they are mainly informal or unwritten. It is the difference between 'fighting to the death' and engaging in stylised, almost ritualistic, conflict that not only discourages – if not prohibits – the adoption of certain moves but endows other moves with symbolic importance.

Paradoxically, the guidelines serve not only to dilute or moderate the bargaining process, but also to make it more effective. In the almost unadulterated form of coercive bargaining described above, everything is subject to manipulation. By the same token, there is little opportunity for either party to assess the seriousness of purpose or the real intentions of the adversary: if it is all a matter of manipulation it can equally plausibly be a matter of bluff. Consequently, the temptation to challenge the opponent's commitments or go one step further up the escalation ladder may be irresistible. In a more regulated form of conflict, where certain courses of action are generally acknowledged to have particular significance, the prospects for understanding are considerably enhanced. As a result, the ability of the participants to distinguish between bluffing and serious declarations of intent should also be improved. But what precise guidelines have been followed? What kinds of rules, regulations and restraints have been introduced into the bargaining process by the superpowers? How have they moderated or overcome the attendant dangers of coercion?

There are at least four ways in which crisis bargaining has been modified, moderated and restrained *in practice*. In the first place, asymmetries in the basic structure of the crisis have been not only explicitly acknowledged, but fully exploited by the participants in a constructive manner designed to facilitate the task of 'disaster avoidance'. A mutual, if sometimes belated, recognition of how important the issue in dispute actually is to each of the participants has been of crucial importance here. The second modification is the introduction of inducements and rewards into the bargaining process. Bargaining in crises does not involve coercion alone. As well as putting pressure on the opponent to force him to yield, it is also possible to make it easier for him to do so – both by limiting one's demands and by offering certain concessions oneself. Thirdly, the more dangerous bargaining tactics described above, although not abandoned entirely, have been used only very sparingly, and then with certain modifications that make them more manageable. The importance of 'communication moves', for example, has been recognised by the two superpowers as an essential part of the bargaining process, and as an acceptable and valid substitute for some of the high-risk techniques.[29] Finally, they have acknowledged the relevance of communication as an aid to understanding and compromise. Each of these modifications and constraints must now be analysed more fully.

V   The Balance of Power, Interests and Resolve

A few analysts of superpower crises have paid considerable attention to the immediate context of each confrontation, highlighting the importance of what has been described as the 'bargaining setting'. Among the factors included in the setting and likely to have some impact on the bargaining process are: 'the conflict of interest which underlies the crisis, the recent relations between the parties, the parties' comparative valuation of the stakes at issue, the relative military capabilities and subjective fears of war, and precrisis commitments'.[30] While this notion of setting is a fairly complex one, the central question is how the various factors within it impinge on the *resolve* of the two superpowers. When the problem is expressed in this way, two factors in the setting immediately stand out as potentially the most important variables. They are the relative balance of military power, both conventional and nuclear, between the two sides, and the balance of interests, or who has most at stake. Indeed, the crucial relationships are those between power and will on the one hand, and values and will on the other.

How does each of these balances affect the relative risk-taking propensities of the two sides? And within the military balance is it most advantageous to be preponderant at the nuclear or the conventional level? Does an overwhelming superiority in local conventional forces, for example, make it easier for the state to run risks? Does nuclear 'superiority' endow threats of escalation with any greater credibility? What if one side has local conventional superiority, but is inferior at the nuclear level? Then again, how does the weight each state attaches to the disputed issue intrude into its calculations about risk-taking? Is this balance more, or less, important than the traditional balance of military power? If there are any asymmetries along either the power or the interests dimension, how and to what extent can these be exploited to bring about an advantageous and peaceful resolution of the crisis? Any serious analysis of crisis bargaining must attempt to answer at least some of those questions if only in a rather tentative way.

A hypothesis that enjoys considerable support is that the military balance, especially at the nuclear level, has a profound influence on the course and outcome of superpower crises. Writing in the mid 1960s, for example, Kintner and Schwarz argued not only that superpower crises were contests of power, but that in these contests strategic superiority was the vital ingredient ensuring a favourable outcome for the United States.[31] Assertions of this kind however should be regarded with some suspicion, as this area of analysis and debate has become highly charged with emotion. In the first place, it is closely related to dilemmas of the arms race. For those who advocate an attempt by Washington either to obtain or to maintain a position of overwhelming nuclear superiority, the argument about crises is a useful one. If it can be demonstrated that strategic superiority endows its owner with significant advantages in superpower confrontations, then the case for it will be substantially reinforced. Thus there is a danger that analyses of crises bargaining will be shaped by extraneous considerations.

Secondly, within the United States defence establishment, and possibly within that of the Soviet Union as well, this issue has become bound up with internal struggles over the allocation of resources, and particularly the conflict over whether emphasis should be put on conventional or nuclear weaponry. After the Cuban Missile Crisis, for example, there was intense debate about the Soviet withdrawal of the missiles. On the one side were ranged those like General LeMay who argued that 'superior US strategic power coupled with the obvious will and ability to apply this power was the major factor that forced the Soviets to back down'.[32] On the other side were many who supported General Wheeler in taking the opposite view and emphasising the conventional advantages as decisive. In one statement on the issue, Wheeler in fact quoted Secretary of Defense McNamara as arguing along very similar lines to himself: 'the forces that were the cutting edge of the action were the non-nuclear ones. Nuclear force was not irrelevant but it was in the background. Non-nuclear forces were our sword; our nuclear forces were our shield'.[33] Both Air Force and Army spokesmen, of course, had a vested interest in demonstrating that their service had played the dominant part in forcing the Soviet Union to back down.

Neither of these problems has entirely disappeared. Indeed, the controversy was rekindled by the Soviet attainment of nuclear parity in the late 1960s and early 1970s. The growth in Russian capabilities has brought with it dire predictions about its effect on both the Soviet and American willingness to run risks during superpower confrontations in the future. It is claimed that Soviet risk-taking propensity has been given a substantial boost while that of Washington has undergone a corresponding reduction. Some argue that parity has provided the Soviet Union with options that were hitherto unavailable and that consequently Moscow is likely to become far more reckless.[34] In support of this thesis, it is argued that in earlier confrontations with the United States the Soviets were almost invariably bargaining and negotiating from weakness and were far more cautious and restrained in their behaviour than would have been necessary had the strategic balance been less unfavourable. Among the most cogent and forceful presentations of the argument is that by Zbigniew Brzezinski, who suggests that in 1962 acute awareness of the inadequacies of the Soviet nuclear posture not only made Khrushchev withdraw the missiles, but also rendered possible counter-moves elsewhere out of the question.

> Had Strategic symmetry prevailed it might have proven much more difficult for the United States to achieve its principle objective in Cuba (the removal of hostile missiles) through the exercise of its own conventional superiority (naval blockade) while simultaneously offsetting its own conventional inferiority in a politically sensitive and vital area (West Berlin) by the inhibiting threat of American strategic superiority. That potential American losses in a nuclear war may have been subjectively 'unacceptable' to the American policy-makers was no reassurance to the leaders in the Kremlin who knew that such a war would mean the almost complete devastation of the Soviet Union.[35]

Now that Soviet leaders know that US policy-makers face destruction of the same magnitude as they themselves, their self-confidence, so it is argued, is significantly enhanced. Consequently, in any future confrontation they will be far less reluctant to adopt highly coercive counter-measures than they were in October 1962. In other words, Soviet risk-taking propensity during international crises is seen by Brezezinski as a direct function of the nuclear balance between the superpowers.

Compelling as such an interpretation may appear, it cannot be allowed to stand without thorough and critical examination. It is suggested here that its basic premise is suspect and that other considerations affect the relative risk-taking propensity of the two sides to a greater extent than fine, discriminating calculations about the strategic balance and the level of casualties each super-power is likely to suffer in a nuclear war. Indeed, Brzezinski's analysis depends on each side not only doing this for itself, but also attempting to gauge the opponent's assessment of the same things. Although there might have been three times as many Soviet citizens as Americans killed if there had been a war in October 1962, it has been estimated that even in these 'favour-able' conditions the United States could have anticipated between thirty and fifty million fatalities.[36] To argue that this assym-metry was a decisive factor seems to be indulging in the kind of number-mongering that Brzezinski himself condemns. For most policy-makers such calculations are almost certainly far less influential than the kind of sentiment echoed in McGeorge Bundy's words:

> A decision that would bring even one hydrogen bomb on one city of one's own country would be recognised in advance as a catastro-phic blunder, ten bombs on ten cities would be a disaster beyond history, and a hundred bombs on a hundred cities are unthinkable.[37]

Thus the suggestion that somehow, nuclear war becomes less abhorrent once the opponent is as vulnerable as oneself does not carry conviction. Nuclear holocaust will hardly be an attrac-tive option even to the side that has the capacity to 'win'. So long as neither superpower regards nuclear war with equanimity, therefore, the strategic balance is unlikely to be the major deter-minant of either side's resolve.

The possibility that there might be other, more powerful influ-ences on each superpower's willingness to take risks is given little attention in Brzezinski's analysis. As a result, the governments of the two superpowers are virtually reduced to automatons whose calculations are dominated wholly and exclusively by the strategic context within which they operate. Not surprisingly, therefore, nuclear parity is held to carry with it serious risks of miscalculation. 'In a setting of parity – whether formalized by SALT or dynamically competitive – credibility becomes largely a matter of will alone and this is dangerous because it could tempt one or both sides to bluff excessively in order to make its determination credible.'[38] Such fears are the penalty for ignoring the possibility that factors other than the strategic balance intrude forcefully into the deliberations of both Soviet and American decision-makers. They also overlook the existence of the tacit guidelines and 'codes' of behaviour that have been developed by the superpowers precisely to enable them to resolve crises *without* excessive bluffing. As one commentator has put it:

> The Cuban experience of 1962 suggests that factors dependent on the particular circumstances of the time and place of the crisis and its development play a central role in determining the actions of governments in a crisis and the final outcome, because they affect, not the remote and difficult-to-contemplate, but the immediate stages of the crisis.[39]

The Berlin Crisis of 1961, where circumstances other than the strategic balance were rather different from Cuba, tends to reinforce this conclusion. A comparative analysis of these two confrontations highlights clearly the importance of the political context within which they occur. It also suggests that it is the immediate circumstances of a crisis that often facilitate implicit acknowledgement of, if not open agreement on, the guidelines within which policy-makers are to operate. Particularly important, of course, are the limits on the bargaining process that are unilaterally or bilaterally imposed as a result.

Such guidelines stem from a mutual recognition of the basic structure of the crisis, together with a realisation of its profound importance in influencing the will of the participants. The tactics of brinkmanship, escalation and the like are in fact dependent for their success on an asymmetry of interests between the protagonists and on the correct perception and evaluation of this asymmetry by them. It may be partially obscured by the attempts of the protagonists to project an image of resolve, as both could hope to gain from appearing to have far more at stake than is actually the case. As J. L. Richardson has put it, 'both sides are interested in appearing to regard disputed issues as vital'.[40]

Although the temptations of temporary advantage are not insubstantial, this type of manipulation is something that, in the long term, could prove self-defeating for the superpowers. Consequently, neither side has attempted to exploit the possibility very far. Such restraint probably reflects not only the common interest in resolving peacefully the crisis of the moment, but the long-term advantages of establishing mutually acceptable ground rules of behaviour.

In the last analysis, therefore, there has been a mutual recognition, and acceptance, of just what the stakes actually were. The importance of this is difficult to overestimate since, in virtually all nuclear confrontations, the greater the interests at stake for any power involved, the greater the risks that power will be prepared to take. Indeed, both Stephen Maxwell and Robert Osgood have laid considerable emphasis on this. Osgood has argued that the 'comparative resolve to use force' or the 'relative risk-taking propensities of the two sides' depends crucially on the relative value each puts on the issue in dispute.[41] Thus, where coercive bargaining techniques have succeeded it is because they have been used almost unilaterally. Although both sides have been willing to enter the 'competition in risk-taking', there has been an implicit, if sometimes slightly delayed, recognition that for the outcome to be decided peacefully, one of the combatants had to be less prepared than the adversary to pursue its objectives vigorously.

The asymmetry of interest may well have been the most important factor in determining the outcome of the Cuban Missile Crisis. It is doubtful if the crisis ever reached the same intensity or had the same importance for the Kremlin as for Washington. In the last resort, the missiles in Cuba were peripheral to Soviet interests, whereas US policy-makers, correctly or not, perceived them as a dire threat to American security. The Kennedy Administration regarded the implications of the Soviet move as far too serious to allow it to go unchallenged. Its willingness to take substantial risks was reinforced by a long history of involvement in the Caribbean, regarded by many as the traditional preserve of the United States. For the Soviets, on the other hand, the stakes were expendable. Although there is still uncertainty about Soviet motives, it may be that they were merely gambling for strategic advantage, hoping that the installation of missiles in Cuba would provide a cheap and easy way to offset American nuclear superiority. What is certain, however, is that Soviet leaders did not regard their security as directly threatened. And, as Hannes Adomeit has argued,

> In accepting or rejecting risks the Soviet leaders have been motivated first and foremost by security considerations. They have demonstrated . . . a close linkage between perceived interests and commitments during crises, making Soviet-taking in this sense basically a 'rational' process.[42]

Since much the same applies to the United States, which in this instance did regard its security as threatened, there was a considerable divergence in their willingness to run risks.

It was this difference that facilitated a peaceful resolution of the crisis. A limited and intermediate deployment of military power combined with a threat of further escalation by the United States 'persuaded' the Soviet Union to withdraw its missiles and thereby brought the crisis to an end. To expect an automatic repetition of this in other confrontations, however, would be to neglect the peculiarities of the Missile Crisis. Yet this is what many commentators did, suggesting that in any future crisis the United States merely had to *up the ante* and the Soviet Union would back down. This argument ignores completely the basic structure of the crisis, which was overwhelmingly in favour of the United States. Kennedy was able to use escalation as a tool of crisis management because the United States had a number of important advantages. Indeed,

> . . . the President himself realised that the Cuban Crisis had three distinctive features: it took place in an area where we enjoyed local conventional superiority, where Soviet national security was not directly engaged and where the Russians lacked a case they could plausibly sustain before the world.[43]

That the second of these features was probably the most important is further indicated by Robert Kennedy's testimony. He argues that the missiles were of vital concern to American national security but not to that of the Kremlin: 'This fact was ultimately recognised by Khrushchev, and this recognition . . . brought about his change in what, up to that time, had been a very adamant position.'[44] Osgood is in total agreement with this and has concluded that the 'distinctly favourable balance of interests' was the greatest advantage possessed by the United

States in the crisis.[45] Indeed, if the situation had been more symmetrical the outcome would probably have been far different. For then the Soviet Union might have been prepared either to challenge the blockage directly or to escalate the conflict horizontally by putting pressure on Berlin. With both sides adopting coercive bargaining tactics and attempting to manipulate the risk of war, the likelihood of uncontrollable escalation would have been increased enormously.

It could be maintained that this asymmetry was a matter of luck for both sides as it enabled the crisis to be resolved peacefully. More convincing is the argument that the outcome of the crisis represented a re-affirmation of the spheres of influence principle, on which the superpowers have based many of their actions during the postwar period.[46] As was briefly hinted at above, something similar occurred in the Berlin Crisis of 1961. Once again, the outcome reflected the underlying structure of the crisis and the relative value each superpower put on the stake at issue. This was manifested most noticeably in the resigned manner with which the Western powers accepted the building of the Berlin Wall. Although the blatant American acquiescence in the Soviet move aroused much acrimonious debate, it was perhaps little more than an overly explicit example of the spheres of influence principle in action. This is almost completely overlooked by those who argue that the Western powers could have demolished the barriers with relative impunity, particularly during the first few hours after they were erected.[47] Other more convincing analyses have arrived at the opposite conclusion. Richardson, in particular, has argued that 'the Soviet stake in the issue in dispute was greater, probably much greater, than that of the West'.[48] For the Soviet Union it was a matter of urgency and importance to stop the flow of refugees from the German Democratic Republic. So debilitating an effect was the exodus having that, had it been allowed to continue, the polity and economy of East Germany could hardly have remained viable. The implications of this were frightening for the Soviet Union: its grasp over the whole of Eastern Europe could have been seriously jeopardised had it allowed the decline of the GDR to continue. Thus any Western counter-move would almost certainly have elicited forceful and vigorous actions by the Soviet leaders. The probability of rapid escalation would have been high. 'The western interest in the freedom of movement in Berlin or discomfiting the East German regime was not great enough to justify risks of this magnitude.'[49]

Thus, even if the 'soft-liners' had not prevailed over the 'hard-liners' within the Kennedy Administration – as Jean Edward Smith has suggested – it is doubtful if a less cautious policy would have emerged.[50] It was almost certainly recognised that the barricades could not be demolished without an immediate expansion of hostilities. Just as in 1962 it was more important for the Americans that the missiles be removed from Cuba than it was for the Soviet Union to keep them there, so in 1961 it was more important for the Kremlin to maintain intact the barriers dividing the city than it was for Washington to remove them. In many respects, therefore, the Berlin and Cuban Crises appear to be the converse of each other, with the major advantages accruing to the Soviet Union in the former situation and the United States in the latter.

Both confrontations, however, demonstrate that it is not so much the immense power that the superpowers wield that really counts but the will to bring it to bear. And this is likely to be dictated above all by the relative interests at stake. That the balance of interests is decisive appears to be borne out by the Soviet erection of the Berlin Wall. Although the strategic balance in 1961 was not profoundly different from that a year later, this did not prevent the Soviets from taking actions urgently required by their own security. Somehow the flow of refugees had to be stopped. Khrushchev was prepared to take the necessary risks to achieve this in the face of an adverse strategic balance. American nuclear superiority did little to deter the Soviet Union from physically dividing the city of Berlin. This is glossed over by those analysts who shout the virtues of nuclear supremacy. It is not ignored, though, by those who brandish the advantages of conventional forces as the most readily usable form of military power. Not only do they emphasise the American conventional superiority in the Caribbean in October 1962, but they argue that Khrushchev was able to take considerable risks in 1961 precisely because the Soviet Union had an overwhelming preponderance of conventional forces in and around Berlin to offset its relative weakness at the nuclear level. If any situation has consistently and dramatically highlighted the limitations of local conventional superiority, however, it *is* Berlin. So long as the Soviets were merely trying to solidify and strengthen the *status quo*, con-

ventional forces appeared useful, but neither conventional preponderance nor nuclear threats have been sufficient support for
attempts to overturn the *status quo*. In the Berlin Crisis the utility
of conventional forces was not constant: up to the point where
Soviet vital interests ended and those of the West began, it was
considerable; beyond that point it was negligible.

Thus, purely military considerations are far from being
dominant in superpower confrontations. The basic structure of
the situation, and particularly which participant has most at
stake, is generally a far better guide to the outcome. It would
hardly be exaggerating to suggest that, although its importance is
not always acknowledged – at least by commentators on international politics and foreign policy as opposed to practitioners of
the art – this is likely to be the decisive factor in determining the
balance of gains and losses among the participants in almost any
superpower crisis.

Many analysts have elaborated at length on the utility of
coercive bargaining tactics in international crises, often depreciat-
ing or neglecting the importance of the context within which such
tactics are used. Yet in the nuclear age these tactics are likely to
prove effective only when they support or emphasise the basic
structure of the crisis. The degree of influence that either superpower can exert on their other's behaviour is probably dependent
more on the characteristics of the situation than any particular
skill in manipulating risks or wielding threats. The structure of a
superpower crisis, of course, is neither wholly out of the control of
the participants nor impervious to their influence. To some
extent, it depends on the objectives the superpowers pursue in
their confrontations and the demands they make on the
opponent. Although this is closely related to the asymmetry of
interests, it is sufficiently important to require separate discussion.

VI   The Limitation of Objectives

The issues in dispute in any superpower confrontation are not
rigidly and unalterably fixed. While they are in part inherent in
the situation, they are also a function of the objectives of the
protagonists and the demands they make upon each other. It is

not inconceivable that one side's demands could be so outrageous as to widen the dispute and transform the crisis from a conflict over a strictly defined and delimited issue to a conflict over the future prestige, power and status of the participants. Indeed, the 'escalation' of objectives during a crisis, although given little attention, is perhaps as serious a problem as the escalation of means. The latter danger tends to be discussed at great length, but the former should not be minimised, especially as the two problems are so closely bound up with each other.

Escalation of means, for example, can result in a corresponding expansion of the objectives sought. An increase in the resources devoted to a conflict – as was suggested above – may commit the government responsible to a position from which it feels unable to withdraw without the very considerable gains that alone can justify the efforts, sacrifices, costs or risks incurred. This could well require more significant concessions from the opponent than one originally hoped or expected to obtain. An escalation of objectives, on the other hand, may have equally profound consequences on the means used. In this case, however, it is the opponent's exertions that are likely to be affected rather than one's own. The more that is asked of the adversary the more intransigent he is likely to become; the greater the concessions demanded, the greater the reluctance to make them.

This was demonstrated prior to American entry into the Second World War, when Washington adopted a policy that threatened not only to contain Japan but to defeat it by a process of 'gradual exhaustion'. Herbert Feis has described Togo's reaction to the American demands of 27 November 1941: 'Japan was asked not only to abandon all the gains of her years of sacrifice, but to surrender her international position as a power in the Far East. That surrender as he saw it would have amounted to national suicide.'[51] In the light of such demands, a Japanese surprise attack against the cutting edge of American forces in the Pacific became a far less unattractive option than it would have appeared had the demands been more moderate. Faced with the dilemma of conceding vital interests or escalating the conflict enormously, Japan chose the latter course, even though it was aware of the dangers accompanying it. To avoid any recurrence of this type of problem, there must be very definite and deliberate restraint on the demands one makes of the opponent. As an eminent social psychologist has put it, 'controlling the importance of what is preceived to be at stake in a conflict may be one of the most effective ways of preventing the conflict from taking a destructive course'.[52]

It has already been emphasised that the crucial differences in the risk-taking propensities of the two sides and their willingness to adopt coercive bargaining techniques are dependent on the mutual acknowledgement of any asymmetry in the crisis. If both sides frame their demands in such a way that the opponent sees its vital interests as being jeopardised, such asymmetry as does exist will be destroyed and *both* superpowers will more likely embark on the kind of competitive risk-taking venture that could so easily end in collision. In such circumstances each participant would almost certainly be prepared to escalate the conflict to a high level before sacrificing vital interests. Thus the asymmetrical use of coercive bargaining techniques must be fostered and encouraged by the moderation of one's bargaining demands. Closer attention must now be given to the manner in which, and the extent to which, this has been done in the major crises of the postwar period.

Through a mixture of good fortune and good judgement, the superpowers have managed to avoid a crisis in which the vital interests of both have been central to the dispute. It is good fortune to the extent that the bipolar world that emerged from the ruins of the Second World War was relatively simple and straightforward. Indeed, it did not take too long before each superpower had carved out its own well-defined sphere of influence. Although there were certain areas of ambiguity, at those places where the superpowers came into direct contact, the point at which the jurisdiction of one ended and that of the other began was usually extremely prominent. Neither was prepared publicly to acknowledge this or (until the recent Helsinki agreement on co-operation and security in Europe) to accept formally the legitimacy of the opponent's position. In official statements each superpower took the opportunity to attack the policies and position of the opponent. Their practice belied their propaganda, however, and a 'rhetorical offensive' by both states hid a tacit acknowledgement and mutual acceptance of the *status quo*.[53] To some extent the superpower confrontations themselves played a part in this process, either by helping to eliminate areas of ambiguity and uncertainty or by accentuating the existing divisions.

It has already been argued that the spheres of influence principle was reaffirmed in the Berlin Crisis of 1961 and aided the peaceful resolution of that crisis; the 1948 confrontation over Berlin had done much to establish this principle in the first place by demonstrating the clear, unequivocal nature of the US guarantee to Western European security. What is perhaps most remarkable though is the cautious way the Soviet Union behaved in 1948 even when faced with uncertainty about the depth of Washington's commitment to Western Europe in general and West Berlin in particular. The build-up to the crisis was gradual and probing rather than dramatic and dangerous. In the crisis itself, Stalin ultimately recognised that US policy-makers attached more value to remaining in the city than he did to evicting them. This is where the elements of good judgement are so important. On occasion, the superpowers have found themselves in a crisis as a result of miscalculating the opponent's determination or underestimating the strength of its commitment. Once having discovered the mistake though they have been prepared to respect the adversary's vital interests and to limit their own objectives and demands accordingly. Even where the challenge has been direct and deliberate, the same kinds of restraint have operated.

In the Berlin Crisis of 1961, for example, Khrushchev reciprocated, at least in part, Washington's tacit acceptance of Russian vital interests. Although the Soviets did not limit themselves exclusively to the purely defensive measure of dividing the city, their probes against the Western position were strictly limited and carefully controlled. Despite some attempt to nibble away at Western rights, basically they respected the American commitment to West Berlin. Moscow had gradually realised that there was no comparable commitment to freedom of movement within the city as a whole and that to elliminate this would not impinge directly on Washington's vital interests. Even if such freedom had been regarded as more important by the Western powers, of course, Soviet decision-makers could hardly have refrained from acting in the manner they did, given what was at stake. Perhaps most illuminating though is the way the Soviet Union made its actions palatable to the West. It was emphasised that the wall did not trespass on the vital interests of the other occupying powers. Simultaneous with the closure, a communiqué was issued making clear that the action did nothing to undermine the basic objectives of France, Britain and the United States. There was no serious challenge to the Western presence in the city; the wall did not interfere with Allied rights of access to West Berlin, nor did it diminish the freedom of the West Berliners to choose their own government.[54]

In marked contrast to the respect shown by the participants for the interests of the adversary, and the consequent limitation of objectives, was the behaviour of the great powers in the Sarajevo Crisis. Although there was far less incentive to compromise in 1914, this crisis nevertheless serves as an excellent example of how states can become committed to incompatible objectives by failing to recognise the sanctity of the opponent's vital interests. The Austrian ultimatum to Serbia that followed the assassination of the Archduke Franz Ferdinand was to all intents and purposes a demand for unconditional surrender. The position of Berchtold, Austria–Hungary's Foreign Minister, was that the Hapsburg monarchy should obtain 'diplomatic victory all along the line or open hostilities'.[55] Thus, neither of the cardinal principles outlined above were acted upon in 1914. Although the Austrian position was understandable, given the precarious existence of the monarchy, it made no allowance to Russian susceptibilities and overlooked the substantial Russian interest in maintaining the integrity of Serbia. 'Austria, in collusion with Germany, had made up her mind to go to extremes and carry out the destruction, material or moral, of her small neighbour, without regard for the prestige, feeling and interests of its protectress Russia.'[56]

The difference between this and nuclear age crises is overwhelming. It has already been demonstrated how both Russian and American aims were kept fairly limited in the 1961 confrontation. The Cuban Crisis is another example of this limitation process. Harlan Cleveland has rightly argued that if objectives are limited enough there is a far greater probability that they will be obtained without recourse to violence.[57] Kennedy recognised this, and rejected the enticing prospect of using the crisis to make a further attempt to dethrone Castro. Although some of his advisers were initially in favour of this, the attendant dangers would have been even more extensive than those involved simply

in getting the missiles removed. Indeed, it would have transformed the structure of the crisis. From being a conflict over
a distinct and limited issue – whether or not Soviet IRBMs could
remain in Cuba – it would have become a much more serious confrontation involving Moscow's willingness to allow an allied
government to be overturned by force of arms. The consequent
loss of prestige would have been enormous and far less tolerable
to the Soviet Union than that incurred by the removal of the
IRBMs. Whether Khrushchev could have refrained from a move
against West Berlin in such circumstances must be doubtful. For
the Soviet Union to have moved against Berlin prior to a United
States invasion of Cuba, however, would have meant that *it* was
willing to transform the crisis from a conflict strictly limited in
terms of both the issue and the geographical area to a confrontation in which such limitations, if not totally destroyed, were
likely to be far less effective. Awareness of the gravity of such
a move probably did more to prohibit the Soviet Union from
making it than any other consideration. As was suggested in the
previous chapter, to adopt this course of action as a retaliatory
move for an attack on Cuba was one thing; to take the initiative
with it was something very different. Thus it was fortunate that
Kennedy immediately perceived the need for a limited objective,
recognising that the United States should not attempt to exploit
the situation to a point where the Soviet leaders felt that the
demands being made upon them were extortionate.

It was merely a small step from this to acknowledging the need
to make it as easy as possible for the Soviet Union to accommodate American demands while bringing the crisis to a speedy
and peaceful conclusion. Indeed, United States policy makers
realised that inducements and rewards are a necessary supplement to threats or deprivations in superpower bargaining during
international crises. As one analyst has succinctly put it, 'making
threats is not enough'[58] Although it was the Soviet Union that
made the major concession by agreeing to withdraw the missiles,
Washington managed to make this a far less difficult and unpleasant task than it would otherwise have been by providing a
guarantee not to invade Cuba. Furthermore, Moscow was
informed that, although the American missiles in Turkey could
not be removed under duress, prior to the crisis the President had
ordered that they be dismantled and would ensure that this

order was implemented once the crisis had subsided and the situation returned to normal.[59] By offering concessions to Khrushchev, Kennedy clearly demonstrated that he was not trying to humiliate the Soviet leader. Such concessions ensured that Moscow would be able to point to the 'substantial gains' it had achieved in return for withdrawing the missiles. Although the outcome of the crisis could have been a lot better for the Soviet Union, it was certainly not a fiasco or an unmitigated disaster.

This demonstrates the need for conciliatory gestures to be combined with a firm stance. So long as a government is able to protect what it regards as vital interests, it can afford to make concessions on more marginal issues or less central concerns. Although many of these concessions may be little more than window dressing, so long as they help to make the choice facing the opponent more palatable they remain significant. Acquiescence in one's demands is made a more attractive option and the likelihood of total intransigence on the opponent's part is correspondingly diminished. This demonstrates the need for flexibility in bargaining. Indeed, a totally uncompromising stance involving a refusal to make any concessions whatsoever will make flexibility and conciliation by the adversary appear too much like surrender. 'Rigidity promotes rigidity.'[60] Fortunately, both superpowers have been aware of this danger and have therefore been flexible rather than rigid in their behaviour.

This pattern can be observed in confrontations other than the Cuban Missile Crisis. It was also evident in the Sino-American Crisis of 1958 over Quemoy. Indeed, the way in which the United States took firm action in support of the Nationalists while almost simultaneously opening up the possibility of negotiations with Peking in a bid to end the artillery bombardment was a textbook model of the 'carrot and stick' approach. The same approach was manifested in the public statements of both Eisenhower and Dulles. Not only did they emphasise Washington's determination not to back down in the face of threats, but they also hinted at the possibility of concessions. As the President put it in his speech of 11 September, 'There are measures that can be taken to ensure that these offshore islands will not be a thorn in the side of peace.'[61] In this way, Washington made it far easier for Communist China to diminish the intensity of the artillery bombardment, and eventually to discontinue it, without feeling that its efforts had been a total failure. The advantages of this dual approach have been summed up by Glenn Snyder: 'Accommodating gestures made concurrently with coercive tactics may defuse a confrontation of much of its emotional overtones of hostility, duress, and engagements of "face".'[62]

Similar combinations were used in the Middle East Crises of 1967 and 1973. In both cases the American response to Soviet threats of intervention was one of *conciliatory firmness*. In 1973 in particular the United States went a long way to meeting the Soviet demands, which were themselves carefully circumscribed. On 25 October Kissinger openly, and almost certainly privately as well, reiterated that the United States was trying to obtain a stricter observance of the cease-fire as laid down in the UN Security Council Resolution 338 adopted three days earlier. He also announced that the United States was willing to agree to an international force to supervise the cease-fire, so long as the permanent members of the Security Council, and particularly the superpowers, did not participate. In his well-publicized news conference, Kissinger, according to his biographers, 'followed a clear two-track policy: soft-talking the Russians out of confrontation after having alerted American military forces to get ready for one'. They add that this was 'classic Kissinger'.[63] It is better seen as 'classic' crisis management. There was little that was particularly novel or distinctive in the Secretary of State's behaviour. Kissinger's dual approach just continued a well-established pattern of superpower behaviour. Merely because it was not an innovation, however, does not render it insignificant. This process of reassurance was essential if a potentially disastrous situation was to be avoided.

Indeed, the Middle East provides a particularly dangerous arena for superpower confrontations since both sides have a great deal at stake. Successive US governments have committed themselves to supporting the state of Israel since its inception in 1948. The Soviet involvement in the area stems from a later date, but has become equally substantial. Mutual disengagement of the superpowers from the area is almost inconceivable, even though Washington and Moscow are sometimes more frightened of their allies than they are of each other. It is easy to understand, therefore, why Kissinger warned that 'the Middle East may become what the Balkans were to Europe – an area where local rivalries . . . draw in the great powers into confrontations they did not necessarily seek or start'.[64] This statement was far from inappropriate, especially when the parallels between the Sarajevo Crisis and the Middle East Crisis of October 1973 are considered more fully. In the latter case both superpowers had a great deal at stake, as did the great powers in July 1914. The possibility that they might become committed to totally incompatible objectives could not be entirely dismissed, especially as the pressures on the Soviet Union to take a firm unyielding stance were enormous. Six years earlier the Soviet Union had watched its client states being beaten, and not even its threats to intervene unless Israel was more restrained had prevented its prestige from being badly tarnished. If this was allowed to happen again, with Moscow making no more than verbal protests, its entire position in the Arab world would be seriously jeopardised. Rhetorical retaliation for the Israeli violations of the initial UN cease-fire was very clearly insufficient, particularly as it did nothing to ease the desperate military plight of the Egyptians.

It was against this background that Moscow made the preparations for intervention that were discussed in the previous chapter. In the event they became superfluous because the United States recognised Moscow's dilemma and, ultimately, may even have sympathised to some extent with the Soviet predicament. This was a major difference between the 1973 crisis and that of 1914. Nevertheless, the brief Soviet–American confrontation that resulted did point to the dangers of a situation in which the basic structure of the crisis is not entirely clear even to the major protagonists. Such was the case in the Middle East, largely because of the ongoing hostilities in which the balance of military advantage could, and did, swing dramatically and quickly from one side to the other.

Although it is obvious that neither superpower would allow the total collapse of its client state or states, the limits of tolerance below this level are not well defined. The extent to which each side is prepared to tolerate gains by the ally of the other superpower is something that not only differs from one Arab–Israeli war to the next, but may fluctuate during hostilities themselves. Both superpowers have been acutely aware of this problem, with the result that they have not only limited their own objectives in the area but have attempted to impose similar limitations on their allies. Nevertheless, so long as the lines are not clearly drawn, each side remains prepared to give help and encouragement to allied states. The potential for superpower misunderstanding or miscalculation in the Middle East is therefore considerable. Nor can the possibility be discounted that another confrontation in the area could involve far less of an asymmetry in perceived interests than other crises, with the result that there is bilateral rather than unilateral adoption of tough bargaining tactics. Fortunately, the superpowers hitherto have recognised not only the need to limit their demands and respect asymmetries of interest, but also the importance of refraining from the more dangerous bargaining techniques wherever possible. The difficulties and dangers of highly coercive bargaining moves have been elaborated above. In those cases where such moves have been adopted in spite of the dangers, it has almost invariably been in support of very limited objectives which the government regarded as vital to its security and wellbeing. On other occasions the superpowers have tended to adopt mild rather than strong forms of coercion.

VII Limitations on Means, or the Dilution of Coercion

The third way in which coercive bargaining has been moderated is through either the deliberate avoidance or the sparing use of the more dangerous techniques. The possibility of exploiting the 'autonomous' risks of crises by making 'threats that leave something to chance', for example, has not found overwhelming favour or quick acceptance. More often than not the manipulation or exploitation of risks has seemed less advantageous to policy-makers attempting to manage an international crisis than many analytical, and somewhat detached, discussions of bargaining would suggest. On the basis of the experience since 1945, it is arguable that the opportunities inherent in superpower crises often appear less compelling than the dangers. The desire to exploit autonomous risks is tempered and discouraged by the need to control them. Similar considerations do much to diminish the attraction of both rationality-of-irrationality tactics and escalatory moves. As has already been suggested, the major problem with the former technique is that it actually requires the government to place its fate in the hands of those whose sense of responsibility and sensitivity to risks is rather less than its own. Indeed, this is something that the superpowers have been preoccupied with avoiding. They regard their freedom of choice and action as a very precious possession and have striven hard to maintain it in the face of serious difficulties and pressures. So any bargaining tactic that demands that they deliberately relinquish it will almost certainly be rejected under all but the most desperate circumstances.

The same type of reluctance to take actions leading to diminished control over the situation militates against the adoption of escalation tactics. It has already been suggested that escalation of issues can obscure the basic structure of a crisis and thereby make it more difficult to manage. Escalation of means has a similarly debilitating effect on the ability of statesmen to end confrontations peacefully. As well as the possibilities of miscalculation, escalation could also diminish or destroy the policy-makers' control over events – particularly if it involved resort to violence.

Thus the considerations outlined in the previous chapter intrude forcefully into the bargaining process, perhaps dominating the calculations of decision-makers. When this is added to the dangers of miscalculating the opponent's risk-taking resolve, the need for caution becomes obvious. That the behaviour of both Moscow and Washington tends to be infused with such caution emerges clearly from another brief look at the Berlin Crisis of 1961, in which the Soviet Union followed what has most appropriately been described as a 'limited risk' policy.[65] In exerting pressure on the West, the Soviets scrupulously avoided the more dangerous forms of coercion. With the obvious exception of the Wall, which was basically a defensive measure, there was no attempt to make firm or irrevocable commitments either by particular deployments of military force or by any other means. Nor did the Soviet Union allow its prestige or status to become totally dependent on the outcome of the crisis, since this would have committed it to a more rigid stance than was desirable. Khrushchev highlighted the dangers and uncertainties of the situation in his public statements, but Soviet actions did not go beyond this in an attempt to exploit the autonomous risks of the crisis. Similarly, although Moscow intimated its intention to hand over the responsibility for Berlin to the Ulbricht regime, nothing was actually done to reduce Soviet control over the behaviour of its ally. The possibility of creating an image of irrationality to frighten the West into submission was rejected as too dangerous. Despite some rather alarming statements about the damage the Soviet Union could inflict on its enemies, and the deliberate and dramatic illumination of Soviet nuclear capabilities by a series of large test explosions, there was no serious attempt to use nuclear threats directly to evict the Western powers from Berlin.

Soviet intimidation tactics, therefore, were mainly in a lower key. Considerable emphasis was placed on the anomalous and anachronistic nature of the Berlin situation, and the consequent need for 'normalisation'. It was probably felt that concessions by the Western powers would more likely be forthcoming to the extent that they could be presented as part of a neat pre-packaged solution to a thorny and long-outstanding problem than as the result of unilateral yielding to pressure. In part this was an attempt to circumvent or loosen the US commitment to West Berlin by defining the situation in a way that not only pointed to the dangers of intransigence, but suggested that flexibility and accommodation by the NATO allies would contribute enormously to a genuine and lasting settlement. It was also an attempt to play up the differences between Western governments by appealing to those who took a moderate stance and were eager to explore avenues of negotiation with the Soviet Union. Thus Moscow's tactics were mild, and seem to have been designed to minimise the likelihood of a violent response by the United States.[66]

It would be misleading, however, to suggest that the prohibition against the stronger forms of coercion is an absolute one. If the situation demands it, the superpowers are prepared to make firm rather than weak commitments. At the same time it is important to remember that such commitments are almost invariably undertaken in support of the *status quo* or where they are regarded as the only way of salvaging a desperate situation. Furthermore, even the stronger forms of commitments made by the United States and the Soviet Union are less dangerous than the irrevocable commitment made by Hitler in 1939, leaving

President Hacha of Czechoslovakia with the last opportunity of avoiding large-scale war against Germany. It is hardly conceivable that either superpower would commit itself to a position where the choice for the other is limited to diplomatic surrender on the one hand or destruction on the other. Even firm superpower commitments are at least one step, and usually many steps, removed from this. They present the opponent not with the last clear chance of avoiding disaster but with the choice of either persisting in or desisting from a course of action likely to lead to a limited clash. The American blockade of Cuba did this. It succeeded because it put the onus for escalation and violence clearly and unequivocally on the Soviet Union, which had no way of circumventing Washington's commitment. A *fait accompli* has much the same effect, as the Soviets demonstrated with the division of Berlin.

So long as these commitments are utilised in support of very limited objectives, the likelihood of their being challenged is not too high. If the intensity of the opponent's interest has not been fully appreciated, however, the state responsible for the commitment may find itself in a far more dangerous confrontation than it either expected or intended. Thus it has been argued that 'commitments must be relatively weak or vague if risks are to be controlled'.[67] There is undoubtedly something to this, but care must be taken not to go to the opposite extreme. A commitment must not be so weak that it is overlooked or misconstrued as implying inaction. Vagueness should not result in ambiguity. Although there might be some merit in keeping the opponent guessing, particularly where the issue is not sufficiently important to evoke a strong reaction from oneself, if there is a serious commitment then the dangers of ambiguity almost certainly outweigh the advantages. A lack of precision about the potential costs that will be inflicted upon the opponent if it challenges the commitment may do little harm, but ambiguity about the commitment itself invites such challenges.

Only if commitments are clear and explicit will the adversary become fully aware of the serious implications of the action he is contemplating. In the Sarajevo Crisis, for example, Sir Edward Grey's diplomatic manoeuvres served only to blur Britain's commitments to the other members of the Triple Entente, and fortified Germany in the mistaken belief that

Britain would remain neutral, a mere onlooker if a European war broke out. The problem with blurred commitments is that they may obscure the basic structure of the crisis. The superpowers, on occasion, have overcome this problem with the adoption of what Snyder has termed 'communication moves'. Such moves differ from commitments in that they 'are not action choices' which reduce or eliminate the freedom of action of the government making them. 'Nor do they change the basic alternatives available to the parties.'[68] At the same time they provide the demonstrations of intent that are essential to clarify the position and interests of each side.

An example of 'communication moves' proving very effective for both superpowers occurred during the Yom Kippur War, with the Soviet Union *preparing* for direct military intervention and the United States adopting a widespread alert of nuclear and conventional forces. It was suggested in the previous chapter that the Soviet preparations for intervention were designed to render it unnecessary, thereby upholding the distinction between coercion and violence. It is now argued not only that Soviet actions respected this distinction, but that they were a *mild*, rather than strong, form of coercion. This has not always been fully acknowledged. Reactions to the Soviet activities and to the American alert of conventional and nuclear forces that followed have sometimes been less restrained than the actions themselves. Both sides have been accused of the most reckless and unnecessary forms of brinkmanship. For different reasons, American and Soviet behaviour has been the focus of considerable debate and controversy. The argument that the superpowers merely made 'communication moves', rather than anything more dangerous suggests a less alarmist interpretation.

Many commentators in the West regarded Moscow's willingness to supply the Arab states with a vast amount of armaments, followed by the proposed intervention, as proof of Moscow's hypocrisy about *détente*. It is held that, far from restraining their allies, the Soviet Union encouraged them to go to war in the first place and then urged them to exploit their early advantages. Only after Arab military setbacks did the Kremlin attempt to impose limits on the conflict. Thus, Soviet behaviour exposed *détente* as a myth: where it saw the opportunity for unilateral gains Moscow attempted to exploit it, regardless of the possible effect on the limited superpower moves for co-operation else-where. Furthermore, it is suggested that the 'intervention' episode demonstrated Soviet willingness to take high risks even when vital interests are not at stake.[69]

These arguments cannot be dismissed out of hand. Soviet behaviour prior to the war, and particularly during its early stages, left much to be desired from the perspective of super-power *détente*. Nevertheless, the wrong conclusions are often drawn about the intervention issue. In the first place, the Soviet Union did have important interests at stake: its position and prestige in the area depended upon it somehow saving the sur-rounded Egyptian Third Army from extinction. Secondly, Moscow's proposal favoured joint superpower intervention over unilateral action. Although there cannot be complete çertainty, it seems probable that Moscow was making a genuine offer and was rather taken aback by Washington's brusque rejection of this proposal, particularly in view of Dr. Kissinger's previous emphasis on the joint responsibility of the superpowers for impos-ing peace and stability on the Middle East. In addition, the Soviet leaders may have felt betrayed at the apparent lack of control exerted by the United States over Israel after acceptance of the UN cease-fire.

The alternative of possible unilateral intervention was probably forced on the Soviet Union, therefore, by the apparent, if only temporary, indifference of the United States to the Soviet pre-dicament. The seriousness of this position had somehow to be impressed upon American policy-makers. This was achieved successfully by the series of elaborate but essentially unambigu-ous 'signals' described in the previous chapter. Indeed, at one point an airlift of Soviet combat forces into Egypt seemed imminent. The skill of Soviet policy-makers, however, was in attaining their objectives without going beyond this preparatory stage. As Kissinger put it in his press conference of 25 October: 'as of now the Soviet Union has not yet taken any irrevocable action . . . . We are not asking the Soviet Union to pull back from anything that it has done.'[70] These comments were perhaps the best tribute to Moscow's dexterity in imparting its determin-ation not to see Egypt crushed while avoiding any actions that would put it in a dangerous and exposed position or bring about a confrontation with the United States that might have surpassed the Cuban Missile Crisis in its intensity.

The United States response caused perhaps even more anxiety, with many critics suggesting that it was merely a dangerous ploy by President Nixon to divert attention from the Watergate affair. Yet the alert of conventional and nuclear forces was in fact eminently appropriate to the circumstances. Although it can be criticised as being overly flamboyant or dramatic – and Kissinger himself admitted that the global nature of the alert was too extreme – it was not highly dangerous or destabilising. At the same time, it succeeded in displaying to Moscow the American unwillingness to remain inactive if Soviet forces intervened against Israel. In many ways it was a *mirror image* of the Soviet 'communication move'. The alert helped both to demonstrate American determination and to highlight the limits of its tolerance, without any serious escalation of the conflict or an undesirable commitment of US resources. As Kissinger again put it, 'The alert that has been ordered is of a precautionary nature . . . it is not in any sense irrevocable. It is what seemed to be indicated by the situation.'[71] By putting US forces in a state of greater readiness, the Nixon Administration amplified its warnings to the Soviet Union not to intervene. It made an American counter-intervention both more feasible and less necessary, and was far from the panic-stricken over-reaction that some critics suggested at the time.

The whole episode, therefore, can be seen as an exercise in communicating one's determination. As Coral Bell points out, the 'signals', particularly those of the United States, were excessively loud, but in this way brought home to the Russians that American resolve had not been undermined by Watergate and, even more importantly, helped to make the Israelis realise the dangers inherent in any further exploitation of their military successes. For Moscow too these 'communication moves' had the advantage of providing 'proof' to its Arab clients of its reliability as an ally and a demonstration of its unwillingness to sacrifice their interests on the altar of superpower *détente*. In other words, the 'signals' 'probably needed to be loud, in order to carry over certain background noises and to reach other ears than those the American and Russian policy-makers concerned'.[72]

In retrospect, perhaps the most significant feature of this short crisis was the adaptability, resourcefulness and imagination of the superpowers in finding actions of a largely symbolic nature that not only succeeded in giving greater effect to their words, but also fulfilled a variety of other necessary functions. An outcome that was satisfactory to both superpowers was obtained with neither government having to resort to stronger and more dangerous forms of coercion. When referring to the *détente* in his 25 October press conference, Kissinger claimed to have 'maintained the integrity of our allies and the security of the United States while reducing the danger of war' between the superpowers.[73] These words provide an appropriate comment on United States policy during the Yom Kippur War, especially as they could legitimately be echoed by the decision-makers of the Soviet Union.

The confrontation illustrates the utility of 'communication moves' as opposed to more drastic 'committal moves'. If either superpower had attempted to go further than it did, or to adopt stronger coercive measures, their tactics could have proved self-defeating as the likelihood of an over-reaction by the opponent would have been substantially increased. Indeed, 'communication moves' depend for their success not only on their coercive impact, but also on their ability to clarify and demonstrate the basic structure of the crisis. When this structure is not entirely clear, 'communication moves' are far safer than commitments. And so long as the adversary ultimately perceives that the state making the move genuinely has important interests at stake, then 'communication moves' are unlikely to be less effective than definitive, but perhaps more contrived, commitments. This reverts to the earlier point, that it is not so much the commitments that matter as the interests on which they are based. It has been argued very convincingly in fact, that:

> Traditional commitment theory has tended to focus on those factors affecting the credibility of commitments and signals that are more readily subject to manipulation. Insufficient attention has been given to the less easily manipulated factor of interests on which credibility depends.[74]

The virtue of 'communication moves' is that, by helping to clarify the structure of the crisis, they also help to reveal and accentuate these interests. They do this not only, and perhaps not even primarily, because they involve threats, but because they *com-*

municate concern: the adversary is made fully conscious of the extent of one's anxiety.

This is to suggest neither that 'communication' and 'committal' moves are mutually exclusive alternatives for policy-makers, nor that commitments play no role in communication, since they very obviously do. In their confrontations it has sometimes been necessary for the superpowers to adopt a variety of tactics, encompassing both types of move. This was so in the Cuban Crisis, for example, when the blockade not only acted as a commitment preventing the shipment of further Soviet missiles to the island, but also fulfilled the vital function of communicating to Khrushchev that Kennedy meant business. In this instance the establishment of a firm commitment made the later 'communication moves', such as Robert Kennedy's ultimatum to Ambassador Dobrynin and the visible preparation for an invasion, all the more effective since it had already established the government's determination and helped make clear that vital United States interests were at stake. Indeed, the crisis exemplifies the old adage that actions speak louder than words. If Kennedy had restricted himself solely to verbal communications, even using the most forceful language, it is unlikely that he would have conveyed adequately either the depth of the American interest or his determination to have Soviet missiles removed from Cuba. Washington's actions compensated for this deficiency.

Similarly, in the 1961 crisis, the decision to send General Clay to Berlin had highly symbolic overtones. As Willy Brandt put it at the time, 'the appointment makes unmistakeably clear the determination of the United States to defend the freedom of Berlin'.[75] This was almost certainly equally apparent to the Russians, although it did not immediately deter them from further low-level probes. Generally speaking, though, actions are rarely self-explanatory and on most occasions are particularly effective when combined with verbal explanations and justifications.

To emphasise that communications, through both deeds and words, lie at the heart of crises is to belabour the obvious, since the whole bargaining process is so clearly based upon communication between adversaries. Nevertheless, its function as an aid to the management and resolution of crises is sufficiently important to merit fuller discussion. In addition to the substitution of 'communication moves' for commitments, there are several other ways in which communication can be used to limit and moderate the bargaining process and facilitate the peaceful resolution of international crises.

VIII The Functions of Communication

The various ways in which communication tempers the dangers of coercive bargaining have been touched upon at several points in the analysis. All that remains, therefore, is to make them a little more explicit and to draw out their implications more fully. In the first place, communication can help to define the structure of a crisis so that both sides perceive accurately the relative values of the interests at stake. Secondly, and following on from this, communication helps to establish the 'rules' of the game in a confrontation, so that the adversaries share common assumptions about the kinds of actions that are legitimate and those that are tacitly, if not formally, prohibited. Making clear to the opponent, for example, that one is refraining from certain of the available options provides the basis for reciprocity. Indeed, it has been suggested above that what is not done in superpower confrontations may be as important as what is done; the avoidance of certain techniques as significant as the adoption of others. Thirdly, effective communication facilitates (as well as depends upon) an awareness of, and a sensitivity to, the opponents' position and problems, thereby making possible more accurate assessments of the implications of one's actions for the adversary. Fourthly, and this is largely dependent on the success with which these three prior tasks are carried out, communication may minimise the likelihood of miscalculation. Finally, it provides the means whereby proposals for agreement and accommodation are transmitted from one participant to the other until a satisfactory basis for a peaceful solution is found.

If these functions are to be fulfilled properly, there must be a minimum degree of trust between the parties and a mutual acknowledgement and acceptance that the communication process is not being exploited by the adversary to misinform or mislead. In the postwar period the common interests of the superpowers in using communications to help terminate their crises has ensured considerable respect for, and faith in, the process. Both realize that they have more to lose than to gain by interfering with it or exploiting it unduly. As Robert Jervis has pointed out, it is even possible for statesmen 'to reach an understanding that when a message is delivered in a given way it indicates their true intention and should be believed'.[76] He also argues that this carries with it serious dangers, since the very fact 'that a channel or method of delivering a signal might, at first glance, make it especially credible, is all the more reason to suspect it. For if the sending state wants to deceive it would use that very method.'[77]

While this analysis seems compelling, it should also be remembered that the particular channel or method of delivery is not the only important variable. Circumstances surrounding the communication also have to be considered. Much depends on the context within which these signals are sent and received. Prior to crises, and even in the preliminary stages before confrontation has been formally joined, secrecy and deception have been legitimate activities enabling one or other of the superpowers to obtain the advantages of surprise and perhaps even achieve a quick, decisive *fait accompli*. As soon as one or both sides have made their initial *open* moves, however, the legitimacy of lying and similar tactics declines enormously. Both superpowers know that they have so much to lose by undermining the integrity of the communications process that the temporary and transient advantages of deception are just not worth it. Each side is aware that if it resorts to these tactics during a crisis the opponent can do the same. The result is that neither really benefits, and the possibilities of misunderstanding and miscalculation are significantly increased. Recognition of this has encouraged them, in a certain sense, to set the communications process apart from their conflicts. Thus the first prerequisite of effective communication appears to have been met.

The attempt to use the various communication channels in a constructive manner still encounters serious difficulties. There are intractable problems involved in both the transmission and reception of information. 'Any communication must pass through an area of uncertainty between "speaker" and "listener" ',[78] an area that is particularly large in relations between states. The first problem with communication is that the 'signals' themselves may not be entirely clear. It is quite easy for a government to mislead itself in the belief that it is transmitting 'signals' that are both easily detectable and plainly obvious and straightforward in their meaning, whereas the 'signals' may actually be obscured or distorted by what has been described as background 'noise'.[79] Even if they are picked up, therefore, the messages may be a mere travesty of those originally intended. To some extent this may be inevitable, because governments are rarely monolithic actors in which the transmission of signals is totally under the control and direction of a single will. Thus a flow of different messages and 'signals', many of which are unintended, contradictory or inconsistent, may emanate from different parts of the government, creating confusion and uncertainty in the mind of the adversary. This is particularly likely if the major decision-makers are either vacillatory in their behaviour or divided on the policy they should pursue. Although the problem of inconsistent 'signals' may be less acute during crises than at other times, because of the high degree of central control exerted over the bureaucracy, it is most unlikely that it can be eliminated entirely.

If anything, the reception and interpretation of signals pose even more formidable problems, many of which are psychological in nature. The strength of pre-existing images or preconceived beliefs held by policy-makers about the adversary is crucial. 'Signals' that run counter to firm expectations about the opponent's future policy are discarded or discounted while those that accord with the expectations are seized upon eagerly as further validation of one's image. There may be a similar tendency to see only what one wants to see, with the result that, if 'signals' are at all contradictory, policy-makers pay attention to those that promise to make things less difficult, and assimilate only very slowly those that suggest the possible bankruptcy of current policies.

These psychological obstacles to clear perception are often compounded and reinforced by cultural blinkers. Policy-makers in each state often hold an image of the opponent that is completely at variance with the opponent's self-image. Indeed, each government tends to see its own state in a more favourable light than it is regarded by others. Furthermore, the past relationship between two nations encrusts and encumbers the perceptions of their statesmen, with the result that they often take time to adjust fully to any radical change in that relationship. The inability of foreign policy-makers to escape from these rigid ethnocentric perceptions and view a situation as it looks to the opponent often has debilitating effects on their policy towards the adversary.[80]

All these difficulties manifested themselves in the Sino–American relationship during the Korean War. Indeed, the war contains a highly illuminating example of how a breakdown or failure of communication can lead to the expansion of conflict. As one analyst has put it, 'Inadequate communication or the failure to convey accurately to an opponent one's intentions and one's probable responses played a pivotal role between August and October, 1950 in precipitating Communist Chinese engagement of UN forces.'[81] Thus, a brief examination of the circumstances and events that provoked the entry of Communist China into the Korean War provides considerable insight into both the causes and possible consequences of communication failures during international crises.

Chinese intervention was a direct consequence of the United States decision to attempt the military reunification of Korea under United Nations auspices. Peking tried to forestall such a move by signalling to Washington that it would not remain idle if North Korea was invaded, but after the Inchon Landing military success was allowed to generate its own momentum as the United States moved beyond containment to the 'liberation' of a Communist state. Why were the Chinese signals so lightly disregarded?

In the first place, the signals were probably neither sufficiently loud nor particularly clear. The lack of direct diplomatic contact between Peking and Washington hindered communication and meant that China had to rely primarily upon diplomatic intermediaries and public announcements. One such intermediary was the Indian ambassador in Peking, who apparently conveyed Chinese anxieties and threat of intervention to the United States. These were not taken very seriously, partly because the channel itself was suspect: the ambassador was regarded as pro-Chinese and therefore unreliable. Firm public statements and warnings by Chou En-Lai were also dismissed as crude attempts to influence United Nations deliberations, rather than given credence as serious evidence of Chinese intent.

This is not to say that there was no concern about Chinese intervention in Washington, for there obviously was. Indeed, the Truman Administration attempted to allay Peking's anxieties by emphasising that its activities were confined strictly to Korea and that it had no ambitions against China itself. These reassurances were designed to eliminate any prospect of China entering the war. Their clarity and impact however, fell far short of Washington's estimate. The effectiveness of the assurances was much diminished by General MacArthur's bellicose statements, which Peking probably regarded as a far more accurate reflection of American policy and hostility. The failure to take account of this possibility had a disastrous effect on the Truman Administration's attitude, causing a degree of complacency that was totally unwarranted. 'Since American declarations of goodwill were estimated as constituting sufficient assurance for China's Communist leaders, the latters' threats of intervention were considered as bluff.'[82]

Even if Chinese 'signals' had been clearer and the United States' assurances less ambiguous, communication would probably have remained ineffective. The gulf between the American decision-makers' own self-image and Peking's image of the United States was unbridgeable. Washington assumed that, because America had traditionally been a benevolent friend and protector of China, the new régime would automatically realise that the United States meant it no harm. Its failure to come to terms with the radical change in the nature of the Chinese government, and to understand the depth of Peking's antipathy towards, and fear of, the United States, is impressive. For Peking, the idea of an American-dominated Korea on its doorstep was intolerable. The new régime was still consolidating its domestic position, and wanted to minimise the possibility of outside interference, particularly from its most powerful and implacable ideological enemy. Consequently, the American advance to the Yalu was viewed with increasingly mounting alarm. Yet United States policy-makers although not totally insensitive to these concerns depreciated their importance. All Washington's calculations were based on outmoded perceptions of the Sino–American relationship and demonstrated the inability of the United States leadership to 'project itself' into the 'frame of reference' from which its adversary operated.[83]

Estimates of Chinese intentions, then, were based on a faulty premise – namely, the belief that the Chinese leaders were calculating their interests in much the same way as we did. Since Truman and Acheson had evidently convinced themselves that legitimate Chinese national interests were not importantly threatened or affected by the US occupation of North Korea or by plans for unifying it with South Korea, they believed that Chinese leaders also saw it in this way or could be persuaded to do so.[84]

While America 'downgraded the seriousness of Chinese concern', Peking in its turn exaggerated the threat presented by the American drive into North Korea.[85] The utter futility of Truman's verbal assurances as a means of closing the gap between the American self-image and Peking's perceptions, therefore, need hardly be emphasised.

The weaknesses of each side's signals, combined with rigid, inflexible images and strong expectations about the others' behaviour, had disastrous implications. The failure of communication could not have been more complete. Thus its potential utility as a means of moderating or even avoiding a military confrontation between the United States and China was wasted. The United States advanced into North Korea with an unjustified equanimity, oblivious as to how this transformed the whole nature and structure of the Korean conflict for Peking, unaware that the drive to the Yalu may even have appeared as the preliminary to an invasion of the Chinese homeland itself. While hostilities were confined to South Korea, the Chinese People's Republic could afford an alert, but essentially passive, stance. To expect it to exercise similar restraint as the war extended into the North and moved towards its borders, however, was wholly unrealistic. So long as Washington confined itself to restoring the *status quo* in Korea, the balance of interests vis-à-vis the Chinese worked for it and militated against intervention by Peking. As a result of its attempt to change the *status quo*, this balance swung the other way: the asymmetry of interests moved in Peking's favour, greatly increasing China's resolve and willingness to take risks. Without knowing it, the demands that the United States was making on the Chinese People's Republic were excessive. The fundamental lack of understanding about the structure of the conflict was exacerbated by the inability of the two sides to establish mutually acceptable ground rules of behaviour, indicating what actions were permissible and what were intolerable. Once again this was a deficiency that might have been rectified by more successful communication.

The breakdown in communication, which itself stemmed in large part from each side's total lack of empathy with the other, ensured that nothing was done to remedy the misapprehensions and misunderstandings that they laboured under. The American government failed miserably to assess either the implications of its actions for the opponent or the response they would elicit. When the Chinese did intervene, therefore, the United Nations forces were caught off guard and suffered an enormous military setback. In short, the United States miscalculation was one of alarming proportions.

Was this miscalculation avoidable? There is no easy or definite answer to this question. The episode has many of the qualities of a Greek tragedy playing towards its inexorable climax. Yet there is also the problem of motivation or will to be considered. Although the Truman Administration obviously did not want a war with China, the almost casual way in which the decision was taken to advance beyond the 38th parallel suggests that US policy-makers were not as concerned about the possible effects on China as they might have been. Had they held a less contemptuous view of Chinese capabilities, far more attention would have been given to Chinese intentions. It was possible to ignore Peking's interests and motivation so systematically only because it was felt that, even if the Chinese did intervene, they would make little impression against the modern well-equipped army under MacArthur's command. The implicit assumption of American military superiority may have been the ultimate basis for many of the mistakes that were made. Certainly a greater respect for Chinese military strength would have given Washington reason to pause, and would have endowed its efforts to assess possible Chinese reactions with a greater sense of urgency.

The fear of disaster that infused United States behaviour during confrontations with the Soviet Union, or indeed later crises with Communist China, was absent in 1950. Had it been present, more deliberate and sustained attempts would have been made to understand Peking's signals and respect Chinese susceptibilities. This is not to imply that such efforts would necessarily have been successful: the obstacles to correct evaluation were considerable, the existing images perhaps impervious to change. Nevertheless, some of the 'misperceptions, miscalculations and inept actions' that brought about a military confrontation 'which neither side wanted' might have been rectified had the desire to avoid hostilities been greater.[86] The United States would certainly have been more thorough in assessing the implications of its actions for the opponent. Indeed, as well as illustrating what may happen when communication breaks down, the episode brings home most dramatically the importance of trying to project oneself into the adversary's 'frame of reference'.

The lesson was not ignored during later confrontations. Although it appears that the Cuban Missile Crisis may have had its genesis in Soviet miscalculations of Kennedy's resolve, further mistakes and miscalculations were avoided during the crisis itself. At every stage of the confrontation each side scrupulously tried to assess the likely impact of its actions on the opponent. It has even been claimed that 'during the crisis President Kennedy spent more time trying to determine the effect of a particular course of action on Khrushchev or the Russians than on any other phase of what he was doing'.[87] Careful attention was devoted to all Soviet communications and an active attempt made to view the situation from Khrushchev's perspective. The knowledge and experience of Ambassador Llewellyn Thompson proved invaluable in this task. It was his emphasis on the Russian respect for 'legality' that prompted the search for a legal basis to justify American actions, a search that came to fruition when the Organization of American States formally approved Washington's position.[88] Similarly, as discussed above, it was Thompson's assessment of how Khrushchev might react to violence that helped determine the choice of the blockade.

This kind of sensitivity to the adversary's position was a great asset. If the Korean War had demonstrated the total inability of United States policy-makers to place themselves in another country's shoes, the Cuban Missile Crisis did the opposite. Its peaceful resolution was in large measure a tribute to the skill and imagination with which the task was accomplished. Soviet policy-makers were probably as adept as their American counterparts and fairly quickly realised the depth of US concern and the seriousness of US intentions. The capacity of each superpower to achieve a high degree of empathy with the adversary was, in retrospect, one of the outstanding features of the confrontation. Successful communication was both a cause and a consequence of this.

Indeed, communication between the protagonists helped to reduce ambiguities and to clarify the basic structure of the crisis, thereby averting further misunderstandings. It also facilitated a mutual awareness of what actions were 'forbidden' and what would be tolerated, as well as indicating the extent to which each side could make 'legitimate' demands on the other. Moreover, it was only through an extended series of communications that agreement was finally reached on the basis for a Soviet withdrawal of the missiles. This is not to suggest that there were no difficulties in the communication process. There were many; but they were not insurmountable and were overcome by sheer perseverance.

All the 'basic channels of communication' between the super-powers were used during the Missile Crisis in an attempt to reach terms that were satisfactory to both parties.[89] Probably most important were unofficial channels, which can sometimes appear very attractive in crises, and the personal exchanges between the heads of government, whether broadcast or by private letter. Indeed, 'trusted emissaries' can provide a valuable if 'extra-diplomatic channel' of communication, and this certainly proved to be the case in 1962.[90] It was an approach by Alexander Fomin – known to be a senior Soviet intelligence officer in the United States 'with his own direct channels of communication to the Kremlin' – to John Scali, diplomatic correspondent of the American Broadcasting Company, that broke the deadlock and first 'suggested a formula for negotiations'.[91] The final agreement was based on the Fomin-Scali conversations and a letter from Khrushchev received by Kennedy on the night of Friday, 26 October. The formal compromise was a Soviet withdrawal of the missiles under United Nations supervision in return for an immediate lifting of the blockade and a pledge by the United States not to invade Cuba. In addition, there was the private assurance about the removal of American missiles from Turkey, given by Robert Kennedy to Ambassador Dobrynin. This went a long way towards meeting the Soviet proposal of Saturday, 27 October, for an exchange between the Turkish and Cuban missiles, while avoiding any appearance of acting under duress. The manner in which this compromise was patched together llustrates how useful the diversity of communication channels :an be.

In fact, normal channels probably proved inadequate to cope with the urgent diplomatic communications during the Cuban :onfrontation and, although estimates of the speed of messages /ary considerably, because of problems of 'decoding and trans- ation' there were almost certainly some delays. The public com- nunications were probably the fastest, but these had the draw- >ack of reducing the leeway for manoeuvre allowed by secret liplomacy. It was not for nothing, therefore, that the hot line :ommunications link was installed between Moscow and Washington in the aftermath of the crisis.[92] The excellent use nade of this during the 1967 Arab–Israeli War has already been liscussed.

To suggest, however, that the hot line has completely super- eded the various other modes of communication would be a nistake. A multiplicity of communication channels can be a vital asset when attempting to resolve international crises, par- icularly in view of the several functions fulfilled by communica- ion. The final agreement that marked the end of the Cuban Crisis is perhaps untypical, in that other crises have just faded away or been terminated more informally. Even when it has not ed to formal agreement, however, communication has played a vital role in superpower confrontations. So too have the other echniques elaborated in the present chapter. Indeed, they have acilitated 'the use of coercive power while avoiding excessive :osts and risks'.[93]

But what conclusions can be drawn from past experience in he use of these techniques? On what basis have the 'conven- ions' or 'rules' of crisis management been founded? Have the uperpowers become increasingly adept in the art of crisis nanagement as their relationship has developed and matured? Are the Soviet Union and the United States nevertheless moving owards the replacement of crisis management by a system of :risis prevention? It is with such questions that the final chapter nust now deal.

CHAPTER EIGHT

Crisis Management: Past and Future

I Crisis Management and Limited War

A major purpose of the present work has been to highlight the central importance of crisis management as a way of controlling and resolving conflicts between the great nuclear powers. Crisis management may have been an academic 'Cinderella' until the 1960s, but it caught and held the attention of 'The Prince' in both Moscow and Washington from the early days of the Cold War. Successive governments in the United States and the Soviet Union have had to learn to cope with tense and dangerous super-power confrontations. Their accomplishments have been impressive and they have demonstrated skill and imagination in devising strategies that enable them simultaneously to continue and to contain their confrontations. Although the risks and problems involved have been real and substantial, the superpowers have succeeded in introducing an element of ritual that has helped make crises more manageable and controllable. As one analyst has written:

> . . . crises perform a surrogate function in the nuclear age – they take the place of war in the resolution of conflict, between great powers at least, when war has become too costly and risky. This notion casts crises in a role somewhat similar to the eighteenth century quadrilles of marching and manoeuvre which produced settlements from superiority of position rather than brute superiority in violence.[1]

Indeed, it is little exaggeration to suggest that crisis management has had far more direct relevance to the evolving Soviet-American relationship than has the much more vaunted concept of limited war.

It has often been argued that hostilities between the super-powers could be controlled and limited, but, as pointed out in chapter four, neither Washington nor Moscow has shown any inclination to put these ideas to the test. Furthermore, as the preceding analysis has demonstrated, the superpowers have scrupulously avoided even very limited clashes between their conventional forces. Nevertheless, it is illuminating to compare some of the features of crisis management as it has been practised throughout the postwar years with the theory of limited war developed by strategic analysts during the 1950s. Although the concept of limited war is free neither of the perspective problems identified in chapter two, nor of controversy about the relative importance or precise forms of particular limitations, it is possible to discern the broad outlines of a consensus on its major features. There is general agreement that restraint on both the objectives *for* which the war is fought and the means *with* which it is fought is crucial. Together with geographical restrictions on hostilities, these restraints provide the essential foundations for limited war. Each of these limitations finds a very close parallel in the management of superpower crises.

The first major prerequisite of limited war is that the com-batants have clearly defined and carefully circumscribed political objectives. Limited war is Clausewitzian war *par excellence* in which political direction and control pervade hostilities. It is a war fought for a definite political purpose in which the aim is not to achieve total victory or the unconditional surrender of the enemy, but merely to influence his behaviour in desired direc-tions. It is an attempt to 'affect the opponent's will not to crush it, to make the conditions to be imposed seem more attractive than continued resistance, to strive for specific goals and not for complete annihilation'.[2] Much the same is true of crisis management that sets out either to make the adversary desist from a particular course of action or to persuade him to acquiesce in one's own actions and policies. It may be possible to extract carefully specified concessions, but unless one's demands are sufficiently limited the adversary is likely to prove obdurate. If the demands are extortionate, then escalation becomes a less unattractive option for the opponent: the potential costs and risks involved in increasing the intensity of the crisis may be outweighed by the costs of giving in. In other words, both crisis management and limited war rest upon a fundamental respect for the adversary's vital interests.

It is possible to go even further than this in relation to crisis management and suggest that similar respect has to be accorded to states closely allied to Moscow or Washington. Indeed, this is one reason why superpower involvement in regional conflicts such as the Middle East is not as damaging as is often feared. Although material support from the superpowers ensures that a war between their clients is fought at a far higher level of technological sophistication than would otherwise be possible, this is offset by the restraints and restrictions that normally accompany such support. Most important, the clear and unequivocal involvement of both superpowers prohibits any serious attempt by their clients to eliminate one another. Consequently, even if there is no formal acceptance of the enemy's legitimacy, his basic integrity and right to exist is not challenged in practice. Any attempt to launch such a challenge would almost certainly provoke the direct intervention of that state's superpower guardian. Whether the other superpower could passively accept this and refrain from a counter-intervention is a moot point. What is certain, however, is that the two superpowers have been intent on avoiding a situation where they have to face this kind of dilemma. Thus, paradoxically, the price the clients must pay for the wherewithal to continue their struggle is a willingness to moderate its intensity. The involvement of the superpowers, therefore, may be beneficial rather than detrimental to the attainment of a greater degree of order and stability in such areas.

In most theoretical analyses of limited war, restraint on objectives is very closely linked to the limitation of means. It is generally accepted that if hostilities are to be kept under control, restrictions have to be imposed on the means used as well as the purposes for which the war is fought. The exact form that such restrictions must take, however, commands far less agreement. At the one extreme is the argument that if war is to be kept limited the use of nuclear weapons has to be wholly excluded. At the other extreme is the idea of limited strategic war involving the homelands of the superpowers, in which targeting is selective and discriminate and confined solely to military installations. Throughout the nuclear exchanges, the continued operation of intra-war deterrence ensures that deliberate efforts are made to avoid the destruction of large population centres.

The gap between these two positions is considerable. Unfortunately it is not possible in the present context to explore every subtlety and nuance of the contrasting ideas. Nevertheless, it is fairly obvious that much of the debate revolves around the importance of the nuclear threshold. To those who emphasise the complete non-use of nuclear weapons, this particular 'firebreak' is sacred and inviolate. They believe that by crossing it the belligerents would profoundly transform the nature of hostilities: escalation would become both massive and automatic, and further attempts at restraint would inevitably prove futile. Their faith in this threshold stems largely from its visibility, from the fact that it is based upon qualitative as opposed to quantitative criteria. The argument is that distinctions based upon differences of kind have greater clarity and effectiveness than those based upon differences of degree. They are obvious stopping places, beyond which the upward spiral of hostilities may be more difficult to control or reverse. Schelling has put the point very well in his observation that any stable limit must 'have an evident symbolic character, such that to breach it is an overt and dramatic act that exposes both sides to the danger that alternative limits will not easily be found'.[3] The experience of superpower crises, in a sense, adds weight to this thesis. There can be little doubt that the qualitative distinction or the salient threshold between different types of activity greatly facilitates the control and management of superpower confrontations. It is relatively easy to agree upon. Furthermore, because transgressions are so obvious, they invite instant retaliation. The coercion–violence threshold certainly has this kind of quality and, as was shown above, provides one of the most important bases for contemporary crisis management.

At the same time it would be foolish to suggest that regulation and control must inevitably be founded on prominent distinctions of this type. The limitation of means does not invariably require bilateral acceptance and observance of salient thresholds. Indeed, one of the most striking features of superpower crises has been the part played by restraints that do not involve mutual and total abstinence from particular modes of behaviour. Some bargaining techniques have been set on one side as inherently volatile: they are far too dangerous to be exploited. Other techniques, however, have merely been used cautiously. There are, in fact, several bargaining tactics that depend for their success on sparing and sometimes unilateral use. They may be rejected under some conditions and for some purposes only to be regarded as permissible in other circumstances and in support of other objectives. The stronger forms of commitment, for example, have been utilised to uphold the *status quo* but not in attempts to change it. Similarly, the superpower with least at stake has generally been less willing than its adversary to use escalation as a bargaining ploy.

In other words, there are certain limits that do not depend upon the existence of simple and obvious distinctions. They are not fixed and unalterable from one crisis to another, but vary according to the basic structure of each confrontation. They may even be asymmetrical in particular instances. Although such limitations are less salient than the other kind, the superpowers have been no less adept at acknowledging, highlighting and exploiting them in a way designed to facilitate a peaceful resolution of their crises. The importance of these limitations should not be denigrated as they have played a crucial part in controlling the bargaining process. The desire to avoid violence has set the outer limits for crisis bargaining, but there are also inner limits which are no less significant merely because they are less immediately and obviously recognisable. Not content with a fairly rigorous and reciprocal observance of the coercion–violence threshold, the superpowers have systematically diluted and moderated the coercive bargaining process in order to render it more malleable and controllable. Although they have not refrained totally from playing brinkmanship, for example, they have tried not to go too near the brink. One commentator on the Taiwan Straits Crisis of 1958 summed up the point neatly when he wrote: 'If this was brinkmanship, it was brinkmanship with kid gloves.'[4] Thus the limitations on the means used by the protagonists in great power crises involve a mixture of prohibition and inhibition.

The third type of limitation often regarded as important in limited war is geographical: many analysts suggest that if escalation is to be avoided hostilities must be confined within a carefully delimited geographical area. Once again this finds a close parallel in the practice of crisis management. It has been recognised by Moscow and Washington that, if the point of conflict is clearly focused and well-defined, confrontations are much easier to limit and control. Consequently, superpower crises in the nuclear era have arisen over specific issues and been strictly limited to one geographical area. They have also been relatively straightforward confrontations in which mutual agreement on the issue in dispute has readily been reached. In each of the crises analysed above, great care was taken by the superpowers to keep the focus of attention on the specific matter at issue – Soviet missiles in Cuba, the status of West Berlin, the offshore islands of Quemoy and Matsu, or the extent of permissible Israeli gains in the Middle East – thereby tacitly acknowledging both the importance of and the need for what Roger Fisher has called 'issue-control'. The exertion of pressure in areas unrelated to the main point of confrontation remained unused, a redundant option that neither government was willing to employ. To have adopted such an option in any of the conflicts discussed would probably have succeeded only in transforming the situation from a *single crisis* over one issue to a *compound crisis* involving several issues and areas. The task of crisis management would have been made inordinately difficult as a result.

The similarities between the theories of limited war that were developed during the 'golden age' of strategic analysis in the late 1950s and early 1960s, and the practice of crisis management as it has evolved throughout the postwar period, are very marked. Because there have been no limited wars directly involving both superpowers, however, debates about the course such wars might take or about their possible outcomes tend to be shrouded in speculation. It could hardly be otherwise. Yet it is not inconceivable that empirical analyses of crisis management can be of assistance by instilling a greater degree of realism into discussions that have sometimes been as impractical as they have been imaginative. Since there is no experience of superpower war, the analysis of situations in which the United States and the Soviet Union have been on, or near, the verge of violent conflict may be highly illuminating. Indeed, there are a number of indications in the present study that, if the superpowers became engaged in open hostilities, limitations would be difficult to impose. To begin with, the very existence of violent interactions would imply scant respect for a threshold hitherto regarded with considerable awe. Furthermore, once they are in the realm of violence, the superpowers might prove unable to resist its pressures and demands: as each side committed more and more of its resources to the struggle, it would probably become increasingly difficult for it to prevent a concomitant expansion of the objectives for which the war was being fought. Gains commensurate with the sacrifices incurred might be necessary. Thus, even if the war remained limited geographically, it would perhaps be transformed from a dispute over specific and narrowly defined issues to a much more far-reaching conflict involving each side's prestige and power.

This would be even more likely if nuclear weapons were introduced into hostilities, especially if they were used on a large scale or against the homelands of the superpowers. Yet the American strategic posture enunciated in the first half of the 1970s by President Nixon and Secretary of Defense James Schlesinger explicitly included options for limited nuclear strikes against missiles and other military installations within the Soviet Union. Its purpose was to provide the United States with maximum flexibility in a nuclear war situation. Sufficient options were required to give an American president choices other than surrender or massive escalation in response to a limited nuclear attack by the Soviet Union.

In terms purely of strategic logic, the rationale of the 'Schlesinger doctrine', as it is called, may be unassailable. Nevertheless, it is difficult to be sanguine about the ability of the superpowers to fight a nuclear war in a controlled and regulated manner. Limited strategic exchanges presume cool, sober, detached policy-makers able to make fine discriminating calculations about the level of damage being incurred and inflicted. The experience of crisis management, however, suggests that this presumption may be totally unwarranted. In a conflict of this kind, stress would be far more intense than in any previous confrontation, and decision-makers less impervious to its effects. Moreover, despite target restrictions, some collateral damage would probably be unavoidable, accidental strikes against densely populated areas inevitable. Consequently, the possibility of statesmen making rash judgements, emotional decisions or unwise choices can not be lightly dismissed – especially as they would almost certainly be harassed and pressured by an emotional public, aroused as never before. Another difficulty with nuclear hostilities is that they would inevitably involve considerations of pride and prestige. It would hardly be surprising if each participant felt that the adversary was attempting to humiliate it. Thus to make the first move in sueing for peace would be seen as an abject surrender; and the incentives for containing and perhaps escalating the war could therefore appear irresistible. In these circumstances the war would fit very neatly into what Morton Deutsch has categorised as 'destructive conflict', that is a conflict which expands or escalates to such an extent that it becomes 'independent of its initiating causes and is likely to continue after these have become irrelevant or have been forgotten'.[5]

It may be, of course, that this prognosis for limited nuclear war is far too pessimistic. But it is indisputable that such a war would be totally alien to the precepts, practices and precautions that have hitherto prevailed in superpower confrontations. One of the main reasons for pessimism is that limited strategic war is outside the realms of practical experience and might well demand conventions or procedures very different from those to which the superpowers are accustomed. Indeed, the existence of certain rules or norms of behaviour has been an important factor in the success of crisis management. Consequently, it is necessary briefly to examine their origins and status.

II The Rules and Conventions of Crisis Management

In chapters six and seven, considerable attention was given to the tacit codes of conduct or rules of behaviour that have helped to guide Moscow and Washington through the perils of superpower confrontations. These norms or principles appear to have arisen through a strange mixture of accident and design. At the *outset* of the Berlin Confrontation in 1948, for example, there may have been little concern with 'concerted crisis management' aimed at establishing mutually acceptable limits of behaviour; but there was 'parallel crisis behaviour' which in the event led to crisis control through the establishment of such limits.[6] The initial avoidance of violence by both sides was perhaps no more than coincidental restraint. Yet the impact was cumulative, with the result that it became increasingly difficult to depart from the norm. If the superpowers hit upon the threshold between coercion and violence almost fortuitously, they were not slow in appreciating its significance. Indeed, they continued to observe it during the Berlin Crisis in a way that suggests a *mutual* recognition and acceptance of its utility in providing a ceiling to the conflict Not only did each government avoid crossing the threshold; it also attempted to avoid actions that could provoke the adversary into doing so. Furthermore, by creating a precedent of this type the superpowers helped to establish a convention of crisis behaviour that has been observed ever since. Although the increasing skill of policy-makers that comes with experience in handling crises should not be disregarded, even more important is the fact that the very recurrence of conflicts that are similar in nature provides an opportunity for them to be institutionalised and regulated. Precedents and traditions help to create expectations about the limits of permissible behaviour and, concomitantly, help define what is intolerable or destabilising. In addition to this, however, there are certain rules or conventions of crisis management that are little more than an elaboration of some of the basic canons of statesmanship. Leaving an adversary a way of retreating without humiliation, or framing one's aspiration and objectives to accommodate the vital interests of others, are central features of skilful diplomacy; in crisis management they are merely writ large and observed with greater diligence. This is not to suggest that they are unimportant, however.

Indeed, one of the most remarkable features of superpower crises is the extent to which the proprieties, conventions and norms have been adhered to almost without deviation. Whatever their source – luck, precedent or traditional diplomacy – the 'rules' of crisis management have been accorded great respect. There are several reasons for this. Perhaps the most fundamental is that it has very obviously been in the interests of the superpowers to establish and maintain mutually acceptable guidelines for behaviour. Both the United States and the Soviet Union have perceived a clear need for regulatory devices and procedures that help them not only to keep control over the situation, but also to moderate or avoid the worst excesses of coercive bargaining. The second reason why the rules have been observed is that they have been equitable and have offered neither superpower permanent advantage or a permanent disability. Against this, of course, it may be argued that the balance of interests has proved beneficial to one side rather than the other in a particular confrontation. There is, indeed, a general 'rule' that the protagonist with most at stake can expect to emerge from the crisis slightly better off than its opponent. But this reinforces rather than undermines the point being made here. The benefits that accrue to this state are not a function of the rule *per se*, but of the structure of the crisis. As the structure varies from one situation to the next the balance of advantage and disadvantage changes accordingly. Neither superpower could reasonably expect the structure to be invariably in its favour or consistently against it. Thus the rule itself is not biased unfairly against either side, and what may be lost by following its injunctions in one crisis may be compensated for by the benefits it bestows in others. There is a crude but effective kind of logic at work here: it is a case of what is lost on the roundabouts being gained on the swings, and vice versa. Each side accepts the rule, even if this is slightly damaging in a specific instance, because it knows that in the future it may work the opposite way, with beneficial results.

A third reason why the tacit ground rules have proved so successful is that they rest upon the operation of a rudimentary system of deterrence: if either superpower violates them the opponent can retaliate by doing the same. Transgression invites transgression. For one side to disregard the conventions is, conceivably, the best possible justification for the opponent to do the same. The probable result would be that both participants would find themselves in a more dangerous position, with neither having made any significant gains.

In other words, the success of the rules or conventions of crisis management has depended on the exercise of prudent self-restraint by the two superpowers. It has also involved a large element of luck. On a few occasions, even the most salient rule, non-violence, has been jeopardised. During the Cuban Missile Crisis, for example, American ships harassed Soviet submarines and forced them to the surface. Although there is no evidence that this spilled over into actual violence, an encounter of this kind is not very far removed from an armed clash and could easily result in one. This highlights both the importance and the weakness of the rules. The pressures and potential for their complete disregard are considerable. They could be abolished, ignored or overridden any time that policy-makers believe this to be more expedient than continued observance. If disregarding the conventions appears to be necessary, then disregarded they will be. An additional problem is accidental violation. Decision-makers in one or other of the capitals could lose control over the implementation of policy. The transgressions that might follow could well provoke retaliatory violations from the adversary who fails to realise that they are unauthorised actions. Thus the effect would be the same as if the rules had been deliberately discarded. In short, they are far from infallible. The fundamental problem is that the only rules likely to have any validity or effectiveness in crises are those based on common consent. By the same token, if that consent is withdrawn the rules are rendered wholly devoid of meaning.

These cautionary comments are not intended to depreciate the importance of these informal rules and conventions. They have, after all, proved highly effective and have been observed with equal diligence by both superpowers. Despite the disturbing asymmetry of evidence, therefore, it seems reasonable to conclude that the crisis behaviour of the United States and that of the Soviet Union differs very little in essentials. The actions of both Washington and Moscow appear to be based on similar premises. Arguments that the Soviet Union will always back down when faced with a firm unyielding stance by the United States are as ill-advised as those that picture the Soviet Union as a reckless state willing to take inordinate risks to achieve its ideologically determined objectives. Although the Soviet Union has occasionally demonstrated a willingness to risk confrontation, its actual crisis behaviour has been marked above all by caution and restraint. It appears, in fact, that the risk-taking propensities of the superpowers during crises are determined primarily by the circumstances: they are a function of the situation rather than inherent properties of the actors themselves.

Equally illuminating is that the rules and conventions developed at a time when the Cold War was intense and super-power interactions were apparently based on unremitting hostility. In retrospect the Berlin Crisis of 1948 is significant not so much because it was the first open and direct superpower confrontation, but because of the skilful way it was managed and controlled. The crisis that led to Chinese entry into the Korean War, on the other hand, was handled much more diffidently. Nevertheless, it proved a traumatic experience, the lessons of which were invaluable in later confrontations such as that over Taiwan in 1958. J. H. Kalicki has argued very convincingly that the pattern of Sino–American crises in the 1950s was one of growing constructiveness even though the overall relationship between the two states remained extremely strained.[8] Much the same is true of Soviet and American crisis behaviour. Far from being sterile, their exchanges during crises helped to highlight areas of activity in which the superpowers had substantial common interests. They also emphasised the dangers of a relationship in which the periodic occurrence of intense confrontations was accepted as inevitable. The Cuban Missile Crisis had a particularly marked effect in this direction. The subsequent efforts to expand, diversify and formalise the rudimentary and tacit co-operation that had facilitated the resolution of superpower crises were central to the subsequent relaxation of tension. But what are the implications of *détente* for crisis management in the future? Has crisis management become redundant or unnecessary? Are the modes of behaviour that have been analysed in the preceding chapters increasingly outmoded and irrelevant?

III Crisis Management in the Future

The answers to such questions depend in large part upon the way superpower *détente* is interpreted and understood. On the one hand, *détente* can be regarded as a pronounced departure from the tensions and conflicts of the Cold War years, as an attempt to establish and sustain a much more amicable basis for superpower interactions. Some of the phrases used by the Nixon Administration in the public presentation of its foreign policy suggested that this was in fact the case: it was claimed, for example, that the 'era of confrontation' had been superseded by an 'era of negotiation'. Implicit in such arguments is the assumption that the superpowers may eventually progress from *détente* to *entente*, that *peaceful co-existence*, with its emphasis primarily on the avoidance of nuclear war, will be replaced by *constructive co-existence*, involving much more positive and far-reaching co-operation and the establishment of a long-term relationship that is not only peaceful but stable and harmonious.[9] In other words, the superpowers may go beyond the fear of collision, to recognise the potential benefits of collusion.

On the other hand, *détente* may be interpreted as merely a continuation of the Cold War by other means. Those commentators who are either sceptical or realistic (depending upon one's point of view) treat *détente* as little more than an attempt by the Soviet Union to lull the West into a false sense of security. It is argued that Soviet moves towards accommodation are based on temporary expediency rather than any fundamental change in Soviet goals or ambitions. And rather than being the precursor to a more constructive relationship, peaceful co-existence implies no more than the avoidance of war. In fact, it presumes an intensification of the competition for power and influence so long as such a course appears unlikely either to lead to military hostilities with the United States or to galvanise the West into concerted opposition to Soviet advances.[10]

Neither of these competing interpretations is wholly implausible. It is argued here, however, that, although the transformation that has occurred under the rubric of *détente* is less profound than suggested by the first interpretation, it is more significant than suggested by the second. Perhaps the essence of *détente* has been the attempt by the United States and the Soviet Union to move from a relationship based on mutual enmity and intermittent crisis management to one based more explicitly – if still only incompletely – on confrontation avoidance or crisis prevention considerations.

This can be illustrated, albeit briefly, by comparing the crises over the Middle East in 1967 and 1973 with earlier superpower confrontations. There are considerable differences, perhaps the most important of which is that the Middle East crises were not brought about by the deliberate policies of the superpowers but were virtually thrust upon them by the actions of their allies. Henry Kissinger put the point very well in his press conference called to explain the alert of American forces during the Yom Kippur War when he stated: 'we are not talking of a missile crisis type situation'.[11] As in 1967 the moves and communications of both sides were precautionary and designed to ensure that the military balance in the Middle East was not disrupted or overturned, a prospect that, had it materialised, would have dragged the superpowers into what could quite easily have been the most difficult and dangerous confrontation of the whole postwar period. Thus the brief crises that did occur on both occasions were intended in large part to avert something far more serious, and the superpowers appear to have been influenced by crisis prevention as well as crisis management considerations.

Perhaps an even better example of crisis prevention, however, is the episode of May 1972 in which President Nixon ordered the mining of Haiphong Harbour, apparently in an attempt to cut off Soviet arms supplies to North Vietnam. Many commentators saw this as a frontal challenge to the Soviet Union and predicted a major confrontation. Yet the Soviet response was almost unprecedented in its mildness. Apart from issuing verbal condemnations it did nothing. This can probably be understood only in relation to Kissinger's visit to Moscow prior to the American decision. It is not inconceivable that during this visit the Secretary of State explained privately to the Soviet leaders that Washington felt compelled to react 'strongly' to the renewed North Vietnamese offensive against the South – if only as a face-saving device. It is equally plausible that he received the green light for an alternative such as the mining, which was almost purely demonstrative, and which helped America's sagging prestige while doing little to alter the course of the war.[12] Although there is little direct evidence to support this interpretation it certainly helps to explain why President Nixon was able to make his historic journey to Moscow within two weeks of his announcement of the mining of Haiphong.

The agreement that was reached during the President's visit and enshrined in a joint Soviet-American declaration on 'The Basic Principles of Relations' also laid considerable emphasis on confrontation avoidance. It explicitly stated that:

> The U.S.A. and the U.S.S.R. attach major importance to preventing the development of situations capable of causing a dangerous exacerbation of their relations. Therefore, they will do their utmost to avoid military confrontations and to prevent the outbreak of nuclear war. They will always exercise restraint in their mutual relations, and will be prepared to negotiate and settle differences by peaceful means. Discussions and negotiations on outstanding issues will be conducted in a spirit of reciprocity, mutual accommodation, and mutual benefit.[13]

In addition, the superpowers acknowledged that attempts by either one 'to obtain *unilateral advantage* at the expense of the other, directly or indirectly, are inconsistent with these objectives'.[14]

The extent to which such principles will affect superpower behaviour in the future is difficult to assess. The declaration of May 1972, together with the Agreement on Reducing the Risk of Nuclear War concluded in September 1971 and the Agreement on the Prevention of Nuclear War of June 1973, certainly suggest that the desire of the superpowers to avoid any reversion to the kind of confrontations that characterised the Cold War is a significant factor in their calculations. Nor is it inconceivable that the superpowers will succeed in avoiding situations in which one side tries to make gains or achieve objectives through a direct frontal challenge to, or assault upon, the interests, prestige and power of the opponent. Yet ideological hostility and the fundamental antipathy between the superpowers that arises from their conflicting social, economic and political systems probably ensures that competition between them is endemic. Adversary partners in Cold War are no less so in a period of *détente*. The emphasis differs, of course; but, just as the superpowers were to some extent partners in the task of 'disaster avoidance' even at the height of the Cold War, so are they adversaries even during a period of *détente*.

Consequently, it would be foolish to ignore the possibility that on occasions the conflicting interests of the superpowers will come to the fore. Similarly, to expect either superpower to refrain from all opportunities to obtain unilateral advantage at the expense of the other is probably unrealistic. In circumstances where both states are unequivocally involved and where a lack of restraint by either would obviously lead to confrontation, then the 'Basic Principles of Relations' are likely to be adhered to and a premium placed on crisis avoidance. Should either superpower believe that it can make substantial unilateral gains without incurring anything more than a verbal censure from the adversary, however, the accords will be observed far less rigidly. This seems to have been the case in Angola. Constraints imposed by the American Congress on the Ford Administration left the Soviet Union with an entirely free hand. The danger is that, in the future, decision-makers in Moscow will calculate that they are in a similar position when in fact they are not. Should such a miscalculation occur, the skill and resourcefulness of the superpowers in the art of crisis management will be put to the test once again.

In spite of the emphasis on confrontation avoidance, therefore, crisis management is likely to be of continued relevance in superpower interactions. Another possibiilty tending to reinforce this conclusion is that the superpowers will be sucked into confrontations by their client states, as they were to some degree in October 1973. The Middle East Crisis in fact suggests what may be a pattern for the future as the superpowers continue to find themselves allied to opposing sides in local conflicts. Successful crisis avoidance may require abstention from involvement in these disputes. But as one analyst has commented:

> The injunction to avoid involvement on opposite sides is difficult to fulfill because present conditions facilitate progressive commitment, because local conflicts often provide opportunities for superpower gains, because local leaders often manoeuver to commit one or both of the superpowers to their side, because secondary powers may make tacit superpower collusion difficult, and because the ideological dispositions of local regimes may naturally divide the superpowers.[15]

In other words, the 'pressures for confrontation' and the 'temptations to conflict' may occasionally prove irresistible.[16] And when they do, skilful crisis management will be indispensable. Nor is crisis management likely to be wholly irrelevant to other states. If nuclear proliferation continues, the crisis management techniques of the superpowers may become a venerated model for other states to copy, adapt and develop. The fear of war that nuclear weapons bring with them will ensure this. The tragedy lies in the price that will have to be paid should such states prove less adept in the art of crisis management than have the Soviet Union and the United States.

Notes

Chapter One

1. Arnold L. Horelick, A. Ross Johnson and John D. Steinbruner, *The Study of Soviet Foreign Policy: A Review of Decision-Theory-Related Approaches* R–1334 (Santa Monica: The Rand Corporation, December 1973), p. vii.
2. See David C. Schwarz, 'Decision Theories and Crisis Behaviour: An Empirical Study of Nuclear Deterrence in International Political Crises', *Orbis*, Vol. 12, No. 2 (Summer 1968).
3. Alexander L. George and Richard Smoke, *Deterrence in American Foreign Policy: Theory and Practice* (New York: Columbia University Press, 1974), p. 95.
4. ibid., p. 96.
5. ibid., p. 636.
6. Laurence W. Martin, 'Crisis Management', paper presented to the Political Studies Association Conference 1967, p. 2.
7. See Glenn Snyder's excellent analysis, 'Crisis Bargaining', in Charles F. Hermann (ed.), *International Crises: Insights from Behavioural Research* (London: Collier-Macmillan, 1972), p. 127.
8. ibid.
9. This thesis is developed further in Trevor Salmon's 'Optimism and Omission in Strategic Theory', *The Royal Air Forces Quarterly*, Vol. 14, No. 2 (Summer 1974).
10. See in particular Thomas Schelling's *Arms and Influence* (New Haven and London: Yale University Press, 1966) and Herman Kahn's *On Escalation: Metaphors and Scenarios* (New York: Praeger, 1965).
11. This clearly emerges in Oran R. Young's major pioneering work on crises, *The Politics of Force: Bargaining during Superpower Crises* (Princeton, New Jersey: University Press, 1968), especially chapter 4.
12. A good example is Thomas Halper, *Foreign Policy Crises: Appearance and Reality in Decision-Making* (Columbus, Ohio: Merrill, 1971).
13. John Garnett, 'The Role of Military Power', in John Baylis, Ken Booth, John Garnett and Phil Williams, *Contemporary Strategy: Theories and Policies* (London: Croom-Helm, 1975), p. 53.

Chapter Two

1. See E. H. Carr, *The Twenty Years Crisis 1919–39*, 2nd edn. (London: Macmillan, 1946). Compare the definition offered by Young below.

2. Charles A. McClelland, 'The Acute International Crisis', *World Politics,* Vol. 14, No. 8 (October 1961), p. 183.
3. Oran R. Young, *The Intermediaries: Third Parties in International Crises* (Princeton: University Press, 1967), p. 9.
4. See in particular James A. Robinson, 'Crisis Decision-Making: An Inventory and Appraisal of Concepts, Theories, Hypotheses, and Techniques of Analysis', in James A. Robinson (ed.), *Political Science Annual Volume Two – 1969* (New York: Bobbs-Merrill, 1970), especially pages 111–16.
5. The idea of 'analytical perspectives' is developed further in John P. Lovell, *Foreign Policy in Perspective: Strategy, Adaptation, Decision-Making* (New York: Holt, Rinehart and Winston, 1970). See also J. David Singer, 'The Level of Analysis Problem in International Relations', in K. Knorr and S. Verba (eds), *The International System: Theoretical Essays* (Princeton, New Jersey: University Press, 1961).
6. This corresponds with the difference between decision-making and systemic approaches, both of which are discussed in Charles F. Hermann (ed.), *International Crises: Insights from Behavioural Research* (London: Collier-Macmillan, 1972), pp. 6–17.
7. This is the classic decision-making definition of crises as presented by Charles F. Hermann, *Crises in Foreign Policy: A Simulation Analysis* (New York: Bobbs-Merrill, 1969).
8. For an elaboration of the notion of 'occasion for decision', see James A. Robinson, 'The Concept of Crisis in Decision-Making', in N. Rosenbaum (ed.), *Readings on The International Political System* (Englewood Cliffs, New Jersey: Prentice-Hall, 1970), pp. 81–90.
9. In fact, this is one of the crises examined by Thomas Halper in *Foreign Policy Crises. Appearance and Reality in Decision-Making* (Columbus, Ohio: Merrill, 1971).
10. See ibid. for a useful and provocative analysis of the way the Johnson Administration perceived events in Santa Dominica.
11. Coral Bell, *The Conventions of Crisis: A Study in Diplomatic Management* (London: Oxford University Press, 1971), p. 9.
12. ibid.
13. This is not to ignore Professor Bell's point that some situations are so complex that they could be fitted into either category: crises between Greece and Turkey are an obvious example of confrontations that cannot be neatly typed. Nor is it to forget that adversary crises may have damaging side-effects on the cohesion of alliance systems. But these qualifications do not invalidate the distinction between the various types of crisis or the point that 'intramural' conflicts are best treated as problems of alliance management.
14. See McClelland, op. cit.
15. Oran R. Young, *The Politics of Force: Bargaining during Superpower Crises* (Princeton: University Press, 1968), p. 15.
16. ibid., p. 14.
17. Herman Kahn, *On Escalation: Metaphors and Scenarios* (New York: Praeger, 1965), p. 63.
18. The following analysis rests heavily upon the discussions by Robinson, op. cit., and Hermann, *Crises in Foreign Policy,* especially pp. 21–36, both of which summarise the twelve characteristics of 'crisis' identified by Herman Kahn and A. J. Wiener in *Crisis and Arms Control* (New

York: Hudson Institute, 1962).
19. Howard M. Lentner, 'The Concept of Crisis as Viewed by The United States Department of State' (Unpublished manuscript, deposited at IISS, London), p. 64. A shorter version of this paper can be found in Hermann (ed.), *International Crises*, pp. 122–35.
20. See F. S. Northedge, *The Foreign Policies of the Powers* (London: Faber and Faber, 1968), pp. 9–10, and Stanley Hoffman, *The State of War: Essays on the Theory and Practice of International Politics* (London: Pall Mall, 1965), p. 135.
21. This point is excellently made in Charles Burton Marshall, *The Limits of Foreign Policy* (Baltimore: Johns Hopkins Press, 1963), pp. 11–34.
22. Thomas C. Schelling, *Arms and Influence* (New Haven and London: Yale University Press, 1966), p. 97. The contrary view can be found in Albert and Roberta Wohlstetter, *Controlling the Risks in Cuba*, Adelphi Paper No. 17 (London: Institute for Strategic Studies, 1965), particularly p. 19.
23. Oran R. Young, 'The Intellectual Bases of "Conflict Management" ' paper presented to the Twelfth S. H. Bailey Conference, January 1970, p. 8.
24. Glenn Snyder, 'Crisis Bargaining', in Hermann (ed.), *International Crises,* p. 240, n. 27.
25. Quoted in 'Crisis Management or Crisis Prevention', *NATO Letter* (August–September 1966), p. 14.
26. William R. Kintner and David C. Schwarz, *A Study on Crisis Management* (Philadelphia: University of Pennsylvania Foreign Policy Research Institute, 1965), Appendix B, p. 21.
27. See Frederick L. Schuman, *The Cold War: Retrospect and Prospect* 2nd edn. (Baton Rouge: Louisiana State University Press, 1967), p. 72
28. Schelling, op. cit., p. 120.
29. See the author's 'Crisis Management' in J. Baylis, K. Booth, J. Garnett and P. Williams, *Contemporary Strategy: Theories and Policies* (London: Croom-Helm, 1975), p. 157.
30. Sir Charles Webster, *The Art and Practice of Diplomacy* (London: Chatto and Windus, 1961), p. 2, quoted in P. C. Fielder, 'The Pattern of Superpower Crises', *International Relations,* Vol. 3, No. 7 (April 1968), p. 499.
31. L. W. Martin, 'Crisis Management', paper presented to the Political Studies Association Conference, 1967, p. 5.

Chapter Three

1. I. F. Clarke, *Voices Prophesying War* (London: Oxford University Press, 1966), p. 75.
2. See Michael Howard, 'Reflections on the First World War', in *Studies in War and Peace* (London: Maurice Temple Smith, 1970), especially p. 103.
3. Barbara Tuchman, *August 1914* (London: Constable, 1962), p. 123.
4. Carl von Clausewitz, *On War* (London: Penguin, 1968), p. 373. See also pp. 374–88 for further elucidation of the argument.

5. See Clarke, op. cit., Chapter 3 in particular.
6. Jay Luvaas, *The Military Legacy of the Civil War: The European Inheritance* (Chicago: University Press, 1959) is an excellent work elaborating this point.
7. Raymond Aron, *The Century of Total War* (London: Derek Vershoyle, 1954), Chapter 1 in particular.
8. Clarke, op. cit., p. 69.
9. This point is made in Henry A. Kissinger, *A World Restored* (New York: Grosset & Dunlap, 1964), p. 6.
10. B. E. Schmitt, *The Origins of the First World War*, Pamphlet No. 39 (London: Historical Association, 1958), p. 18.
11. See Tuchman, op. cit., chapter 9; also A. J. P. Taylor, *War by Timetable* (London: Macdonald, 1969), p. 116.
12. L. Albertini, *The Origins of the War of 1914* (London: Oxford University Press, 1952), Vol. II, p. 516.
13. The alternative thesis, that the war reflected a consistent policy of expansionism by Germany, is presented in the works of Fritz Fischer; for example *Germany's Aims in The First World War* (London: Chatto and Windus, 1967).
14. Coral Bell, *The Conventions of Crisis: A Study in Diplomatic Management* (London: Oxford University Press, 1971), p. 15.
15. Albertini, op. cit., p. 156.
16. See Immanuel Geiss, *July 1914, The Outbreak of the First World War: Selected Documents* (London: Batsford, 1967), p. 366.
17. Schmitt, op. cit., p. 26.
18. L. Albertini, *The Origins of the War of 1914* (London: Oxford University Press, 1957), Vol. III, p. 702.
19. Taylor, op. cit., p. 121.
20. Geiss, op. cit., p. 372.
21. Clarke, op. cit., p. 162.
22. Quoted in Keith Middlemass, *Diplomacy of Illusion: The British Government and Germany 1937–39* (London: Weidenfeld & Nicolson, 1972), p. 15.
23. Quoted in ibid., p. 47.
24. Kissinger, op. cit., p. 1.
25. See M. Howard, 'Military Power and International Order', in *Studies in War and Peace*, p. 20, 5.
26. ibid., p. 205.
27. E. M. Robertson, *Hitler's Pre-War Policy and Military Plans 1933–39* (London: Longmans, 1963), p. 79.
28. ibid.
29. For a convincing and logical critique of policies of appeasement see J. L. Payne, *The American Threat: The Fear of War as an Instrument of Foreign Policy* (Chicago: Markham, 1971).
30. M. Howard, 'Changes in the Use of Force 1919–1969', in Brian Porter (ed.), *The Aberystwyth Papers: International Politics 1919–69* (London: Oxford University Press, 1972), p. 145.
31. Middlemass, op. cit., p. 243.
32. The term 'simple fundamentalism' is taken from M. Howard, 'Changes in the Use of Force 1919–69', where it is used in a discussion of the debates about nuclear deterrence in the post-war world. See Porter (ed.), op. cit., p. 152.
33. A. J. P. Taylor, *The Origins of the Second World War* (London:

Penguin Books, 1964), p. 222.

34. J. W. Wheeler-Bennett, *Munich: Prologue to Tragedy* (London: Macmillan, 1948), p. 269.
35. Taylor, *The Origins of the Second World War*, p. 228.
36. *The Memoirs of Captain Liddell-Hart* (London: Cassell, 1965), Vol. II, pp. 170–1.
37. See George Quester, *Deterrence Before Hiroshima* (New York: Wiley, 1966), pp. 82–105.
38. Robertson, op. cit., p. 136.

Chapter Four

1. See Michael Howard, *Studies in War and Peace* (London: Maurice Temple Smith, 1970), especially chapter 9, 'Bombing and the Bomb'.
2. ibid., pp. 205–6.
3. See Henry A. Kissinger, *Nuclear Weapons and Foreign Policy* (New York: Harper and Row, 1957), pp. 65–72.
4. See for example Walter Millis, *The Abolition of War* (New York: Macmillan, 1963).
5. This particular point is emphasised in Hans J. Morgenthau, 'The Four Paradoxes of Nuclear Strategy', *American Political Science Review*, Vol. 58, No. 1 (March 1964), pp. 23–35.
6. See A. Rapoport's 'Concluding Remarks' to Clausewitz, *On War* (London: Penguin, 1968), pp. 413–14.
7. This matter is superbly analysed by Stanley Hoffmann: see 'The Acceptability of Military Force', in *Force in Modern Societies: Its Place in International Politics*, Adelphi Paper 102 (London: International Institute for Strategic Studies, Winter 1973).
8. This argument can be found in Klaus Knorr, *On The Uses of Military Power in the Nuclear Age* (Princeton, New Jersey: University Press, 1966), which provides a reasoned and comprehensive analysis of the contemporary role of force. See also the same author's *The Power of Nations: The Political Economy of International Relations* (New York: Basic Books, 1975), especially pp. 123–6.
9. John Garnett, 'The Role of Military Power', in J. Baylis, K. Booth, J. Garnett and P. Williams, *Contemporary Strategy: Theories and Policies* (London: Croom-Helm, 1975), p. 59.
10. This is why the theory of limited war has become so important. An excellent discussion of limited war can be found in Bernard Brodie, *Strategy in The Missile Age* (Princeton, New Jersey: University Press, 1959), pp. 205–375.
11. Hedley Bull, 'War and International Order', in Alan James (ed.), *The Bases of International Order* (London: Oxford University Press, 1973), pp. 116–32 at p. 122.
12. William W. Kaufmann, 'Force and Foreign Policy', in W. W. Kaufmann (ed.) *Military Policy and National Security* (Princeton, New Jersey: University Press, 1956), p. 262 (italics added).
13. The term 'adverse partnership' is used by Coral Bell, *The Conventions of Crisis: A Study in Diplomatic Management* (London: Oxford

University Press, 1971), p. 50. See also Marshall D. Shulman, *Beyond the Cold War* (New Haven: Yale University Press, 1966), especially pp. 100–1.
14. Bull, op. cit., p. 125.
15. ibid.
16. ibid., p. 128.
17. This emerges very clearly in Alexander George and Richard Smoke, *Deterrence in Foreign Policy: Theory and Practice* (New York: Columbia University Press, 1974), especially pp. 534–48. The discussion in the following paragraphs owes a great deal to this analysis.
18. The distinction between risks of crisis and risks of war is clearly established in Hannes Adomeit, *Soviet Risk–Taking and Crisis Behaviour: From Confrontation to Coexistence?* Adelphi Paper 101 (London: International Institute for Strategic Studies, Autumn 1973), pp. 3–4. Adomeit also makes a distinction between 'risks of war' and 'risks of mutual annihilation'. It is argued here, however, that this second distinction has been far less important in superpower calculations. They want to avoid *any* violence because of a feeling that it would escalate very quickly to mutual annihilation.
19. See ibid. for a fuller discussion of the determinants of *Soviet* risk-taking behaviour.
20. This also suggests that on occasion the superpowers find themselves in a crisis not as a result of their own policies, but because they are dragged into it by the actions of allies.
21. See Thomas C. Schelling, *Arms and Influence* (New Haven: Yale University Press, 1966), especially pp. 99–125, together with the same author's *The Strategy of Conflict* (New York: Oxford University Press, 1963), pp. 189–203, for a fuller discussion of these tactics.
22. Glenn Snyder, 'Crisis Bargaining', in Charles F. Hermann (ed.), *International Crises* (London: Collier-Macmillan, 1972), p. 240.
23. Stanley Hoffmann, *The State of War: Essays on the Theory and Practice of International Politics* (London: Pall Mall, 1965), p. 142.
24. Kenneth Boulding, *Conflict and Defense* (New York: Harper, 1962), p. 314.
25. Charles O. Lerche Jr, *The Cold War . . . And After* (Englewood Cliffs, N.J.: Prentice-Hall, 1965), p. 113.
26. Robert E. Osgood and Robert W. Tucker, *Force, Order and Justice* (Baltimore: Johns Hopkins Press, 1967), p. 343.
27. John W. Wheeler-Bennett, *Munich: Prologue to Tragedy* (London: Macmillan, 1948), pp. 116–17.
28. Hoffmann, *The State of War*, pp. 143–4.
29. Osgood and Tucker, op. cit., chapter 3.

Chapter Five

1. E. I. Friedland, *Introduction to the Concept of Rationality in Political Science* (Morristown, N.J.: General Learning Press, 1974), p. 2.
2. See J. G. March and H. A. Simon, *Organizations* (New York: Wiley, 1958).

3. W. D. Coplin, *Introduction to International Politics: A Theoretical Overview* (Chicago: Markham, 1971) p. 43.
4. March and Simon, op. cit., pp. 140–1.
5. C. E. Lindblom, 'The Science of "Muddling Through"', in F. A. Kramer, *Perspectives on Public Bureaucracy* (Cambridge, Mass.: Winthrop, 1973), pp. 123–41 at p. 128.
6. ibid., p. 124. See also D. Braybrooke and C. E. Lindblom, *A Strategy of Decision* (New York: Free Press, 1963), especially pp. 20–31. This latter work is a thorough critique of ideas of comprehensive rationality.
7. See G. T. Allison, *Essence of Decision: Explaining the Cuban Missile Crisis* (Boston: Little, Brown, 1971) for a full and critical discussion of the assumptions underlying the often implicit model of rationality used by foreign policy analysts.
8. J. P. Lovell, *Foreign Policy in Perspective: Strategy, Adaptation, Decision-Making* (New York: Holt, Rinehart & Winston, 1970), p. 65.
9. Quoted in J. Garnett, 'Strategic Studies and Its Assumptions', in J. Baylis, K. Booth, J. Garnett and P. Williams, *Contemporary Strategy: Theories and Policies* (London: Croom-Helm, 1975), p. 17.
10. A useful discussion of the problems posed for rational decision-making by such pressures can be found in J. Frankel, *The Making of Foreign Policy* (London: Oxford University Press, 1963), pp. 169–70.
11. Most effectively by Allison, op. cit.
12. I. M. Destler, *Presidents Bureaucrats and Foreign Policy* (Princeton: University Press, 1972), p. 64 (emphasis added).
13. S. Verba, 'Assumptions of Rationality and Non-Rationality in Models of the International System', in H. K. Jacobson and W. Zimmerman (eds.), *The Shaping of Foreign Policy* (New York: Atherton Press, 1969), pp. 179–208 at pp. 200–1.
14. The phrase is Roger Hilsman's: see his *To Move a Nation: The Politics of Foreign Policy in the Administration of John F. Kennedy* (New York: Dell, 1964) for an excellent account of the various ways in which politics impinges on foreign policy-making.
15. Alastair Buchan, *Crisis Management: The New Diplomacy*, the Atlantic Papers, NATO Series II (Boulogne-sur-Seine: Atlantic Institute, 1966).
16. Charles F. Hermann, *Crises in Foreign Policy: A Simulation Analysis* (New York: Bobbs-Merrill, 1969), p. 20.
17. Theodore J. Lowi, 'Making Democracy Safe in the World', in J. Rosenau (ed.), *Domestic Sources of Foreign Policy* (New York: Free Press, 1967), pp. 295–331, especially pp. 300–1.
18. C. F. Hermann and Linda P. Brady, 'Alternative Models of International Crisis Behaviour', in C. F. Hermann (ed.), *International Crises: Insights from Behavioral Research* (New York: Free Press, (1972), pp. 281–303 at p. 288.
19. See Glenn D. Paige, *The Korean Decision* (New York: Free Press, 1968), pp. 81–93.
20. On the problem of information in the bureaucracy, see H. L. Wilensky, *Organizational Intelligence* (New York: Basic Books, 1967).
21. See ibid., pp. 76–7 as well as the same author's 'Intelligence, Crises and Foreign Policy: Reflections on the limits of Rationality', in R. H. Blum (ed.), *Surveillance and Espionage in a Free Society* (New

York: Praeger, 1972), pp. 236–66, especially pp. 238–240.

22. The major exception to this was the American decision to advance into North Korea, which was taken without a thorough scrutiny of Chinese 'signals'. There were particular reasons for this, however, which are detailed in chapter seven below.

23. Lowi, op. cit., p. 301.

24. T. C. Sorensen, *Kennedy* (London: Pan Books, 1966), p. 750.

25. Verba, op. cit., p. 188.

26. Warner R. Schilling, 'The Politics of National Defense: Fiscal 1950', in W. R. Schilling, P. Hammond and G. Snyder, *Strategy, Politics and Defense Budgets* (New York: Columbia University Press, 1962), p. 23.

27. Verba, op. cit., p. 203.

28. The effect on these other issues may, of course, be damaging. The preoccupation with the Cuban Missile Crisis at the higher levels of the Kennedy Administration in October 1962 meant that the Skybolt problem was put to one side, with damaging effect on the Anglo–American relationship. See Richard E. Neustadt, *Alliance Politics* (New York: Columbia University Press, 1970), p. 42.

29. Ole R. Holsti, *Crisis, Escalation, War* (Montreal: McGill–Queen's University Press, 1972), p. 207.

30. A useful discussion of some of these issues is to be found in Morton Deutsch, 'Group Behaviour', in *The International Encyclopaedia of Social Science* (New York: Macmillan and Free Press, 1968), Vol. 6, pp. 265–76.

31. Michael Nicholson, *Conflict Analysis* (London: English Universities Press, 1970), p. 111.

32. Paige, op. cit., pp. 281–6.

33. See Harry S. Truman, *Memoirs. Vol. II: Years of Trial and Hope* (New York: Signet, 1965), pp. 148–51.

34. T. Halper, *Foreign Policy Crises: Appearance and Reality in Decision-Making* (Columbus, Ohio: Merrill, 1971), p. 30, gives full details of the composition of the group.

35. K. Waltz, 'Electoral Punishment and Foreign Policy Crises', in Rosenau (ed.), op. cit., pp. 263–93 at p. 273.

36. ibid.

37. Holsti, op. cit., pp. 11–12, provides a useful summary of the different levels of stress.

38. This is not to ignore the need for caution in the use of memoirs as historical evidence.

39. Holsti, op. cit., p. 12.

40. ibid.

41. As Robert Kennedy put it, 'if we had had to make a decision in twenty-four hours, I believe the course that we ultimately would have taken would have been quite different and filled with far greater risks': *Thirteen Days* (London: Pan Books, 1969), p. 108.

42. For further elaboration see Thomas C. Wiegele, 'Decision-Making in An International Crisis: Some Biological Factors', *International Studies Quarterly*, Vol. 17, No. 3 (September 1973), pp. 295–336.

43. Quoted in Holsti, op. cit., p. 195.

44. Nikita Khrushchev, *Khrushchev Remembers: The Last Testament*, translated by Strobe Talbott (London: Sphere Books, 1971), p. 458.

45. Quoted in ibid.

46. Sorensen, op. cit., p. 791.

47. Khrushchev, op. cit., p. 458.
48. This point is emphasised in Holsti, op. cit., p. 181. Alexander George *et al.*, *The Limits of Coercive Diplomacy: Laos, Cuba, Vietnam* (Boston: Little, Brown, 1971) highlight the tension between the need to slow down the momentum of events and the need to keep the pressure on the opponent; see pp. 232–4 in particular.
49. Irving L. Janis, *Victims of Groupthink: A Psychological Study of Foreign Policy Decisions and Fiascoes* (Boston: Houghton Mifflin, 1972).
50. ibid., p. 5.
51. ibid., p. 3.
52. ibid., p. 6.
53. ibid., p. 9.
54. ibid.
55. ibid., p. 13.
56. ibid., pp. 14–49. A useful discussion of US decision-making for Vietnam can also be found in Townsend Hoopes, *The Limits of Intervention* (New York: McKay, 1973).
57. Janis, op. cit., p. 155.
58. ibid., p. 148.
59. ibid., p. 165.
60. Paige, op. cit., p. 298.
61. E. R. May, *'Lessons' of The Past: The Use and Misuse of History in American Foreign Policy* (New York: Oxford University Press, 1973), p. 86.
62. McNamara initially argued that the missiles would have little impact, but quickly changed his mind on this.
63. Thus, it is hardly surprising that Acheson has been extremely critical of the decision-making procedures adopted in October 1962. He obviously found them very different from those that had prevailed under Truman. See Dean Acheson, 'Homage to Plain Dumb Luck', in R. A. Divine (ed.), *The Cuban Missile Crisis* (Chicago: Quadrangle Books, 1971), pp. 196–207.
64. Glenn D. Paige, 'Comparative Case Analysis of Crisis Decisions: Korea and Cuba', in Hermann (ed.), *International Crises*, pp. 41–55 at p. 51.
65. ibid., p. 45.
66. Truman, op. cit., pp. 381–91 provide fuller details of these discussions.
67. Paige, *The Korean Decision*, p. 292.
68. See Dean Acheson, *Present at the Creation* (London: Hamish Hamilton, 1970), p. 411.
69. See J. E. Smith, *The Defense of Berlin* (Baltimore: Johns Hopkins, 1963), pp. 111–12.
70. ibid., p. 113.
71. That this was the case is argued by Richard Snyder in his 'Introduction' to Paige, *The Korean Decision*, p. xvii.
72. This emerges clearly from some of the questions asked at Kissinger's 25 October press conference. See also M. and B. Kalb, *Kissinger* (New York: Dell, 1975), p. 558.
73. Halper, op. cit., p. iii.
74. ibid., p. 141.
75. Allison, op. cit., p. 194.
76. This is a major theme of both Allison and Halper. It is also fully

acknowledged in Hilsman, op. cit., pp. 196–8.
77. Quoted in J. A. Nathan, 'The Missile Crisis: His Finest Hour Now', *World Politics,* Vol. 27, No. 2 (January 1975), p. 263.
78. Quoted in J. Mander, *Great Britain or Little England* (London: Penguin Books, 1963).
79. I. F. Stone, *In a Time of Torment* (London: Cape, 1968), p. 20.
80. Nathan, op. cit., p. 262.
81. Lovell, op. cit., pp. 64–5.
82. George *et al.,* op. cit., p. 89.
83. ibid., p. 89.
84. Paige, *The Korean Decision,* pp. 193–200.
85. Robert Murphy, *Diplomat Among Warriors* (London: Collins, 1967), pp. 386–7.
86. John W. Spanier, *Games Nations Play* (London: Nelson, 1972), p. 62.
87. Stanley Hoffmann, *Gulliver's Troubles* (New York: McGraw-Hill, 1968), p. 295; quoted in Hermann (ed.), *International Crises,* p. 110.
88. Lovell, op. cit., p. 221.
89. Allison, op. cit., p. 202.
90. ibid., pp. 203–4.
91. Robert Kennedy, op. cit., p. 51.
92. Sorensen, op. cit., pp. 759–60, provides details of other drawbacks of the blockade.
93. George *et al.,* op. cit., p. 94.
94. Hans J. Morgenthau, *Truth and Power* (London: Pall Mall, 1970), p. 158.
95. This theme is developed by Robert M. Slusser, *The Berlin Crisis of 1961: Soviet–American Relations and the Struggle for Power in the Kremlin June–November 1961* (Baltimore: Johns Hopkins Press, 1973). For a short but pertinent critique see Arnold L. Horelick, A. Ross Johnson and John D. Steinbruner, *The Study of Soviet Foreign Policy: A Review of Decision-Theory-Related Approaches,* Rand Paper 1334 (Santa Monica: The Rand Corporation, December 1973), p. 44, and, more generally, pp. 32–7.
96. Glenn Snyder, 'Crisis Bargaining', in Hermann (ed.), *International Crises,* p. 241.

Chapter Six

1. This distinction between bargaining risks and autonomous risks is made by Glenn Snyder. See his 'Crisis Bargaining' in Charles F. Hermann (ed.), *International Crises: Insights from Behavioral Research* (New York: Free Press, 1972), especially pp. 241–2.
2. ibid., p. 242.
3. ibid., p. 242.
4. The extent of this concern is highlighted in Oran R. Young, *The Politics of Force: Bargaining during Superpower Crises* (Princeton: University Press, 1968), especially chapter 9.
5. Robert F. Kennedy, *Thirteen Days* (London: Pan Books, 1969), pp. 72–3 in particular.

6. Snyder, op. cit., p. 241.
7. Carl von Clausewitz, *On War* (London: Pelican, 1968), p. 103.
8. Snyder, op. cit., p. 241.
9. See David C. Schwarz, 'Decision Theories and Crisis Behaviour', *Orbis*, Vol. 12, No. 2 (Summer 1967), and T. C. Schelling, *Arms and Influence* (New Haven: Yale University Press, 1966), p. 221.
10. Ole R. Holsti, *Crisis, Escalation, War* (Montreal: McGill–Queen's University Press, 1972), p. 222.
11. For a full analysis of this problem see ibid., pp. 119–42.
12. Graham T. Allison, *Essence of Decision: Explaining The Cuban Missile Crisis* (Boston: Little, Brown, 1971), p. 79.
13. ibid., p. 89.
14. The notion of 'authority leakage' is developed in Anthony Downs, *Inside Bureaucracy* (Boston: Little, Brown, 1967), pp. 132–6.
15. See Young, op. cit., chapter 9.
16. ibid., p. 14, n. 13.
17. See W. Phillips Davison, *The Berlin Blockade: A Study in Cold War Politics* (Princeton: University Press, 1958), pp. xi–xiii.
18. Robert Murphy, *Diplomat Among Warriors* (London: Collins, 1964), p. 387.
19. Davison, op. cit., pp. 62–72.
20. The way in which the Soviet Union has avoided pushing the Western powers into a corner is dealt with very well in R. Spencer, 'Berlin, The Blockade and the Cold War', *International Journal*, Vol. 23 (1967 68), pp. 383–407.
21. Lucius D. Clay, *Decision in Germany* (London: Heinemann, 1950), p. 374.
22. For the President's assessment of the risks see Harry S. Truman, *Memoirs. Vol II: Years of Trial and Hope 1946–52* (New York: Signet, 1965), p. 151.
23. See Murphy, op. cit., pp. 365–95. The point about resigning is made on p. 388.
24. ibid., pp. 392–3.
25. Howard Trivers, *Three Crises in American Foreign Affairs and a Continuing Revolution* (Carbondale and Edwardsville: Southern Illinois University Press, 1972), p. 6.
26. This is hinted at in Alexander L. George, David K. Hall and William E. Simons, *The Limits of Coercive Diplomacy: Laos, Cuba, Vietnam* (Boston: Little, Brown, 1971), pp. 20–1.
27. Davison, op. cit., p. 68.
28. Spencer, op. cit., p. 390.
29. Elie Abel, *The Missiles of October: The Story of the Cuban Missile Crisis, 1962*, new ed. (London: Macgibbon and Kee, 1969), p. 53.
30. Kennedy, op. cit., pp. 96–8.
31. The possibility cannot be dismissed, of course, that it was not a case of conscious calculation but of the Soviet Air Defence Units acting on 'previous orders, which the leaders had neglected to withdraw'. Allison, op. cit., p. 136, puts this forward as a possibility.
32. Kennedy, op. cit., p. 82.
33. Schelling, op. cit., p. 93.
34. Jonathan Trumbull Howe, *Multicrises: Sea Power and Global Politics in the Missile Age* (Cambridge, Mass.: MIT Press, 1971), p. 99.
35. ibid.

36. Further details of this episode can be found in Lyndon B. Johnson, *The Vantage Point: Perspectives of the Presidency* (New York: Popular Library, 1971), p. 302.
37. See Howe, op. cit., p. 116.
38. Johnson, op. cit., p. 303.
39. ibid., p. 302. See also Howe, op. cit., pp. 105–8.
40. Howe, op. cit., p. 117.
41. See Coral Bell, 'The October Middle East War: A Case Study in Crisis Management during Detente', *International Affairs*, Vol. 50 No. 4 (October 1974), pp. 531–43.
42. A fuller account of the episode can be found in Walter Laqueur, *Confrontation: The Middle East and World Politics* (New York: Bantam Books, 1974), pp. 182–206. Soviet communications are described on p. 200.
43. See official State Department transcript of Secretary of State Henry Kissinger's news conference of 25 October 1973 (United States Information Service), p. 7.
44. Quoted in John W. Spanier, *The Truman–MacArthur Controversy* (Cambridge, Mass.: Harvard University Press, 1959), p. 32.
45. Statement by Deputy Soviet Foreign Minister Andrei Gromyko, 29 June 1950 reprinted in *The Department of State Bulletin*, Vol. 23, No. 575 (10 July 1950), p. 48.
46. Quoted in Dean Acheson, *Present at the Creation* (London: Hamish Hamilton, 1969), p. 452–3.
47. See ibid., p. 463. The text of the American apology is in *The Department of State Bulletin*, Vol. 23, No. 594 (20 November 1950), p. 832.
48. Howe, op. cit., p. 217.
49. ibid., p. 247.
50. Much to Chiang's displeasure: see ibid., p. 246.
51. That Peking might use its bomber force was a matter of great anxiety to Washington early in the crisis. See ibid., p. 227.
52. Young, op. cit., especially chapter 5, is very good on this.
53. Truman, op. cit., p. 149.
54. This incident is described more fully in Jean Edward Smith, *The Defense of Berlin* (Baltimore: Johns Hopkins Press, 1963), pp. 122–3.
55. Kurt L. Shell, 'Berlin', in W. Stahl (ed.), *The Politics of Postwar Germany* (New York: Praeger, 1963), p. 99.
56. Robert M. Slusser, *The Berlin Crisis of 1961: Soviet–American Relations and The Struggle for Power in the Kremlin, June–November 1961* (Baltimore: Johns Hopkins Press, 1973), p. 131.
57. Philip Windsor, *City on Leave: A History of Berlin 1945–62* (London: Chatto and Windus, 1963), p. 240.
58. Trivers, op. cit., p. 27.
59. Smith, op. cit., see chapter 14 for a full account of Clay's actions.
60. ibid., p. 323.
61. Trivers, op. cit., p. 40.
62. Windsor, op. cit., p. 250.
63. Trivers, op. cit., p. 29.
64. Paul Nitze, quoted in Abel, op. cit., p. 142.
65. Abel, op. cit., p. 143.
66. Theodore C. Sorensen, *Kennedy* (London: Pan Books, 1966), p. 783.
67. Kennedy, op. cit., pp. 72–3.

68. Johnson, op. cit., p. 300.
69. Quoted in Howe, op. cit., p. 102.
70. See Johnson, op. cit., p. 300–1.
71. Quoted in Howe, op. cit., p. 102.
72. Fuller details of this episode can be found in R. Hilsman, *To Move a Nation* (New York: Dell, 1964), p. 221. See also Arthur Schlesinger Jr, *A Thousand Days* (London: Mayflower, 1967), p. 640.
73. Kennedy, op. cit., p. 37.
74. Schlesinger, op. cit., p. 622.
75. See David Larson (ed.), *The Cuban Crisis of 1962: Selected Documents and Chronology* (Boston: Houghton Mifflin, 1963), p. 249.
76. L. C. F. Turner, *Origins of the First World War* (London: Edward Arnold, 1970), pp. 91–2.
77. L. Albertini, *The Origins of the War of 1914* (London: Oxford University Press, 1952), Vol. II, p. 309.
78. This emerges clearly in Gerhard Ritter, *The Sword and The Scepter. The Problems of Militarism in Germany* (Coral Gables, Florida: University of Miami Press, 1970), Vol. II, p. 88.
79. Albertini, op. cit., p. 543.
80. A. J. P. Taylor, *War By Timetable* (London: Macdonald, 1969), p. 15.
81. Albertini, op. cit., p. 574.
82. L. Albertini, *The Origins of the War of 1914* (London: Oxford University Press, 1957), Vol. III, p. 243.
83. Barbara Tuchman, *August 1914* (London: Constable, 1962), pp. 85–8.
84. Holsti, op. cit., p. 235.
85. Truman, op. cit., p. 151.
86. Davison, op. cit., p. 103.
87. Johnson, op. cit., p. 298.
88. Abel, op. cit., p. 34.
89. Schlesinger, op. cit., p. 632.
90. Allison, op. cit., p. 130.
91. ibid.
92. Kennedy, op. cit., p. 68.
93. Sorensen, op. cit., p. 785.
94. See Kennedy, op. cit., p. 83.
95. R. T. Loomis, 'The White House Telephone and Crisis Management', *United States Naval Institute Proceedings,* Vol. 95, No. 12 (December 1969) at p. 70.
96. A. Horelick and M. Rush, *Strategic Power and Soviet Foreign Policy* (Chicago: University Press, 1966), p. 133.
97. A. and R. Wohlstetter, *Controlling the Risks in Cuba,* Adelphi Paper 17 (London: Institute for Strategic Studies, 1965), pp. 7–8.
98. See ibid., p. 20, and Hilsman, op. cit., p. 159.
99. Howe, op. cit., p. 74.
100. ibid., p. 145.
101. ibid., p. 275.
102. See ibid., pp. 234–6.
103. Quoted in ibid., p. 245.
104. ibid., p. 222.
105. See ibid., pp. 245–56, for a fuller discussion of the Soviet position.
106. ibid., p. 252.

Chapter Seven

1. Quoted by Paul H. Nitze, 'A Shaky Balance of Brinkmanship', in Ivo D. Duchacek (ed.), *Conflict and Cooperation Among Nations* (New York: Holt, Rinehart and Winston, 1963), p. 394.
2. This is not to suggest that there is always a formal negotiated settlement at the end of each crisis. Often there is not. Nevertheless, it is usually possible to draw up a 'balance sheet' of the gains and losses involved in the final outcome.
3. Thomas C. Schelling, *Arms and Influence* (New Haven: Yale University Press, 1966), p. 2.
4. Glenn Snyder, 'Crisis Bargaining', in C. F. Hermann (ed.), *International Crises* (New York: Free Press, 1972), p. 242.
5. Thomas C. Schelling, *The Strategy of Conflict* (New York: Oxford University Press, 1963), pp. 187–204, provides a detailed analysis of 'threats that leave something to chance'.
6. ibid., p. 200.
7. Fred Iklé, *How Nations Negotiate* (New York: Praeger, 1967), p. 62, clearly establishes the distinction between threats and warnings.
8. S. Maxwell, *Rationality in Deterrence*, Adelphi Paper 50 (London: Institute for Strategic Studies, 1968), p. 13.
9. Snyder, op. cit., p. 242.
10. This is one of the major themes in Herman Kahn, *On Escalation: Metaphors and Scenarios* (New York: Praeger, 1965).
11. Iklé, op. cit., p. 62 (italics in original).
12. Schelling, *The Strategy of Conflict*, p. 22.
13. Daniel Ellsberg, 'Czechoslovakia: Sequel to Munich, March 1939', in *Negotiation and Statecraft: A Selection of Readings,* compiled by the Subcommittee on National Security and International Operations of the Committee on Government Operations, United States Senate (Washington: Government Printing Office, 1970), pp. 39–43 at p. 41. Ellsberg's analysis of this episode is excellent and the discussion in this paragraph borrows heavily from it.
14. This tactic is dealt with at length in Robert Jervis, *The Logic of Images in International Relations* (Princeton N.J.: University Press, 1970).
15. Schelling, *The Strategy of Conflict*, p. 18.
16. This is recounted in A. Bullock, *Hitler: A Study in Tyranny* (London: Penguin, 1962), pp. 422–5.
17. ibid., p. 376.
18. ibid.
19. Albert Speer, *Inside the Third Reich* (New York: Avon, 1971), p. 164.
20. ibid.
21. ibid., p. 160.
22. This was clearly Chamberlain's image of Hitler at this time. See Christopher Thorne, *The Approach of War 1938–39* (London: Macmillan, 1967), p. 72.
23. Schelling, *Arms and Influence,* p. 38.
24. William Kintner and David Schwarz, *A Study on Crisis Management* (Philadelphia: University of Pennsylvania, Foreign Policy Research Institute, 1965), Appendix B, p. 3.
25. Kahn, op. cit., p. 12.

26. James L. Richardson, *Germany and The Atlantic Alliance* (Cambridge, Mass.: Harvard University Press, 1966), p. 144.

27. The argument that the escalation ladder is long and 'controllable' is put forward in A. and R. Wohlstetter, *Controlling the Risks in Cuba* (London: Institute for Strategic Studies, 1965), pp. 17–22.

28. Bruce M. Russett, 'Cause, Surprise and No Escape', *Journal of Politics,* Vol. 24, No. I (February 1962), pp. 3–24.

29. This term is used by Snyder, op. cit., p. 224. It is discussed further below.

30. ibid., p. 221.

31. This is one of the central themes of their analysis. See Kintner and Schwarz, op. cit.

32. Quoted in W. W. Kaufmann, *The McNamara Strategy* (New York: Harper and Row, 1964), p. 273.

33. ibid.

34. This is argued by Uri Ra'anan, *International Negotiation. The Changing American–Soviet Strategic Balance: Some Political Implications,* memorandum for the Subcommittee on National Security and International Operations of the Committee on Government Operations, United States Senate (Washington: Government Printing Office, 1972).

35. Z. Brzezinski, 'USA/USSR: The Power Relationship', in *International Negotiation. The Impact of the Changing Power Balance: Selected Comment,* compiled by the Subcommittee on National Security and International Operations of the Committee on Government Operations, United States Senate (Washington: Government Printing Office, 1971), pp. 8–12 at p. 9.

36. Thirty million is the figure offered by Brzezinski. The higher figure is given by J. I. Coffey, *Strategic Power and National Security* (Pittsburgh: University Press, 1971), p. 68.

37. Quoted by Coffey, op. cit., p. 49.

38. Brzezinski, op. cit., p. 11.

39. Walter Slocombe, *The Political Implications of Strategic Parity,* Adelphi Paper 77 (London: Institute for Strategic Studies, 1971), p. 20.

40. Richardson, op. cit., p. 188.

41. R. E. Osgood and R. W. Tucker, *Force, Order and Justice* (Baltimore: Johns Hopkins, 1967), p. 148. See also Maxwell, op. cit., p. 13.

42. Hannes Adomeit, *Soviet Risk-Taking and Crisis Behaviour: From Confrontation to Coexistence?* Adelphi Paper 101 (London: International Institute for Strategic Studies, 1973), p. 33–4.

43. Arthur Schlesinger Jr, *A Thousand Days* (London: Mayflower, 1967), pp. 642–3.

44. R. F. Kennedy, *Thirteen Days* (London: Pan Books, 1969), p. 124.

45. Osgood and Tucker, op. cit., p. 156.

46. The importance of this principle is fully brought out in P. C. Fielder, 'The Pattern of Superpower Crises', *International Relations,* Vol. 3, No. 7 (April 1969).

47. See for example John Mander, *Berlin: Hostage for the West* (London: Penguin Books, 1962), p. 13.

48. Richardson, op. cit., p. 286. See also P. Windsor, *City on Leave: A History of Berlin 1945–62* (London: Chatto and Windus, 1963), p. 240.

49. Richardson, op. cit., p. 287.

50. Jean Edward Smith, *The Defense of Berlin* (Baltimore: Johns Hopkins Press, 1963), pp. 283–7.
51. Quoted by Bruce Russett, 'Pearl Harbour: Deterrence Theory and Decision Theory', in *Power and Community in World Politics* (San Francisco: Freeman, 1974), pp. 216–33 at p. 227. Russett in this and other works emphasises that the success of deterrence depends on the costs of acquiescence in the opponent's demands. If these are higher than the costs that may be incurred as a result of attacking the adversary, deterrence will be more likely to fail.
52. Morton Deutsch, *The Resolution of Conflict* (New Haven: Yale University Press, 1973), p. 370.
53. Pierre Hassner has put the point very well: 'The Cold War was in fact characterized by the triumph of the defensive, hidden and protected by a verbal offensive.' See his 'Détente: The Other Side' in *Survey*, Vol. 19, No. 2 (Spring 1973), pp. 76–100 at p. 90.
54. See T. C. Sorensen, *Kennedy* (London: Pan Books, 1966), p. 656, and Smith, op. cit., p. 268.
55. See L. Albertini, *The Origins of the First World War* (London: Oxford University Press, 1952), Vol. II, p. 384.
56. ibid., p. 291.
57. H. Cleveland, 'Crisis Diplomacy', *Foreign Affairs*, Vol. 41, No. 4 (July 1963): see pp. 639–42.
58. R. Fisher, *International Conflict for Beginners* (New York: Harper and Row, 1969), p. 27.
59. This is brought out in George *et al.*, op. cit., pp. 101–2.
60. Fisher, op. cit., p. 63.
61. Quoted in J. T. Howe, *Multicrises: Sea Power and Global Politics in the Missile Age* (Cambridge, Mass.: MIT Press, 1971), p. 231.
62. Snyder, op. cit., p. 255.
63. Marvin and Bernard Kalb, *Kissinger* (New York: Dell, 1975), p. 650.
64. Quoted in 'On the Diplomatic Front', *Newsweek* (22 October 1973), p. 20.
65. Richardson, op. cit., p. 246.
66. ibid., pp. 250–5, and Snyder, op. cit., pp. 230–1.
67. Richardson, op. cit., p. 251.
68. Snyder, op. cit., p. 222.
69. This is, of course, a 'worst case' analysis of Soviet policy. A useful and balanced appraisal of Soviet behaviour is made by Malcolm Mackintosh, 'The Impact of the Middle East Crisis on Superpower Relations', in *The Middle East and the International System I. The Impact of the 1973 War*, Adelphi Paper 114 (London: International Institute for Strategic Studies, 1975). In addition, a reasoned, but slightly alarmist, interpretation can be found in W. Laqueur, *Confrontation: The Middle East and World Politics* (New York: Bantam, 1974), pp. 79–86 and 162–206.
70. Henry Kissinger, news conference 25 October 1973, official State Department transcript (United States Information Service), p. 10.
71. ibid., p. 11.
72. Coral Bell, 'The October Middle East War: A Case Study in Crisis Management during Détente', *International Affairs*, Vol. 50, No. 4 (October 1974), pp. 531–43 at p. 537.
73. Kissinger, op. cit., p. 8.
74. Alexander George and Richard Smoke, *Deterrence in American*

Foreign Policy: Theory and Practice (New York: Columbia University Press, 1974), p. 559.

75. Quoted in Smith, op. cit., p. 304.
76. Jervis, op. cit., p. 94.
77. ibid., pp. 94–5.
78. Kintner and Schwarz, op. cit., chapter 4, p. 8.
79. See Roberta Wohlstetter, 'Cuba and Pearl Harbour, Hindsight and Foresight', *Foreign Affairs*, Vol. 43, No. 4 (July 1965).
80. These problems are dealt with more fully in ibid.; George and Smoke op. cit., pp. 580–6; Joseph De Rivera, *The Psychological Dimension of Foreign Policy* (Columbus, Ohio: Merrill, 1968); and John Stoessinger, *Nations in Darkness: China, Russia, America* (New York: Random House 1971).
81. A. S. Whiting, *China Crosses the Yalu: The Decision to Enter the Korean War* (New York: Macmillan, 1960), p. 168.
82. Spanier, op. cit., p. 98.
83. Whiting, op. cit., p. 169.
84. George and Smoke, op. cit., p. 215.
85. Whiting, op. cit., pp. 171–2.
86. George and Smoke, op. cit., p. 184, attribute the escalation solely to 'misperceptions, miscalculations and inept actions'. The point made here is that, although these were important, had the United States been more afraid of war with China, it could have taken greater steps to avoid it.
87. Kennedy, op. cit., pp. 121–2.
88. On the legal aspects of the crisis see Abram Chayes, *International Crises and the Role of Law: The Cuban Missile Crisis* (London: Oxford University Press, 1974).
89. Hilsman, op. cit., p. 216.
90. On the utility of 'extra-diplomatic channels' see Marshall Shulman, *Beyond the Cold War* (New Haven: Yale University Press, 1966), p. 93.
91. Hilsman, op. cit., pp. 217–19.
92. See L. L. Johnson, 'New Communications Technologies and National Security', in *The Implications of Military Technology in the 'Seventies*, Adelphi Paper 46 (London: Institute for Strategic Studies, 1968).
93. Snyder, op. cit., p. 255.

Chapter Eight

1. Glenn Snyder, 'Crisis Bargaining', in C. F. Hermann (ed.), *International Crises* (New York: Free Press, 1972), p. 220.
2. Henry A. Kissinger, *Nuclear Weapons and Foreign Policy* (New York: Harper, 1957), p. 140.
3. Thomas C. Schelling, *The Strategy of Conflict* (New York: Oxford University Press, 1963), p. 262.
4. J. H. Kalicki, *The Pattern of Sino–American Crises* (London: Cambridge University Press, 1975).
5. Morton Deutsch, *The Resolution of Conflict* (New Haven: Yale

University Press, 1973), p. 351.

6. This distinction is made in relation to Sino–American crises by Kalicki, op. cit., p. 100.

7. In thinking about the idea of 'rules' in the regulation of conflict, the discussion by Deutsch, op. cit., pp. 377–80, proved particularly helpful.

8. This is one of the basic themes of Kalicki, op. cit.

9. This emerges to some extent in Henry Kissinger, 'The Challenge of Peace: A Statement of United States Policy towards the Soviet Union', address to the Commonwealth Club of San Francisco, 3 February 1976. Official Text (United States Information Service). Although this was a fairly tough speech, Kissinger stated that the superpowers must attempt 'to transform ideological conflict into constructive participation in building a better world'.

10. See, for example, William R. Kintner, 'The U.S. and the U.S.S.R.: Conflict and Cooperation', *Orbis*, Vol. 17, No. 3 (Fall 1973), pp. 691–719.

11. Henry Kissinger, news conference, 25 October 1973, official State Department transcript (United States Information Service), p. 10.

12. A very different interpretation, which suggests that the decision was a dangerous gamble by Nixon, and that Kissinger probably disapproved, can be found in M. and B. Kalb, *Kissinger* (New York: Dell, 1975), pp. 342–54.

13. 'Basic Principles of Relations', 29 May 1972, reprinted in *Survival*, Vol. 14, No. 4 (July/August 1972), pp. 191–2.

14. ibid.

15. Steven L. Spiegel, *Dominance and Diversity* (Boston: Little, Brown, 1972), p. 236.

16. See ibid., pp. 236–47.

Index